Elana Mira Mizrahi

Stumbling
Dancing
Through
Life
A
Book for
the Jewish
Woman

ISBN 978-965-555-789-3

Layout: ME Design
Cover Illustration: Sarah Tendler

For questions or comments please feel free to contact the author at:
elanamizrahi@gmail.com or +972-2-651-5418

This book
is dedicated to

Jewish Women
of the
*Past, Present &
Future*

My mother-in-law,
Mrs. Frida Ferdose bat Rivka, a"h
A woman of valor. A woman who fears G-d, she should be praised.
Give her the fruits of her hands, and let her be praised in the
gates by her very own deeds.

My grandmothers,
Fruma bat Anshel, a"h
& Chana Leah bat Shmuel Moshe, a"h

May the words in this book elevate
their souls and give them and

my mother,
Mrs. Cherna Silvert

true Yiddishe nachas and may I and my daughters
follow the holy path of our mothers.

Preface

I went on a hike the other day with my students. Olive trees, almonds trees, all kinds of trees marked our path and guided us along the trail. As I walked I kept my eyes on the rocky ground, afraid that if I took them off my feet for one minute I might fall. Unfortunately I was so busy with my eyes looking down that I missed the beautiful trees, the landscape, and the greenery. With my intense concentration I even missed the songs of the birds and the rattling of the leaves as they blew in the wind. All of a sudden I tripped on a rock. I stumbled and fell. And in that moment as I was down on the ground I looked up and I saw it all. Sometimes, it's good to fall.

It's in those moments, when you are on the ground, when you have hit rock bottom or have had the rug pulled out from under you that you realize there is nowhere to go now but upward and forward. It's a moment when you can, with G-d's help, actually see the beautiful world in which we live with clarity.

I stumble, I fall. Another experience in life. Another one of life's lessons. Learning, growing, doing. That's why we are here, right? To learn, to grow, and to do. To make changes and not repeat old mistakes. To get closer and closer to the *Borei Olam* (Creator of the World). We are so afraid, so afraid of falling, but only in those falls do we recognize the Beauty.

These articles, written straight from my heart about life's experiences, were first published on TheJewishWoman.org (a satellite site of Chabad.org) over a period of eight years. For a while now friends have been encouraging me,

"Elana, make them into a book." I wanted to, but I needed the fall in order to do so. It came. My mother-in-law, Frida Ferdose bat Rivka, passed away on 26 Tevet 5774.

I'm down on the ground now, but at the same time my eyes are open to beauty, and I know that my mother-in-law is in a wonderful, holy place. She was a noble woman with an open heart and an open home, a true Woman of Valor. She was a Jewish woman, a Jewish wife, and a Jewish mother. She laughed easily, cried easily and always had a blessing and an encouraging word to say. Her favorite pastimes were serving her family delicious food, preparing with joy for the Holy *Shabbat* and holidays, and going to Torah classes. She was full of life, love, optimism, and smiles. May this book be an elevation for her beautiful soul.

Elana Mira Mizrahi
Jerusalem, Israel
Cheshvan 5775

Acknowledgements

Thank you...

To **Sara Esther Crispe**, former editor of the TheJewishWoman.org for giving me a chance and encouraging me to write more.

To **Mindel Kassorla**, graphic design artist, for helping me to put this book together and for not taking no as an answer. The entire book that you see before you is thanks to Mindel's time, energy and wonderful talents.

To **my parents, Dr. and Mrs. Silvert, Mr. Piller, my father-in-law, R' Avraham Mizrahi, my family and friends,** and **my dear, dear *chevruta*** (who are my family) – you encourage me, support me, and shower me with love and praise.

To **my teachers** – you helped shape, guide and support me, to **Rabbi Dovid Sperling *shlita*, Jajam Rav Mordechai Tussie *shlita*,** and my dearest **Rebbetzin Sima Spetner,** to **my clients** (who heal me) and **my students** (who teach me more than I teach them).

To **my children – Avraham Nissim, Frida Tamar, and Asher Yisrael,** my greatest teachers, my joy, my blessings, my nachas – you have opened doors and worlds of wisdom to me and challenge me to be a better person everyday.

To **my husband, mi querido Salomon – Rav Shlomo Mizrahi** *shlita*, who stumbles with me, dances with me, and walks with me in everything I do – juntos – siempre, Amen. B"H, Solamente hay bueno.

To ***HaKadosh Baruch Hu*** for all the *chesed* He does for me, for making me stumble and catching me when I fall. I thank Him for the beautiful life He gives me and beseech Him to continue to shower *bracha* and *chesed* upon me and *Am Yisrael*.

Contents

Life's Cycles

Life is a Cycle

*I*t was early Thursday evening, and I heard the knocking, but I was in the middle of giving my baby a bath. My son called me, "Mommy, someone is knocking on the door."

"I know, but I can't come now. Don't answer it."

"But they keep knocking."

"I don't care. Tell them that you can't open the door."

I have a rule in my home that my children are not allowed to open the door for anyone unless I tell them that they can, even if the person says it's someone that they know.

The knocking persisted. I took the baby out of his bath, wrapping him in a towel, and made my way to the front door. "Who is it?" I looked in the peephole and saw an eleven-year-old from the neighborhood. I opened the door. The boy had a note: "We are collecting food for a family of ten who doesn't have food for *Shabbat*."

"One second."

I went to my cupboard. "What do I have that I can give?" My garbanzo bean cans called out to me. I grabbed them and put them in the boy's bag. *"Lichvod Shabbat Kodesh"* (for the honor of the holy Sabbath).

Two hours later the telephone rang. My heartbeat raced as I picked it up. I saw the call was from Shelly. Shelly was a friend who was quickly approaching her due date. She had called me months before, asking me if I would accompany her at her birth, like I had done for her at her first birth two years ago.

"Shelly," I told her, "I would love to, but how can I tell you that I can come, when I myself just had a baby?"

The easy solution would have been for me to tell Shelly to find another doula, but I couldn't tell her to find someone else. I know that she and her husband have no money. Who else could be her doula for no pay, as an act of kindness? Also, they don't have family here in Israel where we live, and her husband is an orphan. "All I can do is tell you that I will help you in any way that I can. Maybe you can come to my home before going to the hospital? Maybe I can help you for a few hours between feedings? Don't worry, we'll pray and it will work out."

For the past few months I have been praying for Shelly to have an easy birth, and for it to somehow work out that either I could be with her at her birth or that she shouldn't need me. And here it was, Thursday at 8 PM, Shelly was due on *Shabbat*, and she was calling me.

"Elana, I'm having contractions. They are about five minutes apart." Her voice sounded good, her spirits positive.

"Great. I'm going to a class from 8:30 to 10:00. Unless there is some sort of change, or you need me, please don't call me. We'll talk at 10 PM."

I hung up and turned to my husband. "Shelly might be in labor. Pray!" With my kids sleeping and my cell phone in my pocket on call for Shelly, I went to my Thursday night Torah class. I love this class so much, and it gives me so much spiritual strength and energy that I will do anything possible to make it.

At 10 PM I stepped out of my class, and the phone rang. It was Shelly's husband. "Her contractions are two minutes apart."

"Can she talk to me?"

"Not really."

"That's a good sign that things have progressed! I'll meet you in front of the hospital, but don't enter the building without me…"

I called home. "Everyone still asleep?"

"Yep."

"I'm off to the hospital. The baby will probably wake up around midnight to nurse. Call me if you need me, and I'll come."

At 10:30 PM I was outside the hospital with Shelly.

Her contractions were strong, but I wouldn't let her enter the building yet. We walked. I massaged her back. We breathed together. The baby was on the way.

Between contractions:

"Elana, I'm worried about *Shabbat* and Bracha (her toddler)."

"Shelly, don't worry about that right now. It will all work out, trust me. I'll find a great place for Bracha. Focus on the birth and the baby."

By 11:15 I felt that she was ready. We entered the hospital.

Mazel Tov! A boy! He was born at 11:50 PM.

When her husband walked into the room, it hit me. "You and Bracha will stay with us for *Shabbat*," I told him. "You can walk to the hospital from my home, and visit Shelly and the baby in the afternoon."

"And the *shalom zachar*?"

There is a custom to have a *shalom zachar*, a party on the first Friday night after the birth of a baby boy. At the gathering, people bestow blessings and good wishes upon the parents for their son. There is a widespread practice of eating *arbes* (chickpeas/garbanzo) beans at a *shalom zachar* as well. When the baby is inside the womb, it spends its time learning Torah. As it enters into the world, all the Torah is forgotten. It is customary to serve a mourner round foods, like chickpeas, symbolizing the fact that life is a circle, and thus things will come back around to being good. So we also serve them at a *shalom zachar*, in honor of the baby who is "mourning" the Torah that he lost.

"We'll have it at our home. Don't worry. Everything will fall into place."

I left them at 12:30 AM. I walked into my door. Everyone was still sleeping. That night, my baby miraculously slept until 2 AM without waking up to nurse. There are no coincidences in this world. Everything happens for a reason...

Friday morning. I kept thinking about my garbanzo beans. I told my husband, "We need to buy more chickpeas for the *shalom zachar*."

A knock at the door.

My hands were covered in flour and dough. I was kneading and baking, preparing for *Shabbat*, making *challah* and cakes for the *shalom zachar*.

"I can't come to the door."

Knocking, knocking, persistent knocking.

I looked in the peephole: a neighbor with a bag in his hand.

"Here, this is for tonight." Word had spread fast. He handed me a bag filled with chickpeas...

Life is an amazing cycle.

Thanksgiving

You'd think that I would get the message, but I don't, and so over and over G-d shows me in an infinite number of ways that I, Elana Mira Mizrahi, am not in control. And this, my dear friends ,is very very humbling. I had a week where this message really hit home. I attended two births. Both women were past their due dates and when at last contractions set it and we knew that – yes – this was the real thing, both wanted to know (like every laboring woman) "When will this end? How much longer?" I smiled, I massaged, I encouraged, "A little bit more and it will be over," I reassured them." But really, I didn't know. I never know. No one does, only G-d.

Birth is a humbling, awesome experience. In ten minutes a woman can open up from being dilated 6 cm to 10 cm and in ten hours a woman can go from only 1 cm to 3 cm. There are patterns, but there are no rules. And at last when the baby comes forth from its mother, there is no one – not a doctor, not a midwife, not a doula, and certainly not the mother or the father – who is not completely and totally humbled by the experience. We all saw it: the Hebrew word *leida* (birth) can be read as "*le yad Hashem*" (the hand of G-d) and in birth there is no other, only Him.

Following birth there is a tradition for the mother to say Psalm 100, a psalm of thanksgiving. Of course one feels gratitude upon birthing a baby, but this psalm speaks more than just thanksgiving. It tells us, "Know that G-d, He is G-d [meaning there is no other force]. He made us His and we are His people and the sheep of His pasture..." Birth is a clear revelation of Divine Providence. You see G-d in birth. You know that there is NO other. You understand that He orchestrates everything and guides every event and every occurrence like a shepherd who herds his sheep.

All the birthing courses now available are wonderful: learning to breath in birth, hypnosis in birth, prenatal exercises for birth, etc. I encourage every woman to learn, be informed, and to invest as much effort as she can to make her birthing experience easy and beautiful. I myself did and it helped – tremendously. Nevertheless, a woman must know that you can plan your birth to be one way and it almost never is the way that you plan. In fact, I was never at a birth that went the way it was originally envisioned. Ultimately when the unexpected happens (which is always the case in birth!) the only sure thing that a woman can hold onto is that she's not in control and that G-d Himself is conducting her birthing symphony.

~ ~ ~

The Torah says, "You have been shown to know that G-d, He is the G-d! There is none beside Him" (Deuteronomy 4:35). This verse is not just telling us to believe in only One G-d. We know that there is only one G-d. This verse is telling us to understand and to realize that nothing else exists except for Him and that everything contains a spark of Divinity. However the spark is concealed and our mission in life is to reveal it.

When G-d created man the verse says, "G-d said, 'Let us make man in our image, in our likeness...'" (Genesis 1:25). Rashi explains that G-d used the plural terms "let us" and "our" because he was consulting, so to speak, with the angels in the creation of man. This was in order to teach us the quality of humility – that the greater one should consult and take permission from the lesser one. If the Torah had said "I shall make man" we would not have learned this most important trait.

Birth is from Him and the salvation is from Him. Everything that exists is from Him. G-d created man to reveal holiness. We do this by getting close to Him, by calling out to Him, by knowing Him. We do this by being humble. We were created with the trait of humility, we give birth through humility, and we actualize our potential and ultimate goal through humility.

~ ~ ~

I say the words of Psalm 100 with the beautiful birthing woman who I am supporting...the woman who told me that she was sure that the baby would be born early and the baby decided to make his appearance two weeks late. With the woman who wanted a completely natural birth and who ended up having a life saving cesarean. With the woman who is always late and who, at week thirty-eight, gave birth in my hands in her bathroom (the ambulance finally arrived ten minutes later). I tell all these birthing women to envision a flock of sheep with its faithful shepherd. "Let go. Let G-d guide you and bring your baby into this world. Repeat after me…"

A song for a thanksgiving offering: Shout to the L-rd, all the earth. Serve the L-rd with joy, come before Him with praise. Know that the L-rd is G-d; He made us and we are His, people and the flock of His pasture. Come into His gates with thanksgiving, [into] His courtyards with praise; give thanks to Him, bless His name. For the L-rd is good; His kindness is forever, and until generation after generation is His faith.

~ ~ ~

It's now the beginning of the week and I open my agenda to see what I have scheduled. I think I have my whole week planned. I think again. *"Ein od m'levado"* – "There is none other than Him!" I wonder what He has in store for me for this week and how those sparks of Divinity will be revealed…

"No, I don't want that one! I want this one!" A common phrase expressed by my toddler. He doesn't want a particular shirt, he wants another one. Sometimes, I want to throw my hands up in utter exasperation. He's so stubborn and strong-willed, my son, but as the saying goes, "The apple doesn't fall far from the tree." And I know that my mother had the same conversations with me, twenty-seven years ago. We make our way up the spiraling staircase of life, but we repeat the same patterns, and do the same things. I don't doubt that my son will have the same conversation with his own child twenty-some years from now, G-d willing.

On most days when I take my son to preschool, he runs excitedly to get there. I think to myself, "Time is flying so fast, he's only two and he's already running away from me." At least, for now, he also runs to me when I pick him up, but how long will this last before the table is turned and he becomes so occupied that I'll have to run after him? How long will it be before he decides that he knows more than me, or that I'm no longer fun to be around? Will there be a day in the not-too-distant future when he walks too quickly for me to catch up and talks too quickly for me to understand?

~ ~ ~

For the past ten years, I've made various friends with people who are three to four times my senior. When I visit them, I realize that I have to talk slower and louder. They want me to tell them about my life, but they mostly want me to listen as they unleash years of wisdom and stories. It's true that I've heard the same stories repeated over and over. I've also heard about more aches and pains than, I think, a doctor. But from these acquaintances, I've picked up recipes and learned how to sew. I've been taught invaluable life lessons and been entertained by stories that, if written down, would be best-selling thrillers. I always walk out richer than when I entered.

Have you noticed that the world is speeding up? No one has time anymore. I take my son for a leisurely walk and I catch myself hurrying him along. I see little children dressed up like adults, and made to sit quiet for way too long. I watch people risk their lives by walking against a red light to save a whole minute. And I ask myself, "Where are we rushing to? Why do we push and want to speed everything along?"

Lately, I've been visiting a friend of mine. She's in her mid-eighties. I always take my son along and we affectionately call her "*Savta*" (Grandmother). When I visit Savta, I have to remind my self to speak slower and louder. The last time we went to visit her, she baked us two cakes, one to eat at her house and one for the journey home. Her eyes are always youthful and sparkling with humor, but this time Savta was a little down. She admitted to me that she's a bit depressed. When she visits with her family, she complains to me, they talk too fast and they don't involve her in their lives. No one has any time for her. She feels like an old rag, she admits, one that you keep in the corner. This visit made me so sad, for Savta is a treasure chest with hidden jewels waiting to be discovered.

~ ~ ~

A renowned Chassidic psychiatrist relates how a man was once sobbing hysterically on *Yom Kippur*. The people around him asked, "Why so much?"

He replied, reading from the *Yom Kippur* prayer book, "We came from dust and will return to dust. It's so depressing."

"It's true," he was answered, "But you have a wonderful thing in between – it's called life."

Since my visit with Savta, I've come to look at things in a different light. Life is so short and we're here for such a small amount of time. I ask myself again, "Where are we rushing to? Doesn't time move fast enough without us having to speed it along? I realize one does not live forever. If I don't take the time to be with my elders now, what will I do when they are already gone? If I don't spend time with them, will anyone spend time with me with I'm older?

Growing Old Gracefully

I have some gray hairs. Do I dare to count them? Just the fact that I have enough to count scares me, and turns getting old into a reality. Does having some gray hairs mean that I'm old? I'm certainly getting older. We all are. But why does it have to happen so quickly?

We just celebrated my birthday. I say "celebrated," because we had cake and ice cream. My children even made me a crown. For my kids, any excuse for ice cream and cake is a celebration. Though I'm not sure if to me it was a thing to celebrate. I like the special attention that birthdays bring, but I don't wait for them 364 days of the year like my children do. For them, another number means more privileges, more things that they get to do. For an adult, another number means less things that you can do, like: "I can't run as fast as I used to. I can't see as well as I used to…etc."

I take another look in the mirror. Do I look older? Do I look old? I don't feel old, but I'm actually not sure what old feels like. My grandfather would say you are only as old as you feel. It's the mind that makes you old, not the body.

I go with my children to the old-age home near my apartment building. We walk inside the door. The contrast between my bouncing preschooler and the women sitting in the wheelchair by the door stops me in my tracks. Not so long ago, I was the bouncing preschooler. Not so long ago, these women were the mothers of small children. Fifty years ago they were me, and in fifty years I could be them. The visit, like my birthday, serves as a reality check. "Elana, life is so short and it goes by so fast. Enjoy the moment that you are in, because you will never get it back."

"Enjoy the moment that you are in…" I decide that this is going to be my birthday present to myself. This is also what I want to leave behind to my children after 120 years – the memory of a happy mommy who looked for the good in every situation and in every person. Is that possible? Can I do it? I decide to try and start just by not complaining. In any difficult situation in which I find myself, I am going to try to find the one good thing about it, no matter how small that one good thing might be.

~ ~ ~

When Jacob came to Egypt, Joseph brought him before Pharaoh. The commentators explain that Jacob looked so frail and old that Pharaoh asked him with curiosity how old he was. Jacob answered, "The days of the years of my sojourns have been one hundred and thirty years. Few and bad have been the days of the years of my life, and they have not reached the lifespans of my forefathers in the days of their sojourns." Jacob had a really hard life, and it showed on his face. He wasn't just old in years when he stood before Pharaoh, he was old in suffering, old in outlook and old in misery. When Jacob said that his forefathers lived more, he meant it in the sense that every day of their existence was *living*, and they were able to carry out their difficult missions with a full heart and a positive demeanor.

Abraham, Sarah, Isaac and Rebecca all had incredibly difficult lives with tests and struggles, but we never hear that they complained. Not once does the Torah report them saying that they viewed the days of their lives as being few or bad. In fact, when Sarah dies at the age of 127, the Torah says that she lived "one hundred years, twenty years and seven years." The commentators explain the Torah's way of breaking down her age: at one hundred she was sinless as a twenty-year-old (until the age of twenty one does not suffer from heavenly punishment), and at twenty she was as beautiful as a seven-year-old, whose youthful beauty is natural and without need of any makeup. The only thing that even comes close to a complaint is Sarah's laughter of disbelief about the idea of having a child in her old age. The laughter of disbelief turned into a laughter of celebration, as the commentators expound for us that her menses returned and she bore a child at the age of ninety. Imagine having a son at age ninety, and dying at 127, both sinless and beautiful!

~ ~ ~

I look at my gray hairs once again. Really, there are not so many. I take another look. I tell myself that they are signs of wisdom and maturity. Positive thinking. This is my birthday gift to myself. And really, I have yet to meet a happy person who looks old.

Just Sit Shivah

The large signs in the entryway to our apartment building made it so that even if you didn't want to know, you knew. One of my neighbors had died and as is the custom in Israel, posters announcing his death were hung throughout the neighborhood and within our building.

Whenever there's an announcement of a wedding or a birth, with such ease and good nature I knock on the neighbors' door to congratulate them. For a happy occasion, this isn't a problem for me. But with the notice of death, I didn't know what to do. I think that this is normal. Who likes to hear unhappy news and who knows what to do or what to say in such circumstances? But, it was impossible to pretend that I didn't know.

Days passed as people poured into our building to visit the deceased's family. The initial week of mourning, called "*shiva*," was coming to a close, and soon the mourners would arise from their sitting. The word *shiva* literally means sitting, an appropriate term to use for the seven day period when the deceased's closest family members sit close to the ground, honoring his soul and mourning the loss of the body that housed it.

I chastised myself and walked down the five flights of stairs separating my home from theirs. My eyes instantly fell to the floor, my heart racing.

I didn't really know this neighbor and once again I panicked upon thinking what I would say or what I would do. But then I remembered: the only thing required of you at a *shiva* is to sit. In fact, you're not even permitted to approach the mourners or start a conversation with them. You have to follow their lead. If they want to talk, you talk. If they want silence, you give them silence.

I sat. The wife of the deceased immediately made eye contact with me. She didn't recognize me and of all the people in the room, she decided that she wanted to talk to me. Who was I? Where was I from? What did I do, and what about my husband? How long have I been living in the building, etc? We talked and talked. I could tell that she wanted to talk. I asked her what had happened and let her know that if she needed anything I was nearby, on the seventh floor.

I left a different person, so relieved and glad that I had worked up the courage to share in my neighbor's pain and do the right thing, despite the fact that it made me uncomfortable.

~ ~ ~

After two hundred and ten years of suffering in slavery together, the Jewish nation "Journeyed from Rephidim and arrived at the Wilderness of Sinai and encamped in the Wilderness; and Israel encamped (the term used here is in the singular instead of the plural) there, opposite the mountain" (Exodus 19:2).

"And Israel encamped there – as one man, with one heart" is how Rashi, a Post-Talmudic commentator, explains this verse.

The Jews left Egypt as a huge mass of men, women, and children. Seven weeks later they arrived at Sinai as a united force, as one man with one heart, and this is how they received the Torah. Why wasn't the Torah given to the description of the massive nation, of the many individuals? Because Torah is about unity. To be part of a family, a nation, you need to be together in the happy times, as well as the difficult ones. This is what I learned when I journeyed downstairs to my neighbor's *shiva* and I sat.

Dealing With Challenges

Moving

I can't believe I find myself in the same position, doing the same task: packing. Again, we're moving. Surrounded by boxes, the task appears daunting. "Again, I have to do this?" I ask myself. "Why?" No one answers. We don't want to move, especially not now, in the middle of winter and with a new baby, but our apartment was sold and we have to go. But where? We don't know yet. But the boxes are here and I'm starting to pack. We're moving, again. The same story happened to us just two years before. We've moved five times in seven years.

Moving.

Again.

The first things I pack up are my cookbooks. I know all the recipes by heart and I've changed them anyhow. What else can I pack that we don't need now? Pictures. My toddler stands next to me as I pack, asking me who everyone in the pictures are and "What's that?" Pictures. Memories. Images and memories flood my mind and for a moment I'm transported to a different place and a different time. I look at the pictures. I look at myself in the pictures. Look how much I've changed, look how much I've grown.

Moving.

Again.

Look how much we've changed, look how much we've grown.

What next? I look around the apartment that I still, for the time being, call home. There's so much to pack. Do we really own so many things? I thought we lived simple lives and look how much we possess. I'm overwhelmed with a sense of blessing. Do I really need all this? It's time to sort and give things away.

Moving.

Again.

I'm trying to look on the bright side… At least I'll be ahead for *Pesach* cleaning. I start to laugh because if I don't, then I'll cry.

The phrase "Wandering Jew" pops up in my mind. I feel like I exemplify this title, the wandering Jew. I wonder about the source of that phrase. Upon leaving Egypt, the Nation of Israel traveled for forty years and moved forty-two times, beating even our record. They certainly wandered. I wonder if with each move they thought to themselves, "Oh no, not again." It's interesting that the Torah describes how much the people complained about the food and water, but doesn't mention any complaints about the constant moving. The only thing it says is praise for the nation who camped and traveled by the word of G-d. They didn't see their moving as a bother, but merely as a means of reaching their goal, the way to get from one spiritual and physical place to another.

Moving.

Again.

Each move has a purpose.

We're moving and I don't want to, but I think back to all the times we've moved and I have to say that even when it seemed difficult, it turned out to be for our good. If we hadn't moved, we wouldn't have grown, and with this move, I know we'll grow too.

Moving Again?

We have to move again? Four times in six years. When I first heard the news, part of me was in shock. "I can't believe this is happening to us again! I thought for sure we wouldn't be forced to move this time." The other part of me was calm. "Been there, done that. Did it before, we can do it again. Every time G-d has been so good to us, and it's always for our best."

Six weeks later. We are still looking for an apartment to rent, for a place to call home. It is difficult to find something at this time of year, and whatever is out there is too expensive for our budget.

At night I toss and I turn. A home…how I would love to buy us our own home. But you need money to buy a home. Money…there's no money. Every time I go to the supermarket and I have enough to buy food, I breathe a sigh of relief. "Thank you, dear G-d." I hold my breath as I pay the electricity bill. "Thank you, dear G-d, we just managed to cover it." Wouldn't it be wonderful if someone could help us out? If anyone who could, would just help us out. But no one is helping us out. Wait, did I just say no one?

I'll never forget the sweetness of being completely and totally needed by my babies. Each one I nursed until two, and I never gave them a bottle. For the first six months they ate only my milk. For at least six months, when they were hungry all they wanted was me. They didn't look to anyone else for food. When they were hungry, they let me know. They cried, they screamed, they pulled at me. My milk was abundant, and I was only too happy to comply with their request. We had a connection so strong, it's beyond words. I miss it.

For forty years the nation of Israel wondered in the *midbar* (desert). They had no permanent home. As they wandered, G-d sent down manna, a special type of bread, from the Heavens. Each day every Jew received a portion of manna. The portion allocated was exactly the amount that was needed to satisfy him for that day. No manna was wasted or allowed to be left over. No one was hungry. Every single day the Jewish people felt a direct connection to G-d, and relied only upon Him for their sustenance. He never let them down. Imagine the amount of faith they had – to have only enough for today and never to be allowed to save for tomorrow. To know, to internalize, that if G-d gave me today, He can give me tomorrow. Imagine being so close and so dependent on G-d.

Imagine.

Do I need to imagine? Aren't I living it now? "Salomon," I excitedly told my husband. "We are living in the Generation of the *Midbar*!" Uncertainty – a global depression – it certainly feels like an economic desert. But, do we have a roof over our heads today? Yes. Then G-d can make it so that we will have a roof over our heads tomorrow. Did we find an apartment last time we had to move? Yes. So then G-d will find us an apartment to move into this time as well.

But I have to ask Him for it. I have to call out, and cry, and tell Him, "I need this. I want to nurse, I'm hungry!" Before I open the classified ads or call an agency, I need to say a short prayer or a psalm, not afterwards. Before I look to everyone and everything else, I need to turn to Him. "G-d, let me be to you like a suckling child at the side of his mother (Psalms 131:2) who desires nothing more than what his mother has provided him with, and rests secure that she will continue to provide his needs." I need to rest assured that if He gives me today, He will give me what I need tomorrow. Like the Generation of the *Midbar*, G-d is telling us, "You are closer to Me now than ever before…"

The Treasure Within

We were at it again. My husband and I, the wandering Jews, had to move once again. We had a week to pack up our home, and somehow we did it. It was hard to find movers on such short notice, and all of our previous movers were booked. A friend recommended some movers to us whom she had just used and had been happy with. They were available, and when Thursday – Moving Day – came, we were ready.

The movers arrived, and even from the beginning I could tell that this move was going to be different from than the ones before; and it was. What is usually a four-hour move (we know because we have done this six times in nine years) was going on and on. Nine hours had passed, and they weren't finished. The movers were breaking things left and right. I anxiously looked at the clock. When would this move end?

It was already close to midnight, and they told us, "We're not moving up your couches or your refrigerator. We can't. There's no way that they can come up. Think fast where you want us to leave them, because we are going."

My stomach fell; my heart skipped beats. My throat had a lump in it, and tears were about to burst forth on my cheeks. I was exhausted, worn out and drained. We have no one to call, no one to turn to. I pleaded with them, and prayed. I told my children, who should have been in bed hours before, to pray. I think, after seeing the look on my face and hearing the despair in my voice (and of course, more importantly, the praying) the movers agreed to bring up one couch and the refrigerator, and then they left. The other couch, a couch that had taken me a year of hard work to pay off, was left on the street.

Our new apartment, half the size of the one that we had just moved from, was crowded and packed to the brim. There was no space to move. We managed to get the kids to sleep, and then, just when I thought that our situation could not get any worse, it did…cockroaches!

I spotted one, and then another one. All of a sudden there were hundreds of them, little ones, big ones. This was not just one family; this was an entire nation of cockroaches crawling out of every nook and cranny, every corner and every wall.

It was now 3:30 in the morning, and for the first time in a long time, I broke. I felt destroyed, taken advantage of, and I felt so low. The famous question, "Why?" arose from my throat. Why? I, who am always so strong and focused, who wakes up the in the morning every day with a mission and a purpose, who has faith and clarity – I, Elana, broke. "I don't understand. What does G-d want from me? Why does everything have to be such a struggle? What are we doing here, and why?" And do you know what my husband answered me? "Elana, I don't know why, but I am very calm (someone has to be!). If this situation is such a test for us, it must mean that there is a treasure here."

Before I go on and tell you the end to this story, and what happened to our couch, let me tell you that the words my husband said to me that Thursday night resonated and penetrated my heart. While the dawn was breaking, I kept telling myself, "There must be a treasure here."

~ ~ ~

When you arrive in the land of Canaan (Israel) that I give you as a possession, and I will place a *tzara'at* affliction upon a house in the land of your possession…He [the owner of the house] shall demolish the house – its stones, its timber, and all the mortar of the house… (Leviticus 14:34-45)

Why was it that when the nation of Israel entered the land of Israel, an affliction (called *tzara'at*) appeared on their houses?

The sages teach that from the moment that the Canaanites heard that the nation of Israel was coming, they hid their money and valuables in their houses and their fields. G-d promised Abraham that He would bring his descendants into a land full of all good things, so what did He do? He brought an affliction to a man's house, and when he destroyed it (as the Torah ordained) and knocked down the walls, he found a treasure buried inside of it.

The next day, as we waited for the exterminator to come, my children and I played "chase and hide 'n' seek" with the cockroaches. He came, and we had to leave for an entire week as the apartment aired out. Friends opened their doors to us, and for the first time in I don't know how many years, I had a true vacation! We arrived back home, and within a day we had everything unpacked. The movers came back and brought our couch up. (It was a miracle that nobody stole it!) Things started to look up.

That was a month ago. Since then, we have had two different exterminators come five times. A plumber has had to come twice, a handyman numerous times, and two electricians. Our oven broke. Oh, let me think if I am missing something…I thank G-d that that was it, and this whole time I kept reminding myself about the treasure. And you know what – I found it!

I started to see the light and charm of our new little home. All these externalities – they get fixed and taken care of. (Yes, even the cockroaches are starting to go away at last!) It's a hassle and annoying, but you can't let them deter you from the treasure within. I have a beautiful family, thank G-d, with laughter and domestic harmony, and that is what makes a beautiful home.

We have special people who live on our street, a wonderful mixture of all kinds of Jews, and I must say that in the five countries that I have lived in, and the numerous homes and streets, I have never felt so comfortable and happy. Our location is magnificent. I am a five-minute walk from my children's schools, a three-minute walk from a fun and lively food market, and a thirty-minute walk from the Western Wall – the holiest place in the world. Our apartment, which houses five people in a space that is smaller than my parents' bedroom, is spacious enough for us, and to host my children's friends all the time; more kids come to us in a day than I ever had over as a child in a whole year.

This entire experience has taught me a valuable lesson: it's not the walls that make a home, it's the people. It's not the size that determines wealth or happiness, but the light of holiness and the contentment to be happy with what you have. You can have two people living in a mansion and it's crowded, and you can have eight people living in a two-bedroom apartment where there's always enough space.

Sometimes, what appears as an affliction is really just a message for us to appreciate what we have, and to dig deeper within to find the treasure. You might need to break down some walls first, but the treasure and goodness of every situation is there, just waiting to be discovered.

Unblocking Ourselves

It was one of those months when everything seemed to go wrong – and I do mean everything. The first week we moved into our apartment, it began flooding. We weren't even sure where the water was coming from. Our landlord told us that there had never been a problem before, and he had no idea why our floor was flooded.

A neighbor came over to see the little pool, and concluded that it must be coming from a hole in the water filter. We spoke with the water filter man, who told us that nothing was wrong with it. We then thought that maybe all the water was coming from our refrigerator. Could it be that when the movers had carried it up to our apartment, they had broken something that was now causing it to leak? It was so hard to tell.

We called a refrigerator repairman. He charged us for the visit, and concluded that it definitely was not the refrigerator. Nothing was broken. Again we called the landlord, and again he told us that this had never happened before.

This went on for at least a month. Then my oven broke. As the repairman fixed the oven, I asked him, "Do you have any idea why our apartment floods?" I showed him where we always had water on the floor.

"You must have a blocked pipe," he told me.

"A blocked pipe?" Could all this water on my floor be coming, not from something broken, but from a blocked pipe?

A plumber came to my house – three times. Each time he would unplug the pipe. A week would go by, and again water would flood the floor. My husband was ready to give up. "Let's go," he urged.

"Let's move away from here. We can't live like this."

"We are not going anywhere," I told him. "We are doing all that we can. The rest is up to G-d. I love the area where we live, and we are going to make it work."

I reminded him that we also didn't have any money to move again, even if we wanted to. When our apartment flooded again for the third time, we called a new plumber. He put his de-plugging tube deep into the drain. It went deeper and deeper, and then all of a sudden a big blue pencil sharpener flew out of the pipe. (Yes, this is my real life, and yes, even the plumber was shocked.) That, thank G-d, has been the end of our flooding (at least so far).

I learned a very important lesson from this pencil sharpener.

A person can go through life feeling down and dejected. You make a mistake; you feel terrible about yourself. You don't have a job, or you have a job that you don't like. You have problems with friends or family members. You, G-d forbid, don't have friends or a family. You are missing something, and you can't get what you want. You tell yourself that the reason all these things are happening is because there is something wrong with you.

You are wrong! In those moments of darkness, when you feel like there is nothing about you or the situation that you are in that is right, you always have to remember, "It's not that there is something 'wrong' with me. It's not that I have a hole or a defect. I just have to remove and 'unblock' the thing that is pulling me down."

The Talmud mentions a case where a man bought a house and subsequently found that an ancient treasure lay buried beneath it. After hearing the news, the previous owner argued that he had never intended to sell the treasure. The Talmud rules that since the seller never had reason to suspect the existence of the treasure, it was not his to begin with, and the court must rule in favor of the buyer. The reasoning behind the verdict is that if a person has something of great value but doesn't realize it, it is as if he does not really own it. In order to acquire something of value, it is first necessary to appreciate its true worth.

Every Jew must know that he or she is inherently good, and that within each one of us, we have a direct pipeline – our soul – that goes straight up to the Source of all blessing. Our sages teach us that the Creator searched all of His creation for a vessel fit to contain blessing, and found nothing better than peace: "G-d gives strength to His nation; G-d blesses His nation with peace." When a person has peace within, they become a vessel for blessing.

So how does a person "unblock?" First, value who you are and what you do have. Second, work on freeing yourself from all foreign and unhealthy influences, whether they come from within you or from your surroundings. Depending on the situation, you might need to seek help in order to do this. You might ask a friend, a rabbi or a mentor (or even a plumber!).

Last, remind yourself over and over that you are intrinsically good and that you are directly connected to the Master of the World, in whose hands is contained all the world's blessing.

Letting Go

When we first tried to conceive I asked the doctor if we would have to endure fertility treatments every time we wanted to have a child. I wanted him to tell me that once I conceived, I could put all the injections and pills behind me and from then on conceive naturally. He didn't. Instead he told me honestly, "I don't know."

Treatment after treatment, month after month, year after year, my womb remained empty. Nothing happened except the pain in my heart grew stronger. I felt like everyone around me was pregnant and having babies. In my community especially, it's hard not to feel like you are "the only one" without children.

I cried to G-d, I pleaded with Him. I looked to our matriarchs for guidance and clues as to how to overcome this test. I spoke with rabbis and friends. At last it slowly hit me that I simply had no control over the matter. It was the first time in my life that I had such a clear revelation of the grandeur of my Creator and how I was completely and totally in His hands.

I let myself go. The stubborn voice inside of me that said, "We will have children," never completely faded, but it did quiet down. We put the conventional treatments on hold, we took a break, and then we decided to try a different approach. We changed our diet, tried acupuncture and took herbs. Shortly after I conceived and nine months later I gave birth to our son.

It took me months to realize that I actually had a son. I had a hard time believing that this beautiful life came from my body and that I was his mother. The gratitude that I feel is immeasurable. Why then has the longing returned, as well as the aching and uncertainty?

I pray daily for childless couples and I feel so guilty from my feelings. Why can't I just be thrilled at what I have – the blessing that G-d has given me? Instead my eyes focus on the bulging bellies of pregnant women. I see siblings play together and large families walking down the streets. I hug my son dearly and wonder if I'll ever be able to feel the sensation of life growing inside of me again. I wonder if I'll be able to give him brothers and sisters with whom he can play.

I've returned to acupuncture and stick to my diet. Nothing has happened, yet. So I'm waiting and I find myself in the same situation as I did two years ago; even though now having a son, everything has changed. The little voice inside of me insists, "You have one, there's no reason why you can't have another." But it's fading.

I throw myself once again completely in the hands of my Creator. I admit to Him, to myself, that even with all that I do, I have no control over this, over any matter. I find that letting go helps me get through my darkest moments. A friend of mine asked me how I could do that; how could I give up? I explained to her that letting go and letting G-d take over is not giving up. In fact it's the only way to fight a battle.

Visualizing Our Potential

Thirty-six degrees Celsius.

Another morning I take my temperature. It's the same, thirty-six degrees Celsius. Day after day, morning after morning. It stays the same. I can't tell you how much I want it to change. To go up. A rise in temperature would be a sign that I ovulated which would mean that maybe, just maybe I could be pregnant again. But the temperature stays the same.

Thirty-six degrees Celsius.

I go through phases. Some months go by and I don't bother taking my temperature. It's almost a relief, to wake up and not know what the thermometer says. I've tried hormones, I've performed treatments. I take herbs and try various alternative medicines. I know that something has to work. Some things do appear to help, some things don't.

Some days I feel like giving up. And you know what? On some days, that's okay. I am so very grateful. After many trials and tribulations, I am so fortunate to have two healthy children. And I feel blessed every second of my life. Yet some days I get hopeful that maybe I will be blessed with more. So I take out my trusty thermometer. It tells me the truth, it won't betray me.

Again the thermometer reads: thirty-six degrees Celsius.

I can't remember who told me, but I once heard that if I wanted to become pregnant, then I would have to visualize it happening. I close my eyes, I meditate. I imagine my belly becoming round, my body full and feminine. I try to feel the kicks as my baby moves within me. I pray so hard for this dream to become true. "If nothing else, know Elana that it can happen.

In the past there were two times that I took my temperature and it didn't say thirty-six, but 36.7 degrees Celsius. One rise in temperature was my son, the other my daughter.

People ask me, "What helped? What did it?" Was it the treatments? The herbs? The acupuncture? "Everything" I answer. It was everything and nothing. Each action was another drop of water needed to fill the cup. Without a single one of those drops the cup wouldn't be full.

I sing with my children a beautiful song of hope. A song that Jews have been singing for centuries, "I believe, I believe with perfect faith in the coming of Mashiach. And even though he may tarry, I still will wait for him each day to arrive. I believe!"

~ ~ ~

There was once a king of Aram who sent warriors to a certain location to ambush the Israelites. Elisha the Prophet warned the king of Israel not to pass by that place. The king avoided that area and was saved. This happened many times. The king of Aram was furious and wanted to know who the spy was, who was revealing all his military secrets to the king of Israel. His advisors explained that it wasn't a spy, but Elisha the Prophet who, through prophecy, knew what was going on. The king of Aram then wanted to capture Elisha. He found out Elisha's whereabouts and at night surrounded the town with a large brigade.

Elisha's attendant woke up the next morning shocked to discover that they were in grave danger. "Alas my master, what shall we do?" He asked in panic. Elisha told him, "Do not fear, for those on our side are more numerous than they are" (Kings II 6:16). G-d opened up the attendant's eyes and he saw the brigade of Aram surrounded by an army of angels standing on the hills with chariots and horses capable of destroying the enemy. Aram attacked and Elisha prayed that they should be struck by blindness. They were, and he escaped.

A great rabbi, Rabbi Chaim Shmuelevitz, asks, "Why did G-d send the army of angels if in the end they didn't do anything and played no role in the miracle?" He answers that from here we learn a very important lesson. As long as Elisha's attendant was afraid, no miracle could take place. Faith was lacking. He couldn't imagine any way out and his fear paralyzed the forces of Divine deliverance.

The first thing that Elisha had to do was calm his attendant and show him the truth: G-d was protecting them! When G-d saw that the assistant trusted in Him and no longer feared Aram's warriors, He could then act on his behalf and save him.

"I believe, I believe with perfect faith in the coming of Mashiach. And even though he may tarry, I still will wait for him each day to arrive. I believe!"

~ ~ ~

I walk to the *Kotel* otherwise known as the Wailing or Western Wall. It is the only physical remnant that we have of one of the exterior walls of the Holy Temple. I see stones. There is no building, no glory. I close my eyes and visualize. I imagine the Holy Temple rebuilt, standing tall and majestic. I see an end to all suffering, a gathering of all Jews, and a time of peace and rejoicing. I light *Shabbat* candles, I visit the sick. I take care not to spread gossip or slander. I fill the cup with drops of water. I take my temperature… One day it will be 36.7 degrees Celsius again. I believe!

The Falling Dollar

I was standing in line in the mini-market when the woman in front of me started to argue with the cashier. "That can't be right. Please total up my items again," she argued. He added up the items again: a loaf of bread, a carton of milk, two containers of cottage cheese, and two ice popsicles. No, the amount was as he said. "But it can't be," she again protested as she took the money out of her wallet. "Money is like water, like water." I empathized as I looked at my own items and thought about the dwindling cash supply in my pocketbook.

For the first time, watching the gasoline prices soar, I am actually thankful that we can't afford to buy a car. I'm incredibly grateful that we have food to eat, clothing to wear, and a roof over our heads. Nothing is lacking as I carefully budget, trying to maximize every penny; but I still can't stop worrying and stop the anxiety from creeping into my heart, as salaries are reduced and the cost of living continues to rise. I hear people saying, "What will be, what will be?" Yes – what will be, I too ask myself, as the value of the dollar falls and our income falls along with it.

~ ~ ~

When Adam and Eve, the first Man and Woman, sinned by eating from the prohibited tree, they, along with the serpent who enticed Eve to sin, each received a punishment. G-d punished the serpent saying, "…dust shall you eat all the days of your life" (Genesis 3:14). To the Woman, G-d said,

"I will greatly increase your suffering and your pregnancy; in pain shall you bear children…" (ibid 3:16). And to the Man, "…through suffering shall you eat of it (the ground) all the days of your life…By the sweat of our brow shall you eat bread until you return to the ground…" (ibid 3:19). When you compare the punishment of Man to the punishment of the serpent, it appears that Man received a much harsher punishment. After all, dust is everywhere. The serpent is able to find its food wherever it goes and without any effort, while Man must work and toil and only receives his livelihood by the sweat of his brow. The commentators explain, however, that the serpent actually received the worst punishment of the three.

Ten years ago, my husband worked in the garment industry and things in his business were very difficult. He always paid his employees on Fridays. But one week, there simply was no money to pay his workers. He wrote a check to another merchant and asked him to give him cash for the value of the check which was post-dated for the following Monday. He paid his workers and then came home that Friday with a heavy heart. My husband told me how he turned to G-d in prayer, and said, "Help me." *Shabbat* arrived and my husband received it with the same love as he does every Friday evening. *Shabbat* ended, Sunday passed and Monday arrived, the day the merchant was supposed to cash the check. When my husband arrived at his office there was another check waiting for him from a client. The amount was exactly the same as the amount he needed to cover the check.

When G-d cursed the serpent, it was as though He was saying, "I'm providing you with food everywhere you go so that you will never have to call upon me, because I want nothing to do with you." By making the serpent's life so "easy," G-d was essentially distancing Himself from the serpent, and this is the worst possible curse that there is. Man and Woman, on the other hand, were punished with curses that would require their constant contact with – and direct dependency on – G-d. Their livelihood and their biggest blessing – children – would come only with pain and toil, but a pain and toil that connected them to G-d. Our livelihood and our biggest blessings give us the means to bring us closer and closer to our Creator. I remind myself of this as I see the falling dollar and I call out to G-d, "Help me."

Making Do with What You Have

*I*t was my turn to pay at the cash register in the supermarket. I handed them my debit card. Denied. I handed them my other debit card. Denied. "Will you take a check?" They wouldn't. (I didn't blame them; I wouldn't either want to take a check from someone whose two credit cards were rejected!) I counted how much cash I had with me – not enough to cover the bill.

The people in line were starting to get antsy, the cashier impatient. "Okay, no problem," I told myself. I looked in my cart and started to take things out. "We don't need the juice, or this…" I wanted to get down to what I really needed, get down to the essentials. I paid for what I could, and left the store. Part of me felt embarrassed, humiliated. The other part of me questioned, "What's so wrong with making do with what G-d gives you? If this is what we have, why do I feel deprived if I don't have more?"

~ ~ ~

When Jacob left his parents' home, escaping his brother Esau, he had a dream. There was a ladder. Angels were going up the ladder and angels were going down. G-d appeared to Jacob in the dream and told him, "…Behold, I am with you; and I will guard you wherever you go, and I will return you to this soil; for I will not forsake you until I will have done what I have spoken for you" (Genesis 28:15). When Jacob got up in the morning, he made a vow to G-d and asked Him to "give me bread to eat and clothes to wear."

Jacob had just woken up from a prophecy where G-d Himself had promised to always be with him. Really, he could have asked for anything. Why not ask for riches? Or, at least, for comfort, for a brand-new horse (or a car, in today's language), gold, silver? At least ask for a rib-eye steak! Instead, Jacob asked for bread to eat and clothes to wear. "G-d, give me what I need, not more than I need. Give me what You know is best for me and what will bring out the best in me." Later, we do see that G-d blessed Jacob with great wealth, many children and extreme honor. But Jacob never asked for any of it, and he knew that they were not for him or for the sole purpose of pleasure; they were tools that he was given in order to elevate himself spiritually and get closer to his Divine Source.

The other day I passed a store where there were shoes on a ridiculous sale, for only three dollars. Three-dollar shoes! Can you imagine? Pick your color; for thirty dollars you can have every color of shoe in the rainbow, and more. It was some sort of closeout sale, and people were buying them like crazy. I see this all the time. I, too, am guilty of it. You open up your closet, and you have clothes that you either forgot about or that you have never even worn! The phone, or computer gadget, that was $200 is now on sale for $25! Buy it! Do you need it? Of course not, but you'll convince yourself that you do, because it is such a bargain. People go into debt by buying "bargains." For what? To have your shoes perfectly match your new skirt, which of course has to perfectly match your shirt. There's no end to it, there's no joy to it, there's no elevation in it. If anything, it leaves you feeling empty and craving more.

~ ~ ~

In Gibeon, G-d appeared to Solomon in a dream of the night. G-d said to him, "Request what I should give to you" (Kings I 3:5).

Solomon asked for wisdom and understanding.

It was good in the eyes of the L-rd... "Because you have requested this thing, and you have not requested length of days, and have not requested riches, and have not requested the life of your enemies, but you have requested understanding, to comprehend justice – behold, I have acted in accordance with your words... Furthermore, even that which you have not requested I have granted you – even riches and honor – all your days, such as never has been to any man among the kings like you" (ibid. 3:10-13).

King Solomon is marked down in history, not for his great wealth but for his incredible wisdom. Wisdom and closeness to G-d he asked for, and this is what he got, as well as so much more. This is the same King Solomon who teaches us:

A lover of money will never be satisfied with money; a lover of abundance has no wheat. This, too, is futility. As goods increase, so do those who consume them; what advantage, then has the owner except what his eyes see? (Ecclesiastes 5:9-10).

Sadly, we are influenced by a society that eats not when it's hungry, but when it's bored, and we give cookies and candies to our children just to keep them quiet. We are distracted by access, and it's disheartening, because we are so much more than that. Rabbi Schneur Zalman said, "That which is forbidden is of course, prohibited. But much of what is permissible is unnecessary." It's not that we are supposed to deprive ourselves, or that doing so is the only means to grow and feel good about ourselves. Quite the contrary. In Jewish law we see that, for example, on the holidays one is supposed to have meat and wine, and give candies to their children; in preparation for the holiday, a husband should buy his wife new clothes and jewelry. But this is for a specific purpose. These are supposed to be means of getting closer to G-d. However, by indulging in the unnecessary, too often we get distracted from our goal, not closer to it.

~ ~ ~

I'm about to go to the supermarket now. I sit down with a paper and pen. I make a list of the items that we really need and that we can afford. I do this because I know that it's too easy to go there and get off track.

"G-d, please just give me bread to eat and clothes to wear. Grant me wisdom and understanding, and let me always be happy with my lot."

husband told me to come; he had to tell me something. I had just returned from a run and had gone straight to the kitchen to check on my rising *challah* dough. It looked good. I gave it a punch. "One second, my hands are sticky." He called again, "Come." I went. He looked pale as he held our baby. My son was trailing behind me. He glanced at my son and in the calmest voice he could muster, uttered two words in Spanish that knocked me to the ground: "*Secuestro* David" (They kidnapped David). David? Our David? Yes. Thus began our nightmare which, for David, my husband's brother, had already begun nearly two days before.

In Central and South America kidnapping is big business. Sometimes those who are kidnapped come back unharmed, sometimes they don't. Sometimes a ransom is paid and the person who was kidnapped is let free, and sometimes a ransom is paid and all that is returned is a dead body. It's something that you might have heard about. It is definitely known, but as much as possible – it's not talked about. It's something that happens to "other" people, wealthy people, powerful people, but not something that we ever imagined would happen to us.

It was the day before *Yom Kippur*. David went to work. We even talked to him a few hours before it happened to wish him an easy fast. He left work for his daily Torah class at the synagogue. Upon leaving the synagogue, he was followed as he drove to his parent's home. He drives to his parents' home every night, to visit with them before returning home to his wife and four children. Maybe the fact that his daily routine never changes made him an easy target. We'll never know why or who did it, and it really doesn't matter. Before he could ring the doorbell he was approached by the kidnappers and as he tried to escape they hit him over the head. From that moment on David surrendered, that is physically. He also surrendered spiritually – making a deal with G-d, so to speak, "If this is what You want, I accept it, but don't leave me." And He didn't. David tells us that there was never a moment in the twenty-five days of captivity, blindfolded and trapped, when he didn't feel the presence of G-d with him.

The most important thing for David was not to lose his spiritual freedom. They offered him food, and he told them that he would only eat raw fruit so that he would not violate any of the Jewish dietary laws. They complied. He asked them to tell him when it was 7 AM, 3 PM, and 7 PM so that he would be able to pray the morning, afternoon, and evening prayers. They complied. David was thus able to keep track of the day. He knew when it was *Yom Kippur*, and he fasted. He marked in his head when it was the Sabbath and the festival of *Sukkot*. He tried to do any commandment that he could and this kept him from losing his sanity, and from losing hope.

They mocked him and threatened him, and yet he felt protected.

In the meantime, we prayed and we prayed. My husband and I were so far from our family. We felt helpless. I walked all over my Jerusalem neighborhood putting up signs in apartment buildings and synagogues. I sent e-mails to friends and within hours thousands of Jews from all over the world were praying for the safe and speedy return of my brother-in-law. We gave to charity. In the city of the kidnapping the entire Jewish community was praying for David. Friends, family and mostly strangers offered to help us physically, and spiritually. My husband's parents, brothers, nieces, nephews, and sister-in-law were in constant agony, but every day when I spoke with my mother-in-law I was in awe of her strength. Where did it come from? Her faith. She would tell me, "G-d is with him. David was chosen because he is strong. If he was given this test, it's because he can pass it."

Nearly three weeks had passed and David was still gone. We decided that my husband had to go to be with his family. He left on a Sunday night and the Friday before I made *challah*, along with a group of forty women who made *challah* for David's merit. I put aside a *challah* and told my husband that this one he would take with him on his journey and he would eat it with David. When my husband left to go to the airport I forgot to pack the *challah* in his suitcase. The following Sabbath, the first one that my children experienced without their father, we ate the *challah*. On that Sabbath David was released.

~ ~ ~

In darkness David sat for twenty-five days, as Jews around the world prayed for his safety and return. David tells us that amongst the darkness he felt light. He felt G-d's presence hovering over him, protecting him, and he commented to me that he could actually *feel* the prayers of those praying for his safety. Each observance that people took upon themselves to fulfill on his behalf, whether it be lighting *Shabbat* candles, praying in a synagogue, saying the *Shema*, etc. created sparks of light and protection that reached him.

The twenty fifth word in the Torah is *or* (light) and for twenty-five days David never lacked holy light.

Upon seeing a flower for the first time after so many days without color, David was in awe. He realized how before he would take something like a flower for granted. Now, David sees the colors in everything. When I spoke with him the Saturday night that he was released he kept telling me, "You take care of yourself and the children. Please, hug the children for me." He kept repeating to me to hug the children. Something that we take for granted because it is a daily occurrence, David knows to appreciate. "Don't hold back," he tells me, "show them you love them."

Survivorship

I am a survivor, and if you are Jewish then you are a survivor, too. It took me a while to grasp this. I've never thought of myself as a survivor. My *Bubby* and *Zeidy* (grandmother and grandfather) – now they were survivors: survivors of the Holocaust, survivors of hunger and terror, survivors of life. But me and you, you might ask, what have we survived?

My Bubby and Zeidy were small people. My Bubby didn't even come close to reaching five feet and I don't think that my Zeidy was much taller. But they were giants of greatness and strength. I knew very little about their past. I was told bits and pieces of their stories. I knew that my little Bubby had escaped from death's door and had been a Partisan fighter in the forest. I had heard a story of how all 4' 10" of her had carried her brother on her shoulders, because his feet had frostbite and he couldn't walk. I knew my Zeidy hailed from a very large family, and only he survived. He was shot, starved and tortured – and yet he managed to escape and hide in the forest. The rest was a mystery. Most of what happened will always be a mystery.

The other day I received a treasure. It was an interview that my Zeidy gave in the early fifties. In it, he and another survivor recounted what happened to the people in their village and the final days before my Zeidy was able to escape into the forest. I found out that Zeidy was one of four leaders in a resistance against the Nazi murders. My little Zeidy fought with his bare hands against the enemy's guns, and he lived to tell about it. When I read the interview I shook with emotion. I talked with my mother who cried to me, "I never knew. He never told me about this. I never knew that he was a hero."

Now, there's more to the story. Not the story of their escape or the story of how they saved lives – the story of what they did afterwards. My mother's childhood home was never empty. Zeidy would pick strangers up off the street and take them home with him. Whatever he had, he gave. Bubby would cook and serve food to the strangers that Zeidy brought home: the despondent, the destitute, the poor and the hungry. She would take a cup of flour and turn it into a delicious cake, take a chicken and feed twenty. After being robbed of everything – their family, their homes, their possessions and their health – the only things they wouldn't let anyone steal from them were their desire to live and their desire to give. Zeidy had big blue eyes that always sparkled with a love of life and with laughter. Bubby's hands were never idle; they were always nourishing and healing.

When I read the details of my Zeidy's resistance and a small accounting of his life under torture, I shook with emotion because I realized the greatness of my existence and the miracle of my being alive today. Exiles, the Crusades, the Inquisition, pogroms, the Holocaust, suicide bombers; for thousands of years people have been trying to wipe out the Jewish people – and they can't. G-d won't let them. The blood of survival runs through my veins and the veins of every Jew on the planet. I'm alive, I'm Jewish and I'm a survivor.

After reading the article I ran to my three year old son and told him, "Avraham Nissim, you're a Jew and you must always be proud to be a Jew. You are a survivor and G-d loves you."

All of our holidays, our commandments and our customs are to remind us of this. We are Jews, we are survivors and G-d loves us. I look at my son who now, at the age of three, has lovely *peiot* (side-locks), wears *tzitzit* and, like the prince of the King, wears a *kippah* on his head. Without a doubt he and my daughter are my Bubby and Zeidy's greatest revenge against Hitler. I know that their lofty souls are looking down upon me, their granddaughter, as I live my life in their example, proud to be a Jew.

The Courage to Try Again

I'm tired, really tired – emotionally, physically. I just want to curl up into a ball and go to sleep, and sleep and sleep. In the mornings, when I want to stay in bed, somebody forces me up. "Mommy, Mommy…" It's a new day. I have no choice. I have to get up.

My body is filled with a torrent of hormones, a tornado of emotions. The words go around and around in my head: "The pregnancy isn't right. The fetus didn't develop." Three ultrasounds in two weeks confirm what I don't want to know, but have no choice but to accept.

"First trimester miscarriage is very common." "It doesn't have any implication about future pregnancies." "Thank G-d you have three healthy children at home, right? You'll have more, don't worry." The doctor's kind words replay themselves over and over in my ears, but they don't stop the tears.

I think about my clients. I saw three women just today who had all suffered through a miscarriage at one time. Is this happening to me so that I can better understand them? My husband says not to work today, to stay in bed. But I make myself get up and go. I pray for strength and force myself, because I know that my massaging fingers and hands, my comforting words and empathetic ear, help strengthen me and my faith as much, or more than, it does for them.

One tells me that she is afraid to become pregnant again for fear of miscarrying. "It's safer, less painful not to try than to try and lose it again," she tells me.

I look into her big, beautiful eyes, and as my body bleeds and cramps, I do understand. Suddenly, a name pops into my mind: Rabbi Akiva.

Who was Rabbi Akiva? Akiva, the son of Joseph, was a simple man, an unlearned, illiterate shepherd. He met a woman, Rachel, who believed in him. Rachel was the beautiful, smart daughter of the wealthiest man in the land. She saw great potential in simple Akiva and married him. Her father disowned her, leaving her and Akiva poverty-stricken. She didn't give up or lose her faith. She encouraged forty-year-old Akiva to study and sent him off to learn for a total of twenty-four years.

Akiva came back to his wife twenty-four years later, accompanied by 24,000 students. He had become the greatest scholar of all times, the greatest teacher and transmitter of Torah. He had become the famous Rabbi Akiva. And then what happened to him? In a plague that lasted over a month, all 24,000 students died. In a month's time, he lost it all.

What did Rabbi Akiva do then? Did he think, "It's over. There's nothing left. This is too painful. I will give up because the thought of losing any more students is more painful than the thought of not having any all." Maybe he had those thoughts. I don't know. But if he did, I wouldn't blame him. However, what do we know about what Rabbi Akiva did?

He took five men and he started all over again. From those five students, we have all the Oral Torah that exists – all the Mishnah, Talmud and Kabbalistic works. They all stem from Rabbi Akiva and his five students.

Why does Rabbi Akiva pop into my head as I look into my client's pained eyes? Because Rabbi Akiva left a legacy for every Jew: There is no such thing as staying under the covers. When you are confronted with a test, when you feel like you've been knocked down, you must believe. You have no choice but to pick yourself up and start again. Everyone has the potential for greatness. Everyone, with G-d's help, has the ability to start over again. I know that I can't be afraid to become pregnant again for fear of being disappointed or of losing the pregnancy; instead, I have to focus on the joy and the greatness of the child that will be born, G-d willing.

Motherhood

Laughter & Tears

It was one of those moments when I didn't know if I should laugh or cry. By three o'clock in the morning all my children had migrated to my room, so I went to their room to get some sleep. As I tucked myself into their bunk bed, I wanted to laugh at the situation and cry from exhaustion. Laughter and tears – this is motherhood.

I waited four and a half years for my eldest to come into the world. Before he came, I cried – a lot. When I found out that I was pregnant, I cried and I laughed. When he was born, I cried some more.

In those first few months, he woke up every forty-five minutes. I held him on those sleepless nights, remembering the sleepless nights that I spent wondering if I would ever have children. I held him and kissed him and reminded myself of this over and over, so that the tears of frustration would be tears of joy. Laughter and tears – this is motherhood.

~ ~ ~

"G-d said to Abraham, 'As for Sarai, your wife…I will bless her, and I will also give you a son through her…' *Abraham fell upon his face and laughed…* 'Indeed your wife, Sarah, will bear you a son, and you shall call his name Yitzchak'" (Genesis 17:15-19). *Yitzchak* literally means "he will laugh."

The commentators explain that when G-d told Abraham that Sarah would bear him a son, he laughed as an expression of joy. Later on, the Torah tells us of how three angels disguised as men came to inform Abraham again about the birth of Isaac. Sarah listened to the conversation from her tent, and when she heard their prediction that she would bear a son, she too laughed. But this was the laughter of disbelief. Sarah was an eighty-nine-year-old woman, and her husband a ninety-nine-year-old man. How could they have a child? Who wouldn't laugh? But this laughter was just as prophetic as the angels' words, because a year later, "G-d had remembered Sarah, as He had said; and G-d did for Sarah as He had spoken. Sarah conceived and bore a son unto Abraham...Abraham called the name of his son who was born to him – whom Sarah had borne him – Isaac...Sarah said, 'G-d has made laughter for me...'" (Genesis 21:1-6).

Now Sarah experienced the laughter of joy, the laughter of motherhood. Laughter and tears – this is motherhood.

~ ~ ~

Lying there at three o'clock in the morning in my children's bed, it finally dawned on me why G-d gave the first child born to a Jewish mother the name Isaac, "he will laugh." As we cuddle and kiss, feed and bathe, dress and educate, G-d wants us to always keep in mind the importance of our task and the importance of raising our children with joy. Each time Sarah called her son by his name, she was reminded of how Abraham laughed in faith and joy.

We all know it: being a parent is hard work. It's challenging and demanding. It's physically and emotionally exhausting. It's a huge responsibility. And you know what, with all that – it's so, so rewarding. There's nothing like it in the world. It's blessing and abundance. It's companionship and continuation. It's laughter and tears. And we can choose to laugh and cry, not in hardship or disbelief, but in faith and joy.

Recognizing All That I Do

It's been a few years now, and I had forgotten what it is like, the zombie state when you don't sleep, neither during the night nor in the day. I'm the type of person who can never sleep on an airplane or in the car. I need complete darkness, and for my pillow and the mattress to be "just so." Now I find myself dozing off in any position, my neck contorted, my shoulders hunched. I'm so physically exhausted that I can now sleep at any time. This is the mark of a mother with a newborn baby.

It's eight o'clock in the morning. My husband leaves to take the kids to school. I am sitting on the couch nursing our three-week-old baby. Four hours later he returns and finds me in the same spot, doing the same thing. I have barely moved; I have not accomplished anything that I planned to do. I tell him, frustrated, on the verge of tears, "I didn't do anything this morning!"

"Elana," he tells me. "You're doing exactly what you need to be doing. You're doing Mommy."

How did he know that this was just what I needed to hear? "I'm doing exactly what I need to be doing."

The transition from working outside the home to being at home with a baby, and from a neat and organized home to a messy but functioning one, is enough to get any modern-day "superwoman" down; it's enough to get even a not-so-superwoman like me down. No one (except for my husband) knows what I do all night. There is no public praising for the number of diapers I changed today. The job of a stay-at-home mommy certainly is not going to get me a raise, but I repeat to myself the words of my husband, "You're doing exactly what you need to be doing."

When I have a moment, when the baby is calmly sleeping, I rush to get a load of laundry in, or cook a hot meal. Nursing time becomes reading time with my older children, as I try to balance my time and attention between everyone. I'm tempted to complain as a friend asks me, "How are you doing?" Then I take a moment and think about all that I *am* doing, not what I am *not* doing, and you know what – tired and all, thank G-d, I am doing great.

~ ~ ~

When the Jewish people arrived at Mount Sinai to receive the Torah with all of its commandments, laws and ordinances, G-d said to Moses, "So shall you say to the House of Jacob, and relate to the Children of Israel" (Exodus 19:3). The commentators explain that "the House of Jacob" refers to the Jewish women, and "the Children of Israel" refers to the men. If you notice, G-d told Moses first to speak to the women and then to the men. The Jewish mother has such an important role and high status in education and in the transmittal of our laws and traditions to our children, that G-d put her, and all Jewish women, before the men. Very often, the child spends the majority of his early years with his mother, and she has the most influence upon his development. There is no greater validation, no greater compliment or praise than that – from G-d!

It's funny, because nowadays, really anyone can do anything. Thank G-d, there is formula, wonderful daycare – whatever you need and whenever you need it. The irony is that anyone could do my job. They could stay with, feed, and take care of my baby. But why would I want to give up such an important position? Why would I let someone else receive my reward?

The day before I gave birth, I went to pray at the tomb of the Matriarch Rachel. There is a famous prophecy in which Rachel is crying for her children (Jeremiah 31:14), and the *Midrash* expands on this: When the Jews were exiled to Babylonia after the destruction of the first Temple, Moses and the Patriarchs prayed to G-d to have mercy on the people. At last, Rachel came crying and G-d told her to wipe away her tears and not to worry, for in her merit, the nation of Israel would return to Israel.

As I stood praying to G-d that I should have an easy delivery, a healthy baby and a speedy recovery, I paused for a moment and whispered by Rachel's tomb, "*Mammaleh*, cry, please don't stop crying! Cry for us and pray for us, as only a mother for her children can." I prayed for all the women I know who are waiting and longing to hold a newborn in their arms, and to know what it is to be completely and totally exhausted from a sleepless night with an infant. I pray now that G-d should give me the strength to take care of my family, to educate my children to be upright, and to help me remember that for now I am doing exactly what I need to be doing – and that's great.

My Firstborn

Sometimes I forget how old he is. I know I put more weight on his shoulders than the other ones. He definitely has more responsibilities, and I expect more from him. For seven hours of my day he's the closest one in age to me, and when compared to his younger sister and baby brother, the six-and-a-half years seem so big. After all, he's really the only one with an understandable vocabulary.

I talk to him, he talks to me. I ask his advice and consult with him. He's always the first I turn to when I need help. He's my right-hand man, my companion, my eldest. I love all my children, and each one has his or her special place in my heart, but my eldest, my firstborn, there's no doubt that he has a special status. He's the one who anointed me with the crown of motherhood and gave me the exalted status of Mommy.

I'm sure – partly because he's the first, and partly due to his personality (at least in our home) – that my son is a leader. What he says, the others say; what he does, the others do. He's the example. Yes, I expect more of him than the others, there's no doubt he has more responsibilities, but I don't take it for granted.

With the responsibilities and the extra tasks come more privileges. He gets to stay up later. At the *Shabbat* table, when the others have gone to sleep, he stays and talks with his mother and father. He's the only one who can chew gum or go to the mini-market. He gets to pour his own glass of water, because we trust him and know that he can do it without it spilling and without breaking the glass. And the very chores that I give him bring him closer to me, make him that much more endearing to me and elevated in my eyes.

When I take him over to a friend and his little sister tags along, I look to him to watch out for her. He does. The friend's mother tells me, "You can tell that he's the firstborn. You should have seen how he made sure that his sister was okay, even attending to her by bringing her water!" I smile and nod my head. Yes, he fits the role, the role of the firstborn.

But can you imagine if I didn't give him more privileges? If all he had were more chores and responsibilities, and didn't get any of the perks? I doubt very much whether he would have taken care of his sister with the same affection or attention. In fact, I don't think he would enjoy being the eldest at all.

~ ~ ~

In the Torah, we see that when it speaks about inheritance, the firstborn receives a double portion (Deuteronomy 21:17), regardless of how the parent feels towards him. What does this teach us? A parent can't expect more unless we give more. The oldest, who looks so big in your eyes – he has to want to be big, otherwise it would be better to remain a baby. Getting older has to be fun. The added weight on the shoulders has to be balanced, so that the weight won't topple the person and make him fall. Remember, with his example the others will follow suit. Meaning that, as each child receives more responsibilities, they too should receive more privileges.

"Why does he get a new big backpack and I don't?" the younger one complained when the school year started and my eldest entered first grade.

"Because he's going into first grade and needs one, and you don't. When you start first grade, you'll also get one!"

My answer quieted her and made her more excited than if I were to buy her a new backpack. Why? Because it gave her something to look forward to; it gave her a reason to also want to enter first grade.

My firstborn, he's my right-hand man, the leader. And yes, he lives up to and loves his role.

Mother's Milk, Mother's Faith

"*Because* You drew me forth from the womb, and made me secure on my mother's breast" (Psalms 22:10).

~ ~ ~

It took me a couple of weeks to realize that I could put away my nursing undergarments. It's been two years. Two years of holding my son close to my heart and feeding him from the milk that flowed forth from my body. Two years of sleepless nights and exhausted days. Two years of gazing down at my beautiful baby and delighting in the smile he flashed up at me. Two years of being needed and feeling needed.

My mother nursed me until I was two and a half. I don't remember what it was like breastfeeding. I don't think my son will remember either. But I do hope he feels the same connection that I feel with my mother. No one can take away the closeness and the bond from nine months of sharing a body followed by two years of spending time together physically connected as well. These are experiences that simply cannot be replaced or imitated.

In the beginning it was difficult, and it hurt. I also felt so afraid to step outside of my home. I worried about the logistics and where I would nurse my son and how. I had always assumed that breastfeeding would be a piece of cake. After all, nursing is so natural. But like everything in life, learning how to nurse takes time and patience, and so too a baby doesn't learn to walk in a day and a toddler doesn't learn to talk in an hour. My mother told me, "Give it six weeks.

You'll soon be a pro." She was right. It took me at least a month and three visits with a lactation consultant until I finally started to get the hang of it.

Why did I decide to nurse my son? I had read all the facts. The U.S. Surgeon General recommends that babies be fed solely with breast milk for the first six months of life and say that it is better to breastfeed for six months and ideal to nurse for a year, or for as long as the mother and baby want. A miracle of miracles, mother's milk has just the right proportions of fat, sugar, water, and protein needed for a baby's growth and development. It also contains antibodies that help infants fight against disease, infection, viruses, and protects against bacteria. Breast milk is also easier to digest than formula for the majority of babies and when suckled straight from the breast is always sterile. In addition, studies have shown that touch and physical contact is essential to newborns and enables them feel more secure, warm and at ease.

While not easy in the beginning, after a month or so, the benefits for mothers who nurse are evident as well. Breastfeeding saves times and money. No measuring, mixing, washing bottles or buying formula. Nursing burns up calories, making it easier to shed the pounds put on from pregnancy. It also helps the uterus return to its original size quicker and alleviates any bleeding a woman may have after giving birth. Breastfeeding may also lower the risk of breast and ovarian cancers, and possibly the risk of hip fractures and osteoporosis after menopause. Sounds pretty convincing. But there is something more, something different that I realized after breastfeeding my son. Nursing your child infuses him with faith and security.

Originally my husband and I had talked about nursing my son for only a year. A year seemed like a good time and we had another motive for not wanting to nurse any longer. Before having my son, I had a problem with ovulation and conception. As I nursed, my menses still did not return and the anxiety of not knowing whether my lack of ovulation was due to my initial infertility or due to breastfeeding was very great. It took us nearly four years to conceive my son and we feared another long wait. We therefore wanted to start trying to conceive as soon as possible.

As the year approached its end, I struggled with mixed emotions. I didn't want to stop nursing. I loved the feeling it created between my child and myself and he certainly wasn't showing any signs of wanting to stop either. We know from the *Midrash* that Sara weaned Isaac at two. In the end we decided that since both my baby and I wanted to continue, we would. After all, there was no guarantee that I would become pregnant if I did stop or that I couldn't become pregnant while nursing. What we did have was a healthy, vibrant son, and the best thing for him would be to keep nursing. We realized that we needed to believe that the same G-d who granted us the gift of one child could easily grant us the gift of another.

I was explaining our situation to another mother who I met in the park. She remarked, "Wow, you have such faith, to continue nursing." Her words repeated themselves over and over in my heart. I never thought of nursing my son an act of faith.

> I swear that I stilled and silenced my soul, like a suckling child ("*gamul*" in Hebrew) at his mother's side, like the suckling child is my soul. Let Israel hope to G-d, from this time forth and forever (Psalms 131: 2-3).

The *Midrash* and commentators on this verse explain that just as the suckling child is totally and completely dependent on his mother, so too is man dependent on G-d. I marvel at breast milk and the fact that its composition changes as the baby grows to perfectly fit the child's needs. Other commentaries concur with the translation of the Hebrew word *gamul* as a suckling child, but adds that this word in Hebrew is cognate with the word *gomel*, to perform kindness, for the mother does a great kindness to the child by supplying it with her milk.

Nursing my son taught me that everything that's supposed to come, will come, but its arrival only fulfills one's needs when it comes at the right time. The mother supplies her child with the perfect nutrition. Does that mean that G-d will supply me with what I need as well? It's hard to acknowledge that things are not in your control and that as much as you want to control them, you can't. Can I allow myself to be like a suckling child who feels the security of knowing that everything needed will be provided for him?

Maybe it's this initial act of kindness that ignites the close bond between mother and child – that unconditional love that you give to your child in the beginning when all they can do is take and all you do is give. But what about if you can't nurse or when you stop nursing? Will the connection be there, will it continue? Can I feel security in G-d even when I don't see Him giving me what I think I need?

The commentator Radak writes that the word used here is referring to a child who has already been weaned, as the Torah uses this word in several other places. A weaned child is somewhat independent and yet still hovers close to its mother for security, comfort, and love. More than nursing, I see the love that I infused in my son is what continues to draw him near. We still cuddle and we still snuggle. I shower him with kisses and hugs and stroke his face and hair. I nurse him with my faith and my love.

We've entered a new phase in our relationship and I'm so happy that I had the opportunity to nurse him for two years. It was hard to let go, but I'm also happy that he's weaned, as this act of letting go draws us near. I also realized that I didn't wean him – I never will. With all my capacity to love and give I will never stop infusing in him that love, faith and security. I also realized that G-d won't ever wean me either. He just lets me go to grow on my own.

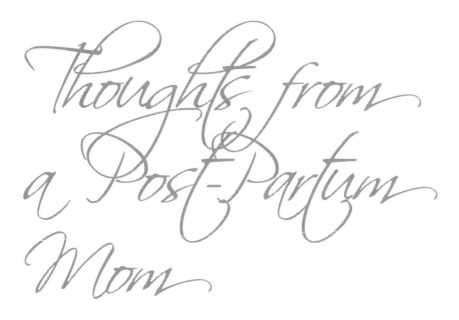

Thoughts from a Post-Partum Mom

I come from a small family and grew up in a world that wasn't made for children, but was surrounded by adults. I always wanted a big family and envisioned myself having many children. I looked with envy at big families, at their noise, their family gatherings, their many siblings playing together. I was even jealous when I saw them arguing. As the first few years of my marriage passed and I didn't conceive, my dream began to diminish. I still held on to it, but it no longer seemed like it was going to become a reality.

Then my son was born and filled our home with a radiating light and laughter that we hadn't experienced before. My husband and I are quiet people, and suddenly there was the glorious noise I had waited so long to hear – crying, laughing, things breaking.

My son became the center of our lives. Taking care of him was so much work and yet it brought me so much pleasure. As he approached his second birthday and the thought of not having more children became too unbearable to imagine, I miraculously conceived again. The pregnancy flew by; I don't even remember it, and I found myself in labor. Frida Tamar, my daughter, was born. Another blessing, another miracle.

Why then did I find myself crying every night after I came home from the hospital? Every day I prayed for children. Now G-d had given me another child, and I felt torn. I didn't quite understand what was going on. I could blame part of it on fatigue and being overwhelmed by the responsibilities of taking care of our home and attending to the physical needs of two children. And part I could blame on hormones which seem to plunge so many women into post-partum depression.

But there was another part that left me confused. I cried over my son. I cried over the fact that I could no longer give him the same attention as I had before. I cried over what this would mean for our relationship and over the fact that he was no longer my baby. Of course, at two-and-a-half years old, he's still got some time before he gets married, but suddenly he seemed so big and grown up to me. I also cried because I would be unable to give to my daughter in the same way as I had given to my son. And I asked myself what so many mothers ask: "How could I possibly love another child as much as I love my firstborn?"

Part of this is fatigue, part of this is hormonal, and part of this is a real feeling of loss in the midst of feeling bountiful.

I spoke with women who have many children and they not only empathized but also pointed something out. I could no longer give my son the same attention as before and my daughter might not receive the same attention as my son had, but they were each gaining and being enriched by the love of a sibling. They also reminded me that things do settle down. The fatigue will pass and the hormones will stabilize and I will be able to find time to give both children the attention that they need. When my son is in preschool, I cuddle with my daughter, and when my daughter is sleeping, I play with my son. There are moments when we all snuggle together, and this is the best of all, because I see how I'm fostering a lifetime of sibling love and friendship.

My son, Avraham Nissim, proudly shows his baby sister to his classmates in preschool. At last, he's no longer the only one without a sibling. He helps me change her diaper and is learning valuable lessons on how to share and how to love. One might have thought that after more than four years of being together with my husband without children, the presence of my son would have put a strain on my marital relationship; but if anything, it only made us love each other more. I suddenly saw qualities in my husband that I had never seen before. His patience, generosity and gentleness when dealing with Avraham Nissim made him even more endearing to me. So, too, when I watch Avraham Nissim conquer a natural tendency toward jealousy and treat the baby with tenderness and affection, it makes me love him, and her, even more.

Within the body of every Jew is a soul that burns like a candle. Each soul that is brought into the world sheds its particular light. Have you ever been in a dark room with a candle? The candle illuminates the room. Take some fire from this candle and use it to light another candle. Does the first candle's light diminish in any way? No. And the room? The room only gets brighter.

Each child whom we are blessed to have illuminates the world and brightens the lives of the others. I tell Avraham Nissim, "I love you because you are my only Avraham Nissim, and I have no other Avraham Nissim," and I tell my daughter, who is barely a month old and yet who has totally captured my heart, "I love you because you are my Frida Tamar, and I have no other Frida Tamar." I didn't know that it would be possible to love another child as much as my firstborn. But if anything, I learned that my love can expand exponentially, and that it is my unbelievable love for my daughter that resulted in me loving my son even more than before. I love him for him and her for her. Every soul is precious, and I feel myself lit up in different ways by each one's particular light.

Every Child Has His Own Song

I should be asleep right now. Everyone else is, but I can't fall asleep. I'm worried I'll miss a precious moment if I close my eyes. It feels like a dream. I stroke his head. I smell his sweet scent. I'm intoxicated as I stare in wonderment at the baby beside me.

I can't believe I was so worried. I hadn't been counting the days left of my pregnancy, or thinking about how many more weeks I had to go. Instead I counted how many weeks, and then how many months, had passed since I conceived. I told myself, "Thank G-d, you made it through the first trimester." Then came the second, and at last, the third. The baby stayed in, he kept growing, and he kept moving.

These were everyday miracles.

There was so much going on during this pregnancy. I worked and had two other children to take care of. We had to move – packing and unpacking. There was no time to sit and sing to this baby like there had been with my previous two pregnancies. There was no time to stand in front of the mirror and marvel at my changing body, at the bulging belly. There was no time for anything, except maybe to worry!

I called a mentor of mine in panic one day. "What am I going to do? I feel so bad for this baby. I have a boy. I have a girl. My boy is the oldest. He's amazing, the best in every way. My girl is our princess; she's amazing, the best in every way. He's our son, she's our daughter. How can this baby ever compare? What will its role be? And will my kids be terribly jealous?"

She calmed me down. "Elana, every child has its place. This baby will too. Stop worrying. Your kids will be fine. This isn't going to be just your baby. They're older; give them responsibilities – this will be their baby too. I'm telling you, the baby will carve out its own path and have its own special role in the world, and of course, in your family."

Her words comforted me, but I still found myself worrying. My husband and I could not agree on any name. How could we come up with something so perfect as we had for our son, Avraham Nissim, and our daughter, Frida Tamar?

As the due date came closer, I prayed and I prayed. *Purim* came and went, and *Pesach* neared. I cleaned and shopped. I kept telling the baby, "Please, just stay in until everything is ready." The first day of the month of Nissan (the month in which *Pesach* occurs) came, and with it the first of my contractions. Every day I felt the contractions come. I prepared my bag to take to the hospital. I told the baby, "I'm not ready. Stay in!" I kept cleaning.

Then the contractions came, and they wouldn't stop, and so I knew that I had no other choice. I submitted to them. This was the day. Whether I am ready or not, I told myself, I have to accept and be ready. I did the last of my food shopping. I started to cook for *Pesach*, giving my husband instructions on what to freeze and what to put in the refrigerator. I breathed, I swayed and I sang.

Of course nothing happened according to plan. No one answered their phones; we couldn't find any babysitters. The traffic was horrific, and there we were in the car: me, my husband and my children. "Stay in, baby. Please, let me make it to the hospital." For nine months I had no time to sing or enjoy. Now was the time. I sang and I sang. Nothing was going according to plan, but I wouldn't let that stop me from singing and from remembering that in the end, G-d willing, I would have my baby.

We arrived at the hospital, and two hours later, with my children in the waiting room, I gave birth to our son. I sang almost until the end, and then, exhausted and breathless, I couldn't sing anymore. But I didn't have to; the first cry of the baby as he emerged into the world was a beautiful song in itself.

After the baby was born I asked my husband, "What is today? Who brought the offerings for the Tabernacle today?" (For the first twelve days of the month of Nissan, a prince from each of the twelve tribes brought offerings and gifts for the Tabernacle in the desert.)

"It is the eleventh day of Nissan. The prince of the tribe of Asher brought them today."

My two days in the hospital, I kept kissing him and gazing at him. What would be his name? I remembered my singing. I remembered the prince of the tribe of Asher.

The Torah commentators explain that when the nation of Israel left Egypt and they walked through the split Red Sea, they walked in twelve rows. Each tribe had his own pathway. In the desert, each tribe had its own flag, and while they all traveled together as one nation, the people of each tribe stayed within their own tribal section. They were separate, yet united.

We know that when the time came to receive the Torah, the nation of Israel was like "one man with one heart." It was the only way we could receive the Torah: in unity. Everyone heard the same commandments and everyone received the Torah with the same will and desire. But what amazes me is that there was unity despite the differences. The majority of Israel had to stand behind a barrier. They were prohibited from coming too close to Mount Sinai. Aaron was closer. Joshua, Moses' student, was even closer, and Moses was permitted to actually go to the top of Mount Sinai to receive the Torah and the two tablets with the Ten Commandments. They were standing at different places, and each had a different role. Some were followers, some were leaders.

I thought about this as everyone asked me, "Who does the baby look like?"

"He looks like Avraham Nissim. He looks like Frida Tamar. I actually think he looks like himself…"

All of a sudden the name fell into place, and my husband and I agreed on the perfect name for this perfect baby: Asher Yisrael (Israel). Not only did we choose Asher because it corresponded to his birthday, but Asher comes from the Hebrew word *ashrei* (praiseworthy). My husband and I picked this name with the hope that this child will fulfill his special mission in life and bring praise to his Creator, to his parents, and to the entire nation of Israel. We also couldn't stop praising G-d for giving us this most precious gift. His first name represents his individual role, and his second name symbolizes how each and every individual is necessary for the whole.

The blessing that Moses gave the tribe of Asher before dying was, "Blessed with sons is Asher; he shall be pleasing to his brothers, and dip his foot in oil." My children are in awe of their baby brother. While his presence does invoke your normal amount of sibling jealousy, they are crazy about him and love him. "Oh Asher Yisrael," I whisper into his tiny ears, "may you grow to be a great man amongst your people, and may your siblings always watch over you and adore you."

Lastly, his name is similar to the word *ashir* (I will sing). We worry so much about everything, but if we can maintain our faith and trust in G-d, if we can just stay focused on the future goal, then we will truly be able to sing in the future. Those who sing praise now will merit to sing praise in the future.

The Juggler

In the middle of what already seemed like a very long day, I looked into my refrigerator and knew I had no choice – we had to go the supermarket. I piled my two children into the baby carriage and we made our way to the market in the sweltering heat. We arrived and started our shopping. As my son was demanding one treat or another, I tried to concentrate on the task at hand.

My one-and-a-half-year-old daughter had managed to escape the shopping cart as I examined tomatoes. I spotted her and whisked her up as she grabbed bags of dry goods. She held on for dear life to a bag of couscous and it ripped. "Oh no," I said to myself as I saw the couscous (in other words, my money) spill to the floor. At this moment my cell phone rang. I answered, trying to be pleasant. But as my daughter squirmed, trying to get free from my arms, and my son continued to talk about whatever it was that he wanted, I had a hard time stopping myself from barking, "I can't talk right now; I'll call you later." "How in the world am I going to do this?" I thought to myself.

~ ~ ~

I feel like a juggler, like the ones I remember from my youth on Fisherman's Wharf in San Francisco: the ones who would stand on a unicycle, their feet peddling fast as they threw three, four, or five sticks of fire into the air. They would catch one stick in the right hand, then two, one in the left, then two, and for the finale one in their mouths as their heads inclined upward.

Yes, I feel like a juggler as I rock one child and hold the other, as I work and take care of our home. And you want to hear the most ironic part of it all? Every day I pray that G-d should bless me with more children. No, I'm not crazy. Maybe you are going to ask me (and I certainly ask myself), "So where are you going to carry a third one – on your head?" Well, if I have to, yes.

~ ~ ~

You see, it all started many years ago when I was first married and a missed menstrual cycle did not equal a positive sign on the pregnancy test. Month after month, year after year the tests continued to show negative. Almost four years of "no" and then all of a sudden – "yes." Can you imagine the yes? I did three tests just to be sure because I could not believe it. During the nausea, the vomiting, and the swollen legs, all I could think of were those negative tests and the curse that was transformed into a beautiful blessing, confirmed by each symptom.

The challenges of pregnancy and labor are nothing compared to those of motherhood. But the broken vase on the floor is just that – a broken vase, and the spilled milk is easily cleaned up. Women who watch me ask me how I have such patience. Others have asked if I already have two, why bother to have more? The patience comes with perspective; when you wait and long for something, your appreciation of its arrival is greater. And why have more? Each child brings his own blessing. Now I couldn't imagine my life without the second child, just as I couldn't imagine my life without the first.

There is something incredible I noticed when I became a mother. Actually, it started even before my first was born, as he kicked and danced in my belly and I was no longer the master of my own body. There is a morning blessing that says, "G-d gives strength to the fatigued." The fatigued, the tired, the exhausted: this is without a doubt, in my opinion, the mother. G-d provides energy to the tired, meaning me. The heavy sleeper suddenly awakes at the slightest whimper; the one who can't function without eight hours of sleep is nursing, preparing lunches and helping with homework on only four.

The incredible thing that I discovered is that if G-d gives you something, He doesn't just give it to you, but He gives you all that you need take care of it. The Sages say that no one is given a test that he cannot withstand – whether it's a test that consists of not having what we want, or a test that consists of having what may seem to be more than we can handle.

The word in Hebrew for baby is *tinok*, which has the same letters as the word *tikkun* (correction). Every person that comes into the world has his special mission in life to fulfill, and every baby brings about a *tikkun*, a correction, for the world and specifically for its parents. The child who is bright or good-looking helps us work on our trait of pride or arrogance; the child who is slow or repetitive helps us work on our trait of patience. This child comes to teach you how to love, this one how to give. This one teaches you how to give in, and this one teaches you how to never give up.

When young brides come to me seeking advice they frequently ask me what I think about putting off having children. I admit to them – I'm not objective. Those four years of longing to have children, longing to when I couldn't, have changed me. They affected me so much that after eight-and-a-half years of marriage and thank G-d two children, I still can't get over the aching and anxiety of not being able to conceive or carry a child to term. Even if I have ten children, I'm not sure if the pain will go away. But I do try to put myself in their shoes and I remember how I felt when I was engaged and how frightening the idea of becoming a mother can be. I tell them with an empathetic and full heart: When it comes to blessing – and each child not only is a blessing, but brings blessing and plenty – never close yourself up or say no. Because whatever G-d gives us (or doesn't give us) is truly for our best and to bring out our best. I tell them to throw the juggles in the air and with their head inclined upward, G-d will give them the capacity to catch the sticks.

The Renaissance Mom

My husband and I were crossing the border from Mexico to the US when we were singled out by the border police. The officer looked at me and asked me what my occupation was. I lowered my eyes and sheepishly replied, "I'm a housewife." He noted the tinge of embarrassment in my voice and scolded me, "Madame, that's nothing to be ashamed about, you're not a housewife, you're a domestic engineer!"

My ten year high school graduation is coming up and I wonder what my peers would say about me – the honor roll student, straight-A, Varsity Captain cheerleader? If I could go – and I can't, if I would go – and I won't, what would I tell them when they ask me, "So what do you do? What's your occupation?"

Of course if they asked me, I would tell them the truth: I'm an actress, a dancer, and a singer. I'm a chef, a nutritionist, and a baker. I'm an accountant, a consultant, and a family doctor. I'm a therapist, a mediator, and a law-enforcer. I have a laundry business and I'm a garbage collector – I mean a sanitation engineer. I'm all of these things and more…I'm a renaissance woman. I'm the woman with many *tichels* (head-coverings). I'm a woman, a wife, and a mother.

Sixty years ago I guarantee you that if I were crossing the border, no one would've asked me "What do you do?" It was enough just to be a woman. But now I have to justify and validate who I am and what I do as a woman, a wife, and a mother. Sixty years ago women worked and today I also work, it's my reality and I have to. But even my working is done as a contribution to my home and family. It doesn't define who I am, or what I do; it's not the title that I choose to go by.

You might ask me, "Aren't you bored? What do you do all day? Why not send your kid away so that you'll be free to actually *do* something?" And I'll tell you, I've never been as physically or emotionally challenged as I am being a wife and a mother. Everyday I discover something new. I've never had to work so hard on being patient and creative. And to be free to actually do something...What more important thing could I do than what I'm doing? I manage a household, I hold down a fort, I'm raising and building the future.

~ ~ ~

My son looks up at me with his big eyes and giggles when I hold him in my arms. I play on the floor with him, dance with him, cook with him and clean with him. He goes where I go and if I can't bring him along, I simply don't go.

I had the honor, the luxury to be there when he took his first step, said his first word and blew his first kiss. He's our greatest investment for the future and I'm willing to invest – it's worth it, every sleepless night and exhausted hour. It's all worth it.

When I was pregnant I walked with my head held high, reminding myself that I was carrying a *Yiddishe neshama* (Jewish soul), and that this baby was the *mashiach* or the one to bring the *mashiach*.

Oh I remember holding him in my arms when he was a newborn. That sweet, precious smell of innocent beauty. Every two hours he awoke and I got up to breastfeed him. I would look at him and tell him, "I love you. You're going to be a great *tzaddik* (righteous person)." It was my way of dealing with the lack of sleep. We so easily lose sight.

Don't you see that the stage passed and as your children grow bigger and bigger you realize, "What happened, where did it go? How can I get the time and the moment back?" But you can't, so you have to tell yourself over and over, "It goes so fast. Enjoy it!"

I'm my husband's wife, the woman of the house, and I'm my son's mommy. No one can take that away from me...unless I let them. And I won't. So I prefer to cutback and live modestly. I prefer to work from home and not chase after a futile career or meaningless title.

I'm home when my husband arrives from *kollel* (Torah learning group) and I see him off when he leaves in the morning. I'm my son's world – for the time being, until he gets married! I'm a *bat melech* (daughter of the King), a Jewish woman. I encompass the essence of Sarah, Rivka, Rachel, and Leah. I cook and I clean, I iron, and I bake. I work and I read. I nurture and I love. I pray and I talk to Hashem. I sing and I sweep. I do all these things.

So if you want you can call me a domestic engineer, but I don't need the title. I'm a woman, a wife, and mother – they're titles that I'm proud of and that's enough.

I've been told that there are miracle babies who sleep twelve hours straight through the night, enabling their mothers to rest. My son certainly wasn't one of them and judging from the dark circles under the eyes of almost every mother I know, I'm doubtful those babies and toddlers really exist. (Or maybe *I* did something wrong, and two years later I'm continuing to do something wrong.)

When my son was younger, there was a time he would go to sleep without a fight, but that was before he learned how to jump out of his crib. If it's not one thing, it's another, and I still haven't found a real solution. I've had hours upon hours of discussions about this topic (my lack of sleep, how to get my child to sleep and stay asleep) with my husband and friends. I've read countless books and asked countless people for advice. Some suggestions have worked. But ideas that work for other mothers don't work for me. And what's worked for me never seems to work for them. I think I've tried almost everything.

Every night, my toddler refuses to sleep unless either I or my husband lay down with him. I wouldn't mind if it didn't involve laying there for over an hour as he tries to tickle, pinch, and attack me, and of course, escape from his room. Also, I can't help but admit my sense of anxiety over having to sit down to work which I can only do after he falls asleep. I pray that he should go to sleep for the night, but it seems that I am not readily answered.

Last night however, something changed. Not with him, but with me. As I lay there, I perked up my ears and began to listen. My son was having a monologue. It's a ritual he does before falling asleep. He goes through all his favorite words, "Belly, slide, friends, fun, elephant, let's go!, nose, one, two, three…" At last he came to the words that melted my heart, "Mommy, mommy, mommy, I wuv (love) you." And then my heart really began to race with emotion when he sang, "*Shemaaa Yisrael Hashem Elokeinu Hashem Echad* (Hear O Israel the L-rd is our G-d, the L-rd is One)."

For the first time I realized, "Elana, *this* is spending quality time with your child. Instead of seeing it as a struggle and dreadful event, see it as a precious moment and enjoy it." Moments are only fleeting seconds, and in twenty years I'm not going to remember or miss the work I had to do or the clothes I had to iron or the cake I had to bake. I'm going to remember *this* moment and wish I had it back.

The Torah places a huge emphasis on teaching children, and the important role mothers play in the education of their children. When G-d told Moses to give the Torah to the Jewish people (Exodus 19:3), He instructed Moses to do it in the following manner: "So shall you say to the house of Jacob and relate to the children of Israel." Our Sages tell us that the "House of Jacob" is the Jewish women, while the "Children of Israel" are the Jewish men (*Mechilta* 19:3, cited by the commentator Rashi). Why does G-d speak to the women first? Because, as our Sages tell us, the woman is the home, and the first opportunities for education and teaching of conduct are in the home.

After the Second World War, Rabbi Yosef Shlomo Kahaneman traveled throughout Europe searching for Jewish children that had been left for safekeeping in Catholic convents and orphanages. These children had lost their families in the Holocaust, and he was determined to find as many of them as possible and place them in Jewish homes. When he came upon one particular orphanage, the priest told him that he wouldn't find any Jews there, and if there were, he would need proof of their Jewish identity. Rabbi Kahaneman asked for permission to see the children. The priest allowed him to enter, knowing that the children would have no recollection of their Jewish roots after so many years of separation.

The rabbi walked into the sleeping quarters of the children and cried out, "*Shema Yisrael Hashem Elokeinu Hashem Echad!*" Suddenly, from throughout the room, some of the children began stirring and sitting up in their beds. Cries of *"Mameh"* (Mother) and *"Tatte"* (Father) could be heard as the children remembered the familiar prayer their parents instilled in them years before. One by one, he was able to pick out the Jewish children while the gentile children remained sleeping.

Imagine the mothers who sat with these children before going to sleep each night, teaching them those precious words that later enabled them to return to their brethren. This true story came to mind when my little impossible sleeper sang these words that have come forth from Jewish lips for thousands of years. It still doesn't change the fact that he won't go to sleep on his own, but at least it helped me see bedtime in a new light. Afterwards, I kissed and hugged him and blessed him to have many children who will give him many sleepless nights.

Teaching Children Not To Lie

It was early one *Shabbat* morning. My two oldest children wanted ed me to take them to the park, but the baby was sleeping. I looked at my oldest, my six-year-old, and instructed him, "You can take Frida Tamar (his younger sister) to the park for ten minutes and then come back." (The park is within eyesight of my kitchen window, and getting there doesn't involve crossing any streets. Also, in the neighborhood where I live, in terms of taking care of younger siblings, a six-year-old is like a sixteen-year-old!) I gave him my watch and they were off. About three minutes later they were back, arguing.

"Wow, that was quick. What happened?"

"He made me get off the swing."

"I pushed her on it until one hundred, and then she had to come off, just like you do, Mommy."

"But I do that only when other kids are waiting in line. Were there other kids waiting?" I said the last part a bit accusingly, and I realized that the moment I put the question out, there I was: provoking someone not to tell the truth. My daughter answered no, my son answered yes. I thought to myself, "Why did I just do that? Couldn't I have just left it by giving them the information needed, and by not setting a trap for them to lie?"

It's something that I am working on. I catch myself all the time. It's those little questions. Your child went to the bathroom: "Did you wash your hands?" You see them eating: "Did you say the blessing before eating that cookie?" One of your children comes crying: "Did you hit your sister?" "Did you give the teacher the note I sent with you?"

Let me ask you: when a person puts you on the spot, what is your instinct? Defend yourself, of course, whether you did it or not. Can we expect our children to behave any differently?

The Torah teaches us an alternative approach. Tamar, the widowed daughter-in-law of Judah, was being inaccurately accused of a crime. She had evidence to prove her innocence, but didn't directly confront Judah with it (which would prove not only her innocence, but his guilt). Instead, "she sent word to [Judah]: ...'Recognize, if you please, whose are this signet, this wrap and this staff [the evidence].' Judah recognized; and he said, 'She is right; it is from me...'" (Genesis 38:25-26). The commentators explain that Tamar reasoned, "If he will admit on his own, let him admit. And if not, let them burn [punish] me, but I will not embarrass him."

What was the result of this incident? It was decreed that the kings of Israel would come forth from the offspring of Judah and Tamar – from her, for her modesty and her way of handling the situation; and from him, for his full recognition of his mistake.

Telling the truth is a fundamental Torah principle. So how do we get our children to do it? The first step is by building trust. They need to trust us and we need to trust them, and show them that we do. The second step is to accustom them to telling them the truth, or at the very least, to not let lying become a habit. How? By not asking confrontational questions like, "Did you wash your hands?" Instead try, "Don't forget to wash your hands!" If they already did, they will most likely say, "I already did."

Your child comes home with an incredible story. Preschool and kindergarten children are not yet capable of distinguishing between a true and a fictional story. For them, fantasy is reality. He tells you that the teacher told him he has to bring ice pops tomorrow for his entire class. Try not to express disbelief: "Really? Are you sure? Is that true?" Instead say, "Wow, I would have loved it if my teacher told me that when I was in school." Later, simply call the teacher and find out if you really do need to send those ice pops or not. This way, if it's not true and he was only expressing what he wished the teacher had told him, you don't trap him by making him answer in a lie such as "Yes, she really said that."

It's those little things, those daily things, that make all the difference. You are careful with your own words. You fulfill your promises. You buy the ice cream when you say you will. You tell him, "I can't talk right now," instead of "Tell them I'm not home." Our children will learn from this. They'll realize that words are important, and become accustomed to telling the truth.

Parenting Advice from a Survivor

Sometimes I don't know who helps whom more, the "healer" or the one who comes for "healing."

Lily sat in front of me, her leg swollen, hot and red. I put my hands on it. All I did was touch it. Her reaction surprised me. She sighed, a good sigh, a tired sigh that one lets out when finally home after a long journey. "Why didn't I come to you sooner?" she asked. "It feels better already."

"But I didn't do anything yet."

"Of course you did: you are giving attention to it. Nobody does, and the little massage I can do to myself isn't enough."

As I worked to get the blood going and the energy and lymph flowing, Lily spoke. She spoke about the past. She spoke about the present. I was shocked to find out that the woman in front of me was a Holocaust survivor. Her mother bore her in the beginning of the war. She survived terror, hunger and disease. She survived the camps. By the time she was four, Lily had survived and lived more lives than a person of a hundred and twenty.

I massaged; Lily spoke. I listened; Lily taught. As Lily told me about her childhood, she taught me an important lesson. Lily was the eldest of three children. She was the tall one. She was the smart one. She was the strong one. She was the eldest. Lily kept repeating to me, over and over, "I always had to give in to the others. My mother told me, 'You are the tallest, the smartest, the strongest. You are the oldest. You must give in to them.'" That meant Lily never got to go first. She never had a toy of her own. She was never right when it came to a quarrel with one of her siblings. And even if she was, it didn't matter, because after all, she was the oldest, and the oldest has to give in to the younger ones. She was the oldest, and the oldest always has to know better.

Suddenly, in the midst of her storytelling, Lily became quiet. And then she told me: "You have three children. Don't make the oldest always give in to the younger ones. Don't think that the eight-year-old knows better than the five-year-old. He doesn't. Don't expect them to play together and be friends if you treat them differently. Because if you do, you will turn them into enemies instead of friends."

These were the words of Lily.

They were strong. They were straight. They were right.

How many times is the eldest playing with a ball when the toddler comes along and wants it? The eldest doesn't give it up – after all, he was playing with it. So the toddler starts to cry, and you say, "Can't you just give him the ball?" Wasn't it his ball? Why does he always have to give in to the toddler just because the toddler knows how to cry?

Or, you are in the park and everyone is hungry. You always give the middle one food first. Why? Because she's thinner than the rest; because she cries more than the rest. She always gets first. Do you really think it is possible to measure hunger? Why do the other ones always get served second just because she's thinner?

The examples from our lives go on and on. Lily is right.

We see this in our holy Torah:

> **This is Aaron and Moses**, to whom G-d said: "Take the children of Israel out of Egypt according to their legions." They are the ones who spoke to Pharaoh, king of Egypt, to take the children of Israel out of the land of Egypt; **they are Moses and Aaron** (Exodus 6:26–27).

On these verses, the famous commentator Rashi writes:

> **This is Aaron and Moses:** Who are mentioned above, whom Yocheved bore to Amram – [these two] are [the same] Aaron and Moses "to whom G-d said," etc. In some places [Scripture] places Aaron before Moses, and in other places it places Moses before Aaron, to tell us **that they were equal**.

> **They are Moses and Aaron:** They remained in their mission and in their righteousness from beginning to end.

Even though they were both great, Moses was without a doubt the leader of the nation of Israel. Aaron was older than Moses, but G-d chose Moses because He saw that Moses was the most qualified one to be the leader.

Moses' mission in life was to lead Israel. Aaron had a different mission, and even though Moses worried about offending his older brother's honor, Aaron wasn't jealous. The Torah relates that G-d told Moses that Aaron "will see you and rejoice in his heart."

I think that there was no jealousy and that they had such respect for each other because no one ever compared them with each other. Despite the fact that they had different missions and roles, they were given "equal significance." Sometimes Aaron went first, and sometimes Moses went first.

As a parent, it's so hard not to fall into patterns. You don't even realize it, but if you take a step back for a moment, you might see how you always give one child first, or you always give one child more than the others. It could be the one who cries loudest, and you just want to quiet him. It could be that you do it to the one with whom you most identify. Or it could be to the one you identify with the least, and you are trying to make up for it by overcompensating. Your intentions are good; you don't even notice that you do it, but you do.

~ ~ ~

By the end of our session, Lily said that her leg started to feel better. I attribute part of her pain to exhaustion. Lily's tired. She's tired of always having to be the strongest and tallest. She's tired of always having to give in. She's tired of standing on her own. I squeeze her toes and massage the leg one more time before thanking her for sharing her stories with me.

The next time the five-year-old is jumping rope and the two-year-old comes along and wants her rope, I stop myself from saying, "Can't you just give it to him for a little bit?" Instead I tell him, "She was playing with it first." I let him have a tantrum over it, and I pick him up, kiss him, and try to distract him with another toy. My five-year-old smiles at me with a look of gratitude.

Thank you, Lily, for your words of advice.

A Sweet Education

I sat in the park near the bottom of my apartment building, watching the scene unfold in front of me. A three-year-old boy, whose mother had just given birth, came to the park with his older twelve-year-old sister. The sister sat on a bench chatting with a friend, while her little brother went to sit by the bottom of the slide. I didn't catch what he was doing, but every time kids slid down the slide, he bopped them on the head as they came out. I watched child after child cry, and thought to myself, "What is going on?"

Another mother, who was more aware than I, then came and started to scream at the top of her lungs at the little culprit. She insulted him, rebuked him and yelled at him. He didn't flinch, or even bat an eyelid. The mother then walked over to the boy's sister and screamed at her, insulted her and rebuked her. The girl, shamefaced, walked over to the slide and tried to get her brother to move. He wouldn't budge. He held fast to his spot – hurt, not fully grasping the wrongdoing of his actions. She threw up her hands and walked away.

Another mother, who had been blowing bubbles with her children, walked over to the little boy and said, "Sweetness, come to the bench and see if you can catch the bubbles." She gave him a smile, patted his head and said, "What a sweet boy you are, I'm sure that you didn't realize you were hurting the other children. We don't hit. Here, now, come with us and catch the bubbles." He jumped up from the bottom of the slide in a second and walked over to her bubbles. I didn't see him hit or "bop" another child the rest of the day. In fact, he even played nicely.

I later went over to the mother with the bubbles, and complimented her technique. "Children," she told me, "will take medicine only if it's coated with honey first." It took me a minute, but I understood what she was getting at. However, I wanted to add, "It's not just children. We all do!"

~ ~ ~

We see in Jewish law how Judaism favors the right over the left (this is for right-handed people, while for left-handed people, they begin with their left as this is their "right" hand). For example, when you wash your hands before eating bread, you wash first the right, then the left. When you put on your shoes, first the right shoe is put on, then the left. The left shoelace is then tied, and then you return to tie the right. So you start with the right and end with the right.

The right, which is (for the majority of people) the dominant side, represents *chesed* (kindness); the left, the weaker side, represents *din* (strict judgment). The Torah, which was given to the Jewish people by G-d from a place of incredible love and out of *chesed*, teaches us that while strict judgment exists and is necessary, it's not the way G-d runs the world, nor is it the way we should always act in our lives. One must first approach each situation from the right side, the side of *chesed*, and then it can be approached with the left. We start with *chesed* and end with *chesed*.

In the text of the *Ethics of the Fathers*, the sages ask how one defines strength. They don't mention how many muscles you need to flex, or how many pounds you need to bench-press. The sages define strength by the ability to conquer one's *yetzer hara* (evil inclination), one's bad character traits. Strength can't be physically measured; instead, it is measured by control. Are you strong enough to be patient? Are you strong enough not to get angry? Are you strong enough to take a deep breath and think before you yell or say those damaging words that you can never take back? Are you strong enough to judge your fellow favorably? The one who is strong, the one who dominates, is the one who uses their right side, their side of *chesed*, first.

~ ~ ~

Every night, before I put my children to sleep, I say with them the *Shema*: "Hear O Israel, the L-rd is our G-d, the L-rd is One." I then recite with them the three paragraphs found in the Torah that follow the *Shema*, which begin:

> You shall love the L-rd your G-d with all your heart, with all your soul, and with all your might. And these words which I command you today shall be upon your heart. You shall teach them thoroughly to your children, and you shall speak of them when you sit in your house and when you walk on the road, when you lie down and when you rise....

One of my teachers once explained that as parents, we have an obligation to teach and to transmit. The question is: how do we know that our children will continue to do any of things that we teach them when they are no longer in our presence? How can we ensure that the values we instill in them will stay with them when they "sit in their own houses" or when they "go out onto the road?"

The following parable sums it all up:

There was once a boy who wanted to be king. At first he bullied and yelled. He instilled fear into the hearts of all those around him, and got everyone to do what he wanted. But the moment that the king went away, no one followed his orders or obeyed his rules. The boy, now king, realized that obtaining power through fear doesn't work in the long run. He decided to try a different way. He treated everyone with respect and kindness. He was sincere, giving, caring and kindhearted. They honored him and performed his will. Even away from his presence, they continued to follow his orders and obeyed his laws.

~ ~ ~

I understand the first mother in the park. If my child had been bopped on the head, or if I had understand what the little boy was doing, I too might have arisen and yelled at him. But, if you notice, all the yelling and screaming didn't help anything. The boy didn't stop. The only thing that stopped the boy was kindness and distraction. Of course, the boy needs to learn that what he is doing is wrong, that his actions required a punishment; but he wasn't going to accept the lesson from a place of disrespect and anger. It takes a lot of strength to overcome physical exhaustion, irritation, frustration. It takes a lot of strength not to yell or get upset, but everyone was endowed with the strength to do so. It's the dominant strength, the strength of one's right hand, and if you really want to get someone to learn or do something, it's the only way to do it so that it will make a lasting impression. After all, medicine goes down so much better when it's coated in honey.

Pulling Away to Draw Close

I'm not sure who suffers more, the parent or the child. After two full years of nursing, I'm weaning my daughter. This process of letting go is so difficult. She comes to me to nurse her, but I have begun to say, "No." When I weaned my son I also had a hard time dealing with it. I found myself running away from him or passing him on to his father. It's so much easier to run away then confront, isn't it?

Now I have a little more experience and I think maybe I'm a little wiser. Instead of running away from my daughter I hold her close and wrap my arms around her. I kiss her precious face and tell her over and over that I love her as I say no. She cries, but she clings to me and I see as I continue holding onto her and kissing her that the sobbing becomes quieter.

I wonder if she is comforted knowing that as our relationship evolves Mommy is still here for her. Even though it appears that I'm pushing her away, my distance or separation is only to help her grow and develop. In fact I feel just as connected and in love with her as when I nurse, if not more. Her crying, while heart-breaking, also comforts me because it shows me that she loves and needs me. I am saying no to her, but at the same time I am telling her, "Mommy is here, I love you and I'm here."

Her birthday was yesterday and I didn't nurse her the night before. I just held her. When she woke up this morning I was so scared. She came to sit on my lap as I drank my coffee. As crazy as it sounds I was scared that if I didn't nurse her, I wouldn't know how to comfort her and if I am at a loss as to how to comfort her, she won't love me anymore. She didn't ask to nurse. She just wanted to sit and be with me. I started to cry as I thought to myself, "She still loves me."

I remember as a child reading a book, *Are You There G-d? It's Me, Margaret.* I can't remember the details of the story, but the title has never left me. How many of us have asked, "Are you there G-d? It's me, So-and-so." "Mommy," my son asks me, "Where is G-d? In the sky, up there?" "He's everywhere," I answer him. "So why can't I see him?" Why can't I see Him? Good question. Sometimes His presence is obvious and sometimes we have to look harder. But the one who seeks it will find it.

~ ~ ~

I walked quickly down the street on my way to class when suddenly I heard a crash and saw a motor scooter driver fly into the air. He did a somersault. I saw his body twist and his head crashed into the pavement. Everyone stopped. Cars screeched to a halt. I put my hand to my mouth in horror. Thank G-d he had been wearing a helmet. We all watched as the young man picked himself up and cried out to all the spectators, "Nothing happened. Nothing happened." I couldn't believe what I was hearing. Nothing happened? Was this boy crazy? He almost died. "Will you stop for a minute? You almost died!" I wanted to shout out to him as I saw him pick his scooter up and collect all the broken pieces. "Will you at least thank G-d that you are alive? Do you see how He saved you?"

"Go, go, go." I feel like this is the watchword of the day; "Go, go, go, don't stop, don't think, don't feel. Don't see and don't make any connections. Just go throughout your day as though nothing has happened."

The Baal Shem Tov, the founder of the Chassidic movement, was once sitting with his disciples. He was telling them that a person can learn a lesson in how to better serve the Creator from everything that he hears or sees. At that moment, there was a knock at the door. A handyman asked, "Do you have any broken utensils that need fixing?" The Baal Shem Tov answered, "Thank G-d everything in my home is in excellent shape. Nothing needs fixing." "Are you sure?" The man persisted. "Check carefully. Maybe after looking though everything, you will notice something that needs to be fixed."

The Baal Shem Tov turned to his disciples. "Of course, this man is talking about pots, pans, and furniture. But from my standpoint he is really a messenger of G-d, sent to reprove me to remind me that much in my life is not the way it should be. This handyman has made me realize that I must carefully search my actions and life-style and make a reckoning of my spiritual condition."

It is also told of Rabbi Leib of Shpoli that he was travelling down a road when a man approached him and asked him for help. "Help me pick up my overturned wagon," he begged. "I'm too weak for this task. I can't help you," Rabbi Leib said.

The man began to shout, "You can help me, but you don't want to!"

Rabbi Leib stood still as the words penetrated his heart. He understood them in a spiritual light, "Righting the wagon of one's life is something that one can do – if he only wants to."

G-d is here and there. He is within us and above us. Every day He sends us messages. The people that we encounter are His messengers and the events that take place are those messages. As we grow and pass through different stages of life, different stages of exile and redemption, like the parent to the child, our relationship changes. At times it appears as though He is pushing us away, like the mother weaning her child. But as He weans, enabling us to grow, He holds us even tighter. "I am here. I love you and I am here," He whispers.

Chickens & Childrearing

Last week I spent twenty-four hours with two chickens. Live chickens. You know, the ones with feathers, that squawk. You might be asking yourself, "So what's the big deal?" Well, first of all, I don't live on a farm. I don't even live in a house. I live in an apartment, in the middle of the city, without a yard, balcony or patio. You get the point.

Twenty-four hours of two chickens in my apartment.

My one-year-old was petrified. My four-year-old was intrigued, and my seven-year-old had a blast, but he wouldn't touch the chickens. They ran around my apartment for over an hour, making a mess, until I finally was able to catch them and put them back in their box.

Are you laughing yet? I wasn't. Especially when it took me three hours of mopping to clean up the mess. But now that they are gone, I have to admit it *was* hysterically funny.

How did I get two live chickens in my home? They arrived due to a lack of clarity, a lack of boundaries and a lack of clear goals.

My eldest told me he wanted chickens. I told him I loved the idea. I myself would like a chicken. I would also like a goat. What could be better than fresh organic eggs and milk? I spoke in a language of dreams and wishful thinking. He spoke in a language of doing: wishing and wanting are not words of fantasy, they are words of reality. Every day he mentioned that he wanted to buy chickens. "Sure, sure," I kept telling him. I was very unclear.

I didn't realize how determined he was – and really, part of me wanted a chicken. I myself lacked clarity.

"There is a boy who lives two blocks from us who sells chickens."

"Really?"

"His name is Zvi. I'm going to buy one."

"Really?"

Uncertainty. Lack of clarity. Lack of clear goals.

I didn't talk about responsibility, or go into details about what you need to take care of a chicken. I didn't mention that just because we want something, it doesn't mean that we can have it, or that it's even good for us.

I learned that if a child wants something and we can't let him have it, we can't be vague about it, because with children there are no gray areas. Unless it's absolutely forbidden, it's permitted.

My son came home with two little chickens.

"I can't believe he bought them!"

Believe it!

~ ~ ~

Right before Moshe died, G-d showed him the entire Land of Israel. The Torah writes:

G-d showed him the entire land: the Gilead as far as Dan; all of Naphtali, and the land of Ephraim and Manasseh, and the entire land of Judah as far as the western sea; the Negev and the Plain – the valley of Jericho, city of date palms – as far as Zoar (Deuteronomy 34:3).

Why would G-d show Moshe the entire land of Israel and specify its borders, when it was decreed that Moshe would never enter Israel? Why was the Torah so careful, in an earlier chapter (Numbers 34:1–12), to list each and every one of the borders of the land of Israel? The Torah spells it out for us in clear and precise language to teach us that borders and boundaries have to be made clear. If they are not clear, then "anything goes," and you are left with a lot of gray areas. Moshe, who was, and always will be, our greatest teacher, was shown the boundaries of the land of Israel to teach us a very important lesson when it comes to educating our children: we need to be clear, set boundaries and have clarity.

~ ~ ~

As a parent, our job is to encourage and bring out the best in our children (and in ourselves). We need to give our children the freedom to explore, discover and grow. We have to give them flexibility, and at times let them stumble and fall on their own as a part of life's learning process. However, this all has to be done within a certain framework, because rules and boundaries protect and give security. G-d created a beautiful world to know and explore, and He created the Torah to give us boundaries and to give us clarity.

So, back to our chickens: needless to say, they were returned. My son was disappointed at first, but I allow him to go to his friend Zvi's every day to help feed and care for the baby chicks. He is thrilled, as am I, and all thanks to some clear boundaries.

Always Asking for More

Do you ever stop and catch yourself? Maybe it was the tone of your voice, the expression that you used, the words that you said. You stop yourself mid-sentence and gasp, "I sound exactly like my mother. I'm turning into my mother!"

The other day I had one of those moments, but it was in the reverse. I overheard my children talking. One had received a goody bag of treats from a birthday party. The other asked, "Can I have some?" Then she asked again. The first one, the owner of the treats, told her, "I don't want you to ask me again. I told you that I will give you some, but if you ask me again, then I won't."

Ouch, my child sounded just like his mother. Oh no. What have I done?

Just the week before this incident, I worried and worried. Why do my children *always* ask me for *everything* all the time? "Mommy, buy me this. Mommy, can I have that? Mommy, I want. Mommy, give me." It's never-ending. At least it feels like the requests are never-ending, and I worry that my children are over-demanding.

I don't remember being so demanding of my parents. I wonder if they will ever be "happy with their lot"? Maybe all of their requests are an indication that they feel deprived? Am I depriving them? But they have so much, too much. Maybe they are spoiled? I'm told that it's the generation, a generation of never being satisfied, of always wanting more.

I had to really think about this.

Are my children so wrong to ask? Maybe it's me who is wrong by becoming angry that they ask so much? Am I teaching my children that it's not okay to want, that's it's not acceptable to ask? Is that the message that I want to give them?

All of a sudden it hit me. If my child can't ask me – his mother – for things, then whom should he ask? He sees that I feed him, bathe him, and clothe him. I tuck him in at night and buy him toys. I play with him and teach him things. Whom else should he turn to if not me – a stranger? His asking me is his way of telling me that he believes in me, of connecting to me.

~ ~ ~

In Hebrew the word for giving is *natan*, spelled with the hebrew letters *nun, taf, nun*. The first letter and the last are the same, indicating that the one who gives actually receives and vice versa; therefore, by receiving we also give. The process of giving and receiving is like the cardiovascular system of the body. Oxygenated "giving blood" pumps into the body from the heart. The blood circulates through the body and "receives" carbon dioxide. This "receiving blood" then goes to the lungs, becomes oxygenated, and at last returns back to the heart as "giving blood" once again. The cycle continues, endlessly. If it stops, the body collapses.

From the very first moment that I conceived, I started to give. Whether it was my strength, my sleep, my body, I was giving – and, thank G-d, I haven't stopped. It's the single most important act that bonds me to my child. I also haven't stopped receiving, whether it's happiness, joy or love. The heart-melting way my baby looks up at me when I nurse – there is no gift sweeter than this. I get and I get and I get, and through this I have an unbreakable bond with my children. When they are small babies it's easier to see this, but for some reason, as they grow, the vision becomes blurred.

I realize that not only is it not too much to ask, but my child has a right to ask. And I also have a right: I have a right to say no, pleasantly, compassionately and confidently. Everything seemed to clear up in my head. I don't feel anger or ingratitude; I just say no when I don't want to (or feel that I should not) give.

But even when I say no, I continue to give. If I'm asked for an object or to do an activity that I don't want to give or permit, I will still say no, but at the same time will give – a warm smile, a hug, and try to find an alternative. You can never spoil by giving too much love. So, "let him ask and want," I tell myself. It gives me the opportunity to give, and only by giving can we grow close.

Discovery

I have two telephone cords that extend all the way from my telephone in the living room area to the computer in my kitchen. The living room's phone socket is the closest to the kitchen and I have no other way of using the Internet unless the two are attached to each other.

Knowing that these longs cords would attract the curiosity of my one-year-old, I taped them high along the wall, out of reach from his inquisitive fingers. Everyday he jumped for the cords, trying to pull them down. The other day he succeeded.

One-year-olds love to knock things down. My son spends half of his day on his tippy-toes trying to reach whatever is above him. He uses all of this effort just for the satisfaction of knocking the item down.

What amazes me is that now that they're down, he's not interested in them anymore. He didn't want the cords, just the challenge. Babies don't look down, they look up. After achieving his goal, he's ready to move on.

I love how babies and toddlers live each moment to its fullest and they live in the present. When they're hungry, they need to eat "now." When they're tired, they need to sleep "now." When they're lonely they need cuddling and to be held "now." They forgive and let go easily.

I also love their curiosity and the way they get so excited about everything. Everything fascinates them and everything merits exploration. They need to touch, handle, taste, and see, using all of their sensory organs.

My husband says that there are no "free rides" with our son. You can't hold him without him trying to leap out of your arms, grabbing the nearest object on his way. He opens purses and bags for investigation, pick-pockets pockets, removes eyeglasses and hats and either puts everything in his mouth or throws it on the floor.

I tidy up after him, putting his toys in order, just so that he can discover and throw them all over the place once again. I watch my little hurricane with delight (and exhaustion) as he wreaks havoc and I ask myself, "What happens to this sense of curiosity? What happens to the excitement of life and the beauty of discovery?"

Life becomes routine, making it easy to take even the grandest miracles for granted. We awake with the assumption that the sun rises in the morning and sets in the evening, but it isn't a given – it's a miracle.

Sometimes I take my son out of his carriage so that he can walk along the sidewalk with me. I do this when I know I'm not in a hurry. He stops along the way, every couple of steps or so, picking up things, showing me leaves and fallen flowers. If he didn't point them out to me, I probably wouldn't even notice that they were there.

There is a series of blessings that one recites every morning and one of them is: Blessed are You L-rd, King of the universe who gives sight to the blind. When I watch my son I understand this blessing. Seeing his emotions, his excitement, the way he investigates, observes, and grows with each moment, opens my eyes that are blinded by habituation, giving me new sight.

One Step at a Time

"I don't want to go to school," my son protested. "I'll go if you come too." I felt myself in a dilemma. I didn't blame my son for not wanting to go. Not only was he facing a new school and a new teacher, but new peers, and most difficultly, a new language. I debated, "Should I go with him?" How I wanted to go and hold his hand and sit beside him, or even place him on my lap. But was this the best thing? Would he grow and blossom, could he adapt quickly and learn the language if I kept holding onto him?

I held his hand until he went on the school bus; I kissed him and then sent him on his way, alone. The whole time he was in school, I found myself thinking of him, worrying about him, praying for him. The phone would ring and I'd grab it, thinking that maybe it was his teacher telling me to come pick him up.

"Why G-d, do You stand at a distance, do You conceal Yourself in times of distress?" (Psalms 10:1)

There is a famous parable about a child who is learning to walk. First, the child held on tight to its father as they walked together ever so slowly. The father let go of one hand and then the other. The child stumbled and fell. The father picked up the child and repeated the process. This time, the child took a step on its own. The father moved further away from the child, motioning for the child to come. Again, the child took a step forward. Again, the father took a step back, away from the child. The child's steps became steadier. Farther apart and yet closer together, the child and father walked until the child was able to walk on its own.

I remind myself of this parable when I think about the same time last year, when my son started preschool. The group was smaller, the language was familiar, but it was scary and challenging for him just the same. In those first couple of weeks, the teacher called me, worrying, "He doesn't speak. Your son doesn't say a word to me." Patience, patience, one step at a time. Soon, she called to tell me what a joy he was, that he was the one who always answered the questions.

I often find myself in a situation where I feel so distant and far from G-d. I look up to the sky and I call out, "Are You there? *Tatteleh* (Daddy), are You with me?" Like the father in the parable, G-d gives us His hand to hold, but in order for His children to grow and learn to walk, He then lets go and takes a step back. Like the mother who sits at a distance by the phone, He is always waiting to hear from us, always alert and on call.

The Beauty of Silence

As a mother of two small children I worry when I hear silence. Whether it's laughing or screaming, to me, noise is reassuring. Noise means that everything is okay. Well usually, anyways. Yet I recently learned a different lesson about noise and about silence. I learned that just as silence can sometimes be a warning flag, it can also be an opportune moment to shower praise and to appreciate all the good that I have.

Picture the scene: My five-year-old was playing with his two-and-a-half-year-old sister. They were actually playing quite nicely. No one was hitting, biting, pushing, or saying not-so-nice things. It was pretty silent. The phone rang. It was a friend. We began to chat. All of a sudden there was noise. This one took that one's toy and the other one hit this one. Screaming, crying. Urrrghhh. "Why is it that every time that the phone rings or that I try to have a conversation, you have to fight?" I asked them in a not-so-nice voice. I felt like exploding. I felt so frustrated. I told my friend that I had to go as I complained about my disruptive offspring. The silence and the playing nicely from the previous five minutes were instantly forgotten.

Now press the rewind button. You know, the one that we all wish that we had. The children are playing. Again, no hitting, biting, pushing, or saying not-so-nice things. Silence. I go to check out what's going on because like I mentioned before, silence worries me. I see that wow – everything is great. The children are playing so nicely.

"Wow, you guys are playing so nicely. Mommy is proud of the way that you are sharing. I really appreciate that you are letting Mommy work without making a lot of noise. Thank you!"

The phone rings. It's a friend. Before I start chatting I mention to her in a loud voice (so that my children can hear of course) how nicely and quietly my children are playing together. I have a really good conversation. I'm even able to chat for ten whole minutes!

Why did the second scenario end so differently than the previous one? What were the keys that made it a parenting success?

First, my children got their Mommy's attention without having to act out.

Second, they received well deserved praise for positive behavior.

Third, the praise was a motivating compliment that encouraged them to continue with their positive, compliment-provoking behavior.

So now let's move on from childrearing lessons to raising myself, and from relationships with our children to relationships with everyone and with our Creator.

I'm worried that we won't have money to pay our rent this month. "G-d please help us out with this one. I don't want to have to borrow money." My daughter has an ear infection, again. "Please G-d, let her stop crying. Take away the pain." My students are not listening to a word that I say. "I need You to help me. How can I get through to them?" Noise, noise, and more noise. I see that G-d is trying to get my attention. He's got it. I keep talking, and asking, and pleading.

Silence. Everyone is healthy. We were able to pay all of our bills this month. The clerk in the supermarket smiled at me and told me to have a nice day. The taxi driver didn't scream at me and I actually arrived at work on time. The weather is nice. I'm walking on two legs. I have a beautiful family.

Silence, silence, silence.

Now here's the big test. I remember G-d when things are shaky, but what about when things are going good? Do I remember to say thank you? To appreciate and to praise? It's not enough to just talk when I need to complain or ask or beg. Rather, I must recognize the beauty of silence and use that as an opportunity to recognize and acknowledge. So thank You G-d for giving me life! Thank You G-d for opening my eyes and letting me see goodness today.

Mommy, Will You Understand?

What was it that my son said to me? I can't remember and it made no sense, but I understood what he wanted to say and I answered him accordingly. He himself admitted that it made no sense and I saw the look of relief on his face when I understood without him having to repeat himself or explain. I reassured him, "Mommy understands. Mommies always understand."

Catching a glimpse of myself in the mirror, I had a flashback of myself ten, twelve years ago speaking with my mother. I certainly didn't feel like she understood what I was saying, even though I felt that I was speaking clearly. Even today there are subjects that I decide that it is better not to bring up or speak about because when we do it only creates tension and miscommunication. Maybe every child has moments of feeling "they don't understand!", no matter how hard the parent tries. Does the parent feel the same way?

Without a doubt, the most challenging thing about becoming religious is the feeling of loneliness and frustration that accompanies you as you try over and over again to explain to family and friends what you are doing and why. I'm not talking about the technical aspects of Jewish observance – not why I won't eat a McDonald's hamburger or why I won't go in a car during *Shabbat* – but the nitty gritty of why I changed directions in life and why the path that I am taking appears so different from the one that family and friends are on.

Now, as a mother, I admit my lenses are different. Before I could only see my perspective and think about my feelings and desires. All I wanted before was for my family to embrace, or at least accept me and approve of my life decisions. The pain still exists as does the strong desire to share, but it's not the same. I no longer seek approval like I did before, and now I've come to understand that many of the things that separate us were really brought about by a lack of communication. If only I understood back then what I'm beginning to understand now, I would have saved myself many fights and arguments. If only I had known that the biggest fear my mother had, or has, is of losing me to some unknown. Knowing this, I could have reassured her that becoming religious would only bring me that much closer to her, that the values she instilled in me are still the base upon which I grow.

~ ~ ~

My mother-in-law took me to her garden to see her tree. Once tall and big, the tree was now a small stump. It had broken in half and the gardeners had to cut it down. "What a shame! It was beautiful, but look – from the stump, branches are sprouting and the tree is still alive. It will grow tall once again." When the roots are strong and firmly planted in the ground, the tree will grow and rejuvenate. It will produce flowers and fruit.

You are my roots, Mommy, you and over three thousand years of laws and traditions. I'm holding your hand and you are holding your mother's and the line continues, from Jewish mother to mother, all the way back to our Matriarch Sarah.

Oh Mommy, why didn't I tell you before that I wasn't rejecting you? If I say no to your food, or no to that beautiful outfit that you want to buy for me, I'm not saying no to you, but to things that no longer correspond to me. Instead of saying no, I should have said, "Come with me here instead of there, let me cook for you, I would love it if you bought me this instead of that." I should have invited you more and shared with you more. I never wanted to preach to you or make you do something against your wishes. I just wanted you to know me more and the life that I live, and this way you wouldn't feel so estranged.

I know that there were times when I overreacted, when I accused you of judging me when more likely it was I who was judging you. I see now that those times that I interpreted as attacks, were really just moments of you crying out to me, "I love you and I'm scared of losing you. I don't understand what you are doing and why; it's foreign to me." Why in those moments didn't I just take your hand and kiss your cheek? Why didn't I comfort you?

It's true that I didn't say these words to you before, but Mommy, I'm saying them to you now. Look at me and my children. Look at the radiance and joy. Look at our friends and the people who surround us, the warmth and kindness that you thought no longer exists. Don't worry, Mommy, I won't push you away, but I do invite you to come close and be part of my life. Hold my hand, Mommy, and the hand of your mother and granddaughter. Hold my hand tight; you see – I'm not going to let go.

Suegra

A person's whole life can change with a phone call. Ours did, many times. This past week it happened again.

The phone rang. I saw my husband speaking. He sat down heavily in a chair, the color draining from his face. His voice grew quiet. I knew that something had happened.

My mother-in-law didn't feel well and went to the doctor, who ran some tests and told her to go to the hospital immediately. Suddenly our lives changed, as the woman who bore my husband, the grandmother of my children, the matriarch and pillar of our family, was diagnosed with leukemia. Overnight, my mother-in-law went from never needing an aspirin to undergoing chemotherapy.

I recall the first day that I met her. She immediately welcomed me into her home and into her heart with her smile, her radiance and her beauty. I'll never forget the day I sat down with her to shape *kippe*, the traditional Syrian meatballs eaten every Friday night and at every holiday meal. Hers were perfectly oval, all the same size and shape. Mine were a mixture of circles and balls, snail shapes and sticks. She proudly showed them to everyone, "Look, Elana made *kippe*!" She invited us to six-course traditional dinners, and lovingly tried my tofu stir-fry or whole wheat cake. The little that I made became the center of her attention. When my father-in-law was sick, I suggested making him chicken soup. She got to work, and when she served it to him, she told him, "Elana made you soup. You see how she always thinks of you!" Everything we do, she loves and praises. And this is just a taste of my mother-in-law's spirit.

In the beginning, I had a hard time understanding her. I was young, naive and immature, and she seemed, well, foreign. You know the ways of mothers-in-law and daughters-in-law. Too many phone calls, and it's an invasion of privacy; not enough, and you say she doesn't care. She's always telling you what to do, or she doesn't take an interest. I fought over petty things and thought that I knew so much better. Then, as the years went by, as I myself became a mother, I began to appreciate her more and more. Her silly sayings became words of wisdom. I find that I quote her all the time. We share recipes and tell each other about beautiful Torah classes that we attended.

I don't fight anymore when she gives my children sugary candy. I realized these past few years that the love infused in those treats is healthier and more important for the growth of my children than the healthiest of fruits and vegetables. She has her ways and I have mine, but she respects me, she adores me – what more could I ask for? A few months ago, I told her, "I'm not calling you *Suegra* ("Mother-in Law") anymore, but Mama." And I know that I'm not her "daughter-in-law," I'm her daughter.

And then the phone rang, and we received news that changed our life.

Our sages teach us, "Repent one day before your death" (*Ethics of the Fathers* 2:15). Does one ever know when he will die? Rather, explain the sages, one must always assume that today is the last day of his life, and not push anything off. I ask you: what if the sages are not just speaking about the day of your death, but the day of your beloved's death? Or the day of your friend's or your relative's death? Did you tell them how much you loved them? Did you forgive them for those petty things? Did you ask forgiveness for those words said without thought, for those actions done? Did you sit and talk as much as you needed? Did you listen to what they had to say? If not, you must know that you need to live now as though it's your last day – or theirs – and enjoy them, learn from them, be with them.

There is a beautiful image described in *Kohelet Rabbah* (9:8) of a sailor's wife who dressed in her finest clothing every day. When questioned about her practice, she replied, "My husband is a sailor. A strong wind can bring him into port at any moment, and I will be very ashamed if he finds me ungroomed and unattractive."

We need to live our lives like the sailor's wife, never wasting a moment, always ready and attractive for our loved ones.

Now, I'm glued to the phone. I jump at its ring and run to answer it. We call my mother-in-law night and day. Just hearing her strong, positive voice, so full of faith and love, gives us strength and hope. "I love you, Mama," I tell her over and over. "May G-d bless you with a full and complete recovery." *Refuah sheleimah*, Frida Ferdose bat Rivka.

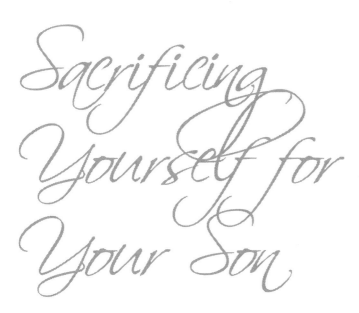

Sacrificing Yourself for Your Son

For the first time in my one-and-a-half years of motherhood, I went clothes shopping for my son. Our parents and families have been so generous that there was no need to go before. They bought us everything from socks to hats, pants to shirts, long-underwear to mittens. But he needed new shoes for his fast growing feet and shirts for the winter.

I set out for my shopping mission excited. As I arrived at the store I walked up to a salesperson and held out my son, "I need shirts for him. Point me in the right direction." Half an hour later I walked out of the store with a huge shopping bag, having bought my son a shirt in nearly every color. I felt so much joy and *nachas* (pride) as we made our way home, the big shopping bag dangling from his carriage and his feet sporting "only the best" boots that the store had to offer.

Today I sat watching him play with the children of our apartment building. I felt like I was bursting with joy as he screamed in delight, running with them from one side of the play area to the other in his new boots. They were playing with a hanging sheet, running into to it, under it, around it. I was so happy to see him happy and so pleased for him that we lived in this children-filled building.

As a parent, all you want to do is give to your child and make him happy. My days are consumed with entertaining him, feeding him, praying for him. My nights are filled comforting him, breast-feeding him, worrying over him. He is the highlight of topic of conversation and my husband and I are crazy about him.

All this has led me to understand what the test of Avraham really was, when G-d told him to sacrifice his son.

Parents want only good for their children and they want only good from their children. You become so engrossed in doing things for them, saving for them, working hard for them; and as you fantasize about the greatness that you want them to become, you begin to forget about yourself and the great person that you need to work on becoming.

When G-d told Abraham to sacrifice his son, Isaac, it was as though He was telling him that all the joy and pleasure that he derives from his son, and all the expectations that he has for him, are useless – if he isn't constantly working on himself, on Abraham.

It's much easier for a person to sacrifice himself then to sacrifice his son. It's much easier to put everything into your child, than it is to put it into yourself and your own self-improvement. Abraham, who loved his son and had waited a hundred years for him, was willing to sacrifice his son for his son – to teach him and send him the message, to send us all the message, that we can't live for our children, or through our children, but only as examples to our children. If you want your child to be great, you must strive to be great.

Call Me Baby

My son, who, depending on the moment, is *already* three or *only* three, has recently asked me to call him a baby. I looked at him carefully when he first asked. It was just after I had told him, "Okay, Avraham Nissim, it's clean-up time." He responded, "Call me baby. I'm the baby. Right, Mommy? I'm your baby?"

I looked at him and then at his six-month-old sister and my mind started to analyze the situation. "Did he want me to call him baby because he's jealous? Is he feeling sad about the end of the school year? Is he afraid to move on from his safe, small pre-school to next school year's bigger pre-school? Am I not giving him enough attention? I really don't want to call him baby; I don't even call my daughter baby."

My son, the practical one, brought me back to reality.

"Mommy, call me baby."

I acted fast. "Okay. Baby, it's clean up time." In two seconds he cleaned up all of his toys. For whatever reason, he just wanted me to call him baby. And throughout the rest of the afternoon, I called him baby. At times, I slipped up, letting out an occasional "sweetie" or "cutie" but I quickly corrected myself and told him while wrapping him up in a big hug, "Yes, you *are* my baby." It amazed me how cooperative he was and how happily he went to sleep that night.

~ ~ ~

The other day, I was sitting in the park and I saw a little girl fall. Her caretaker instantly rushed to her, picking her up. The girl screamed hysterically as the caretaker hugged her and told her, "It's nothing. Nothing happened." The girl only wailed louder. I can't tell you how many times I have been in the same situation. My child falls and all I want to do is say, "It's nothing. You're fine." No one wants to see someone in pain and the easiest way to deal with is it to pretend to make it go away. However every time I refrain from saying those words and instead, offer words of empathy such as, "It must hurt so much. Where does it hurt, where is it ouchy?" I find my child instantly calms down and in two seconds is off running again.

"Teach a child according to his nature" (Proverbs 22:6).

When I first read this wise advice of King Solomon about childrearing, I thought that it only had one meaning: to teach a child knowledge according to his talents or inclinations. If your child is artistic, teach him with pictures, and if he is musical, teach him with song. Teaching, however, goes beyond knowledge. If you can teach a visual person the ABC's with pictures, that's wonderful. If you can teach math to an active child with measuring cups while baking, then I'm sure the child will learn more arithmetic then if he were sitting at a desk with pen and paper.

But what about loving and teaching a child to love? Shouldn't this too be according to the child's nature? As parents, spouses, relatives, and friends, all we want to do is give. But too often we give what *we* want to give and how we want to give and not in the way the person wants or needs us to give.

King Solomon continues: "Just as water mirrors the face to the face, so does the heart of man to man" (ibid 27:19).

One might ask why King Solomon chose to use water as a metaphor for reflection, and not a mirror. I was told it is because when you look at yourself in water, you must bend. In order to reflect the emotions of others and love them in the way they need to be loved, you, at times, are forced to bend and bow down to your own feelings and desires. You're forced to love according to others' nature. When they laugh, laugh with them; when they cry, cry with them. When they need to be a baby, baby them.

Living in the Moment

We were sitting on the sidewalk right in front of our apartment building, our clothes dirty, our hands covered in colored chalk. I closed my eyes, savoring the moment – of being filthy, of sitting on the floor, of coloring and laughing with my children. I wanted more, but as always I pulled myself in another direction. "Time to get up, time to eat dinner, time to take a bath, time to go to sleep, but children, time to play? Maybe tomorrow, there's no more time today…"

There is a blessing that we say upon eating a new fruit (the first time you eat a seasonal fruit in the season) which praises and thanks G-d for enabling us to be in the present moment. The blessing is also an expression of appreciation for all the wonderful things that G-d creates for us to enjoy in this world. The text of the blessing is:

Baruch atah Ado-nai Elo-heinu melech ha'olam shehecheyanu v'kiyemanu v'higiyanu lizman hazeh – "Blessed are You, G-d, our G-d, Master of the world, for allowing us to live, sustaining us, and allowing us to reach this time (season)."

In the Jerusalem Talmud (*Kiddushin* 4:12) it says:

[When a person will stand in judgment before G-d after he or she leaves this world], he will have to give a *din v'cheshbon* (reckoning) for anything (i.e. food that G-d created) he saw which, although permissible, he did not enjoy.

There are references in the Torah where man is compared to a tree. Children, which are the offspring of man, are thus the fruits of the tree. Hours after my children went to sleep on the day we played with chalk, I couldn't help thinking to myself, "Elana, these moments with your children, you have to savor them now; if not, you will look back and be held accountable for missing them. You will so wish that you had them back, and regret that you didn't appreciate them. This is the season!"

"Thank you, G-d, for allowing me to live and have this time, this moment."

~ ~ ~

We live in a world that is caught up with the body. As a mother, you worry so much about physicality: the cooking, the cleaning, the shopping, and the never-ending pile of laundry. "Are you cold? Are you hot? Did you eat breakfast this morning? Go to sleep, get some rest. Wake up, wake up!" Do we take enough time to look into our childrens' eyes, to touch their hand, to really talk? Do we worry, and seek to find out, about what is going on in their hearts, their souls? "In one minute, when I finish this phone call." "Let me just clean up and I'll be right with you." The problem is that "one minute" is never just one minute, and that the one minute might be a minute too late.

In Hebrew the word *zman* (time) has the same root as the word *lehazmin* (to invite) and *hazmanah* (invitation). If only we could take the same amount of time getting to know and enjoying our children as we would for an important guest. I shudder to think what will happen in the future if I don't make that time now. Will they ever invite me into their lives, their hearts? Will they trust me and confide in me, turning to me when they need me, or will they run to someone else because I am always too busy?

I simply don't have the time…

But that's not true! If it's a priority, I'll make the time. I linger for just one more minute as they give me another hug and kiss goodnight (and not get stressed thinking about all that I need to do when they are asleep). I'll sweep the floor only once at the end of the day, and not each and every time they make a mess (every five minutes!). I'll sit down with them to a dinner of cereal and milk, instead of cooking and having them sit down to eat while I stand up. I'll ignore the phone when it rings, and turn the music on to dance with them instead. I'll laugh with them, I'll cry with them, I'll play with them. I'll be with them, and I'll bless, "Thank You, G-d, for allowing me to live and have this time, this precious moment that I will never get back."

Letting Go

In the hours after giving birth, due to the mixture of emotions and hormones, I didn't know if I was dreaming or awake. I held my precious baby in my arms. What a miracle! How could it be that this human being had been inside of me? And now that he was out, why was it that my hands instinctively rubbed my belly as though he was still inside? When it was time to hand him over to the nurse, I felt like I was handing over a part of me. And with each child, I felt that same connection, and the same question popped into my mind: How is it that they were inside of me, and now they are not? How is it that they were a part of me, but now they are separate?

When you look at your children, you search for similarities. You can't help it. "He has my nose, my eyes, my laughter and love of life." Some of these similarities you love, and some of them you don't. "He's so stubborn, she's strong-willed...why does she have to take after me in that quality?!"

As a mother, you worry. "What is he eating?" "Is she sleeping?" "How is he doing in school?" "Does she get along with her classmates?" They succeed, you feel you succeed. They make a mistake, you feel that it's your mistake. It's confusing. Are your children a part of you, or are they separate?

The other day, my daughter and I were braiding *challah* dough. I pinched the three ropes together, and quickly braided one *challah* after another. My daughter took her three ropes, braided them, and then flattened the dough down with her hand. Don't judge me, but my first thought was, "What are you doing? We're not making pitas, we're making *challahs*!" I kept quiet. At least, I tried to. I finally asked her, "What are you making?"

"*Challahs.*"

"I never saw anyone flatten the dough like that before."

"This is how I do it."

"Okay."

This is just one example out of a thousand interactions that transpire in the course of a day. And as I watched her flatten and make pancakes out of her *challahs*, I realized this is what King Solomon was speaking about when he taught, "Educate the child according to his way" (Proverbs 22:6). In the past, when I had heard this teaching, I understood it to mean that if children are artistic, they should learn with art; if musical, teach them with song. I understood that King Solomon was instructing **me** how to teach my child. But I think that there is more to this teaching from the wisest man in history.

Let children learn according to their way, not your way! Let children learn from their **own** trials and errors, from their **own** successes and failures (obviously, while establishing boundaries and rules, and instilling Torah values). My grandfather used to say, "Life is the best college education." This means that I don't have to interrupt and interject when they are trying to do something new. This means that I don't have to direct them as they clean their room or draw a picture. This means that I can let them learn that if you put your jacket on inside-out, it won't button, and if you put the key in upside-down, it won't turn the lock. This means that I can spare a few minutes of my precious time to wait while I let my children figure out how to do something on their own.

The parent-child connection is beautiful, and yes, there are so many similarities (and differences) between us and our children, but we are not the same. G-d didn't create us to have children through osmosis. The baby growing inside of you is not part of you in any way. It's attached to you, it's protected by you and it receives its nourishment and oxygen from you, but even as an unfertilized egg, it's not you. As we love and worry, as we educate and nourish, we have to remember that our children are their own separate beings, have their own special mission, and will ultimately learn according to their own way.

The Jewish Woman's Year in a Nutshell

Rosh Hashanah

Sweet Beginnings

You don't have to be a mathematician to figure out that one cranky and tired pre-schooler plus one cranky and tired baby, equals one very cranky and tired mother. This was the equation of the morning I had the other day. A morning that started at five o'clock and lasted for four hours until my son entered pre-school and I put my daughter down for her nap. Mornings like these have the power to put a damper on my entire day until night falls and I can hope for a better tomorrow.

Today began in a similar way, yet I decided to do something different. I looked at my equation. Why not make two negatives equal a positive? Could I do it? Judaism places such great emphasis on the female role that the Sages equate a woman to her entire home. In Hebrew, the woman of the house is called the "*akeret habayit*," the essence of the home. *Akeret* comes from the word *ikar*, which refers to the central part or core. This word also comes from the same root as the word *akar*, to uproot. So on that difficult morning, I was in the midst of tears when I suddenly asked myself, "Elana, do you want to infuse your home with a lovely essence by being the *akeret* habayit, or are you going to fall into the trap of being angry and be the *okrut bayit*, an uprooter? Is this really how you want to start out your day?"

I knew what I had to do. I swept up my crying baby with one hand and grabbed my whining son with the other, and I started to dance and sing at the top of my lungs. The distraction worked, and before I knew it, we were laughing instead of crying, singing instead of screaming. The rest of the day has gone smoothly, and tonight when I fall asleep, I can assure you that I'm going to say a little prayer that tomorrow should be like today. It's amazing how beginnings really do make a difference.

~ ~ ~

Have you ever wondered why there is a custom to dip an apple in honey on *Rosh Hashanah*? To eat the head of a fish (or sheep, depending on your custom) and not the tail? On *Rosh Hashanah*, the Jewish New Year, many also have the custom to refrain from eating bitter foods and specifically try to eat sweet ones. The Sages also caution that on *Rosh Hashanah*, one should make an extra effort to refrain from arguments to help ensure a peaceful year. One might ask, "Why does this one day have so much significance that it has the power to influence the rest of the year?"

~ ~ ~

Hagar and Ishmael were on the brink of death because of their thirst in the desert, when "G-d heard the cry of the youth (Ishmael), and an angel of G-d called to Hagar from Heaven and said to her, 'What troubles you, Hagar? Fear not, for G-d has heeded the cry of the youth in his present state. Arise, lift up the youth and grasp your hand upon him, for I will make a great nation of him.' Then G-d opened her eyes and she perceived a well of water; she went and filled the skin with water and gave the youth to drink" (Genesis 21:17-19).

The commentary (*Bereishit Rabba* 53:14) explains that at this moment, the angels in Heaven went before G-d and declared, "Master of the World, the one who in the future will cause Your children, Israel, to die of thirst, for this one you are providing a well of water?"

G-d asked them, "In this moment, is he (Ishmael) righteous or wicked?"

"Righteous," they answered.

"Judgment is passed in this world based on the present moment," He proclaimed.

Rosh Hashanah isn't just any day of the year. As its name describes, it is the *rosh* (head) of the *shana* (year), and beginnings set the tone. With each dipping of the apple in the honey, and with each moment that we are able to control ourselves by not getting upset, we can add a special prayer that this action set the precedence for a sweet and peaceful year. We can also use this time to open our hearts and pray for the strength to let go and forgive, and pray to be forgiven, allowing us to embark on the path for a new and bright start. *Shanah tova u'metuka*, a good and sweet year that is ignited with a good and sweet beginning!

The Power of Speech

I had a woman come to me this past month for a massage. She's been going out on dates for over a decade: looking, wanting, hoping to get married. As I worked on her I took a chance, I opened my mouth, and you know what I told her? I told her that she was beautiful, desirable and attractive. I told her that I could see her standing under the wedding canopy with her husband. I told each one of her muscles and limbs, all the parts of her body that have given up, that the search was nearing its end. I told her to envision herself in a white flowing gown. She listened, in silence.

"Tell yourself that you are going to get married."

"I can't."

"What do you mean you can't? Of course you can. I know you can. You will."

"You really think that I will?"

"Yes."

Before she left, I asked her for her Hebrew name so that I could pray for her, and I told her to call me when I should change my prayers from finding her soul mate to peace in the home. She just called me. She's a bride. Over a decade of searching – he's found.

When I was a little girl, my Bubbie (grandmother) would never say bad things out loud. If she had to say that, G-d forbid, someone had an illness, she would whisper it. I was thought that this custom was one of those silly things that old ladies do – you know, a *bubbe maise*. Then I read something that is written by written by the Rema (Rabbi Moshe Isserles of Cracow, 1525-1572), which changed my thinking. He writes in the Codified Book of Jewish Law (*Shulchan Aruch, Yoreh De'ah* 376) that one should not say something that could create a negative reality.

A person should not speak about events that he does not wish to transpire, such as disasters and catastrophes, as words have the power to cause these misfortunes to happen. The sages teach, *"Berit kerutah lasefatayim"* – there is a "covenant" made with the lips whereby they have power to cause that which they speak about. The word *dibbur* (speech) is derived from *davar*, which means both "word" and "thing." Speech creates things. It has substance and force, and therefore we must use it with great caution. If a person must be careful to refrain from saying negative things, all the more so should a person be careful to say positive things, so that these things *will* happen.

~ ~ ~

Rosh Hashanah, the New Year, is also called the Day of Judgment. Every human being passes before the King of Kings, G-d, and his actions throughout the year are judged. What's interesting is that unlike on *Yom Kippur*, which is the Day of Atonement, there is no verbal confession of sin in the prayer service on *Rosh Hashanah*. Not one time do we mention our wrong-doings or ask for forgiveness on this awesome day.

Why? Because on this Day of Judgment our words have a powerful effect, and our prayers have the strength to transform.

On this day, our only obligation is to make G-d our King. We tell Him: "You are our Father, You are our King. Remember us as Your children. Think of us as good. Let good come forth from our lips, and we will do good." We mention the righteous acts of our forefathers. We tell G-d, "Don't forget that we are the children of Abraham, of Isaac, of Jacob. Don't forget what they did to prove to You their loyalty and love for You. Don't forget the promise that You made to them – that their offspring would forever be Your chosen people."

We blow the *shofar*. In silence we stand, and the voice of the *shofar* pierces our hearts. We hear the *shofar*, whose name has the same root as [*mei*] *shafir*, the fluid that protects and nourishes the baby in the mother's womb. It cries out, "G-d, let us connect to You. Bring us back to You, to when we were one with You. Remember those times and know that this connection is what our hearts truly desire. Let our desire come forth from our lips in prayers, and let our prayer become tangible. Let us say good things, and good things will happen!"

Every day, but even more so on *Rosh Hashanah*, we speak positively. We don't get frustrated and angry with our stubborn, defiant child, but instead we tell him, "You have such tremendous strength and ambition.

You are going to be a great and noble leader!" And it will be so. You tell the spacey, passive child, "You are so easygoing and flexible. People always enjoy being around you." And it will be so. Don't hold back with good. Never tell the lazy one that he is lazy. Instead, bless him in a loud voice that he should be hardworking. To the difficult one, tell him that he is sweet.

Tell the unemployed that they will find a good job. Tell the singles that they will find their spouse, the homeless that they will find their home, the childless that they will have children. These are not lies. We create reality through our speech. And then we pray that our words will come to fruition.

Dip the apple in the honey, turn to our Creator, the King of Kings, and say, "Let this be a sweet and good year." And, with G-d's help, it will be.

The Missing Shofar

Have you ever gone to the supermarket and seen two products that appear exactly the same, but are two completely different prices? This happened to me the other day. I had two boxes of crackers in front of me, one for 9.90 and one for 4.90. The cracker in the picture looked the same, the brand name was the same; however the price was drastically different. I turned the boxes over to look at the ingredients. "Let's see what's inside," I thought to myself.

The more expensive cracker had two ingredients and the cheaper one had five. Hmm, more money for less ingredients, what was this about? I looked at the ingredients. The expensive cracker had water and organic spelt flour. The cheaper cracker had water, wheat flour, some sort of extract, some sort of sweetener, and one more ingredient that I didn't recognize. Believe it or not I put the cheaper cracker back and placed the expensive one in my cart. My motto is pay a bit more to eat healthy now and you'll pay a lot less in the future with G-d willing a longer, healthier life. And you do pay for what you get. The organic spelt flour is more difficult to cultivate and protect from pestilence and bugs. Its fiber, vitamins, and nutrients are carefully intact and it is easier for the body to process and digest. The refined product is stripped of its nourishing content and artificially sweetened. One is satisfying and nourishes, the other is filling while at the same time leaves you hungry.

They cried out and G-d listens, and from all their troubles He rescues them. G-d is close to the brokenhearted; and those crushed in spirit He saves (Psalms 34:18-19).

G-d supports all the fallen ones, and straightens all those who are bent. The eyes of all to You do look with hope, and You give them their food in its proper time...Close is G-d to all who call upon Him, to all who call upon Him sincerely. The will of those who fear Him He will do; and their cry He will hear, and He will save them (Psalms 145:14-19).

There is a famous story about a little boy who went to synagogue on the High Holidays to pray. This boy didn't know how to read and he didn't know the formal way to pray. The only thing he knew was how to recite the aleph bet. He closed his eyes and concentrated. He lifted his voice in song and sang, "*Aleph, bet, gimmel...*" as he directed his heart to Heaven. Those around him were very annoyed and wanted to quiet his singing, but the rabbi of the synagogue stopped them and explained to them that this boy's sincere and simple prayer reached higher spiritual levels than any of the prayers that they offered. He assured them that the letters of this boy's heart would be received as complete sentences.

~ ~ ~

I'll never forget what happened to me two years ago. It was my first year not going to synagogue on *Rosh Hashanah*. I was at home with my son. Even the previous year before that I had been able to go to synagogue because then my son had been a small baby who could easily be quieted with something to suck. But now he was too big, too active, and too noisy. I knew I couldn't take him with me and so I stayed home.

My husband and I had a plan. He went to a synagogue that prayed very early and he was going to come home during the break so that he could stay with my son while I went to a different synagogue that started later. This way I could at least hear the blasts of the *shofar*. The time came for me to go and my husband hadn't come back yet. Little did I know that my husband had thought that we had agreed to meet by the park and was waiting for me there while I had thought we were to meet at home. I wondered where my husband was and thought that maybe I should go out and look for him, but my son was taking a nap. Why did it have to be at that precise time that my son needed to take a nap? I debated, "Should I wake him up?" That also happened to be the year when getting my son to try to sleep and nap consumed me. It was always a constant battle and now here he was, napping at the exact time when I was supposed to hear the *shofar*.

The time passed and there was a knock at the door – my husband. We both spoke at once, "I've been waiting for you." We realized what happened. I ran out to try to find a synagogue that hadn't yet blown the *shofar* but I couldn't find one and didn't know where to go. I felt absolutely horrible. It was the first time in my life that I hadn't heard the *shofar* blast on *Rosh Hashanah*. Tears streamed down my face as I returned home to my son and words of prayer poured out of my heart. Without a doubt I am sure that those prayers were as dear to G-d, if not more, than any prayer I could have said in the synagogue. Due to circumstances beyond my control, I wasn't able to hear the *shofar* and go to synagogue, but I was able to offer up to G-d the best and purest ingredients of my heart. While my children are young I know that going to synagogue might not necessarily be an option, but as King David writes, "Close is to G-d to all who call upon Him, to all who call upon Him sincerely." In any moment and in any place He listens to the supplications of our heart, He hears us.

New Year's Resolution

Promises, promises, promises. As *Rosh Hashanah* approaches I always find myself making promises. "I promise I will not get angry ever again!" "I will never eat sugar again!" "From now on my home is always going to be spick and span!" "I will not raise my voice." "I'm going to call my mother-in-law everyday just to say hello." "Mommy is going to make fresh bread daily!" Promises, promises, promises.

The first week I actually fulfill my promises. I manage to control my temper, the floors of my home are so clean you could eat off of them, and I'm the perfect mother, daughter, wife, sister, boss, employee, you name it. The second week into my New Year, my resolutions are not so successful. I feel overwhelmed, overtired, and even resentful of my promises. I certainly don't feel like the perfect anything, let alone the perfect mother, daughter, wife, sister, boss, or employee. What went wrong? How is it that I got back to where I started, if not worse? Now I even feel like a failure and don't want to do anything.

The Sages of the Talmud (*Chaggigah*) tells us that when a person tries to grab a lot, he ends up with nothing, but when he tries to grab a little, he ends up grabbing it.

~ ~ ~

He [Abraham] lifted his eyes and saw: And behold! There men were standing before him. He saw, and he ran toward them from the entrance of the tent, and bowed toward the ground. And he said, 'My lords, if it pleases you that I find favor in Your eyes, please pass not from before Your servant. Let some water be brought, please, and wash your feet, and recline beneath tree. I will fetch a morsel of bread of bread that you may nourish your heart' (Genesis 18:2-5).

Abraham told his guests that he was going to bring them a glass of water and some bread to eat. He didn't make them any big promises that he would bring them a glass of wine and a gourmet meal. His words were small, but his actions were big. He ran into his home and asked his wife Sarah to help him. They made cakes brought cream, milk and a lavish five-star meal to their guests. "Say little, do a lot" was Abraham's motto.

Now let me try to apply this to myself as the New Year gets closer and closer and as my desire to grow and improve pours forth from me. Let me take one thing that I realistically think I can try to accomplish. This year I am only going to select one negative character trait that I want to work on and focus on turning it into a positive one.

I look around my home. There's so much to do and so much that needs to get done. I close my eyes and take a deep breath. "Elana, choose one thing." I feel calmer.

Instead of the need to make baked goods every day, how about just once a week for the Holy *Shabbat*? Let me start off my exercising twice a week instead of telling myself that it has to be every day and instead of cutting out chocolate completely, what if I only eat a square a day? There are a million things that I want to change or make better.

My list is long. I'm not perfect. But I know that if I tell myself I need to fix everything, I'm not going to do anything. If I take one thing at a time my list will shrink as I actually get things done. Say little, do a lot. If you grab a lot, you will end up with nothing, but when you grab a little, you actually end up with something in your hands.

New Year New Person

Leah first came to be about a year ago. She had been married for eight years with unexplained infertility. Both she and her husband are healthy and not a single test that they did gave them a bit of hope because every test came back that everything was fine with both of them. When you are told that you have a problem, you feel hopeful because you have something to fix. When you are told that there is no problem, you feel helpless and desperate, not sure what to do or what not to do.

As funny as this sounds, I massage women's bellies. That's what I do for a living. I massage and get the blood and lymph to flow. I massaged Leah's belly. She started to flow. Not just the blood and the lymph, not just energy, but words started to flow from her mouth.

Leah was unhappy and frustrated. She felt unhappy at work. Her husband was also miserable with his job. Since they married they lived in the same apartment, had the same jobs. Everything was the same everything. They were stuck and unhappy.

"Leah," I said boldly. "You need a change. Change! Something, anything! I don't know what, but change. Maybe your job? Your husband's job? Your apartment? Change!"

Leah's reaction: "I'm too scared…"

A few months went by. I kept insisting and encouraging. "You can do it! Encourage your husband as well. Make a change!"

How many times did she hear that word from me? At least a dozen.

Leah came to me excited. "I did it!"

"What?"

"I went on a job interview! It all happened so fast. My sister told me about the job on Thursday. It was to replace someone going on maternity leave. I knew that I didn't want the job if it was only for short term, but I sent my resume anyways. They called me that night. Sunday I went to their offices. Elana, the interview was a half hour long and the whole time all they did was ask me questions about my current job. Question after question. The more I told them, the more I realized what a great job I have. I work with wonderful people. My boss pretty much leaves me alone. I have a variety of tasks and responsibilities. I feel fulfilled because it is working for a non-profit that really helps people. I left the interview so appreciative and happy with my current job."

"Wonderful!" I share in her excitement. "You made the change!"

~ ~ ~

Sometimes we don't have to change our "location," our "job," our "surroundings," in order to make the change.

Life, for most people anyways, is a routine. We go through the year with the same seasons. We go through the calendar with the same holidays. *Rosh Hashanah, Yom Kippur, Sukkot, Purim, Pesach, Shavuot.* We start the year. We end the year and we arrive once more at *Rosh Hashanah.* It's the same apples dipped in honey. The same date and honey cake. The same holiday, as we stand before the King of Kings, our Creator and He asks a question, "Are you the same?"

The word for year in Hebrew, *shanah,* has the same root as the word for change, *shinui.* This word also shares the root for the word sleep, *shaina.* As the days draw closer and closer to Rosh Hashanah the shofar blasts can be heard loud and clear. Used like an alarm clock to arouse us of our of sleep, they wake us up from our routine.

"Toot toot toot…"

"Wake up! Change! It's the start of a new year!"

The change doesn't have to be big or drastic.

The change doesn't have to be a new job, a new home, a new place.

The change has to come from within you. It's your outlook, your perspective, it's you.

The phone just rang. I see it's Leah. I'm so happy, thank G-d she's called me to tell me good news….

Yom Kippur

A Day of Joy

I remember my first *Yom Kippur* in Israel; it amazed me to see everything stop and yet at the same time to see everything come alive. There were no buses, no cars; there was no noise from restaurants or stores as they were all closed. From every street corner I saw people walking with a lively gait to various synagogues. The air was so festive and electric. Why was everyone happy? My perception of *Yom Kippur* from my youth was nothing like this. I knew it as being a heavy day; a long, solemn day of fasting.

There are few things that I can actually say I hate. One of them, without a doubt, that I can say I hate is punishing my children. Maybe "punishing" isn't the right word. It's more like I hate that there is a negative consequence to an inappropriate or dangerous action that they do, such as hitting. Let's say that one sibling hit the other one. Regardless of the reason, we have a rule in our home: hitting is not allowed. Usually, when a child hits, he has to go to his room. There are times when instead of sending the child to his room, I go to *my* room and the "punishment" is that he doesn't get to be with Mommy. They are still young enough that they actually *want* to be with me and this is at times more effective then sending them to their own room. Either way, if you hit you are in "time-out." Now I certainly do not want to send my child into "time-out." I would much rather have him be playing and happy than "punished" and sulking in his room. But I look at playing with a sibling as a privilege and if you can't play nicely, then you have to be alone.

Every minute my child is in "time-out" I look at the clock, waiting for the time to be up. To me, two minutes feels like four and five feels like ten. My heart is so heavy when I show disapproval to my children. I love them; I adore them. I only want them to be happy and happy with me. But my job as a mother is to educate them and guide them, which at times means going against what would make them happy. I can't always say yes; sometimes I must say no. I can't always praise, sometimes I must rebuke. A voice calls out from the other room, "Mommy can I come out?"

"Are you willing to apologize and play nicely?"

"Yes."

I run to the child's room, "You can come out." I embrace him and pray that he learned the lesson and am thankful that he at least feels enough remorse to admit that he needs to give an apology.

When the prophet Isaiah prophesized the end of the exile he told Israel, "Comfort, comfort My people," says your G-d. "Speak consolingly of Jerusalem and proclaim to her that her period of exile has been completed, that her iniquity has been forgiven; for she has received double for all her sins from the hand of G-d."

The end of the prophecy isn't logical. Why would G-d punish Israel doubly for her sins? He didn't. After all, as the Torah states and as we repeat over and over in the *Yom Kippur* prayers, G-d is "Compassionate and Gracious; Slow to Anger and Abundant in Kindness and Truth; Preserver of Kindness for thousands of generations; Forgiver of Iniquity, Willful Sin and Error; and Who Cleanses." When G-d punishes, at the most it is measure for measure. That is, at least from our perspective, but from the "perspective" of G-d, two minutes are four and five are ten. To Him, the punishment is double because He doesn't want to castigate in the first place. Like a parent, His goal is not to "punish" but to teach. He shows us that each action has a consequence. The moment we apologize and show even a minimal amount of remorse, He opens the door to forgiveness and embraces us.

When I tuck my children into sleep at night, regardless of what happened during the day I tell them, "I love you. I love you just because you are you. I love you when you are complaining and I love you when you are thankful. I love you when you listen and I love you even when you don't. I love you when you are happy and I love you when you are sad. I love you when you are laughing and I love you when you are crying. I love you just because you are you and because you are my children."

Yom Kippur in Israel – the streets are alive with energy on this holy, holy day as people walk around festively, knowing that G-d loves us unconditionally, that He bears no grudge and does not hold any bad feelings. He loves us and all He wants is for us to be close to Him and to be happy. On *Yom Kippur* He is especially near: waiting by the door like a loving parent, in eager anticipation, to hear us, His children, say "I'm sorry."

Learning to Apologize

I sat on the park bench and watched the familiar scene. A little boy hit his sister. The mother grabbed the boy's hand and reprimanded him, "Tell Sarah that you are sorry."

"Sorry," he quickly shouted and then ran off to play. I don't think the "sorry" appeased his sister, but it did his mother. Given my own personal experience with my children, I can guarantee you that this incident was not the first, nor will it be the last. It will repeat itself over and over. So I ask you: what good is it for us to teach our children to "say you are sorry"?

There is a commandment in the Torah to do *teshuvah*. The word *teshuvah* is commonly translated as "repentance," but it also comes from the word "to return." Rambam (Maimonides) explains that in order to do *teshuvah* for a sin committed, you must:

1. Regret (and deal with) what you have done wrong

2. Commit yourself to not repeat the act (complete *teshuvah* would be when you encounter yourself in the exact same situation and you refrain from committing the sin), and

3. Verbally confess the wrongdoing committed

A child does not have the emotional maturity to understand his act, let alone regret it. Most five-year-olds who smack their baby siblings know exactly what they are doing – they just might not understand the consequences of it – and as much as the baby cries, they don't feel a single ounce of remorse. They also certainly cannot be trusted not to do the act again. When we tell them, "Say that you are sorry," we are essentially teaching them that "sorry" doesn't mean anything.

How many times have I, as an adult, mumbled the words "I'm sorry" without even really thinking about what I have done? At the moment of the apology, did I commit to not repeat the wrongdoing? If I could go back, would I do it again? What am I teaching my children, as their mother, when I say "I'm sorry" and then repeat the same act over and over again?

Obviously, the first step to doing *teshuvah* is to stop the act and abandon the wrongdoing. The child hits his sibling. We define the wrongdoing: "Mommy doesn't allow you to hit Sarah." We punish, calmly and without anger (I know that it's difficult!) by taking away a privilege: "Because you hit, you can't play at your friend's house today." Or, "…we are not going to the park." We offer an alternative: "If there is a problem, instead of hitting, you have to come to me and I will take care of it." Hopefully, by constructively punishing, you get rid of the bad behavior. Then, when the child is older, when emotional maturity has set in, then we can teach our children what it means to be sorry and feel remorse.

Of course, we start by doing so ourselves.

You arrived late to the meeting. Everyone waited for you to arrive before they began. "I'm sorry," you say. You were a bit embarrassed, but did you really feel so bad that the next time there is a meeting you will leave earlier? Or will you make the same mistake? If so, then are you really sorry? We make the same mistakes over and over. Do we realize that by doing so, the person we are harming most is ourselves?

When a person starts living a Torah-observant life, he or she is called a *baal teshuvah*, a "master at returning." How is this so? Chassidic teachings explain that nothing in the universe can exist without some nucleus of G-dliness within it. Even sin or evil, therefore, has a spark of divinity that enables it to exist. When the righteous triumph over evil, they withdraw this spark of divinity, causing the evil to disintegrate into nothingness, and the spark returns to its origin.

When people becomes more Torah observant, they are doing just that. They observe their actions, their thoughts and their speech more. This observation is a catalyst for thought and *teshuvah*. "Am I doing the same act over and over again? Can I eradicate this bad behavior, and return to the same situation and not repeat the act? By returning, am I able to withdraw sparks of holiness and return them to their Source? Am I really sorry?" If I am, then I can say it, verbally admit it. "I'm sorry."

This "sorry," this remorse, this example of regret, of *teshuvah*, will penetrate into the hearts of our children and teach them that "sorry" is not merely a word.

The Day is Short

close relative of mine is very ill, and I go to the *Kotel* (Wailing Wall) every day to pray for her recovery. One morning, as the sun rises and the birds sing sweet melodies, I call her. "I am here at the *Kotel*," I tell her. "You are here with me. Speak into the phone and pray to Hashem, for it is as if you are here beside me."

In a tearful voice, this loved one says, "Please, G-d, give me another chance. All I am asking for is a second chance. Give me another chance to live! Another chance to be with my husband and children. Another chance to do good. Please, G-d, give me another chance."

Her words break me. I hang up the phone and sob. *Another chance.* How many times do I push off asking for forgiveness? How many times does pride get in my way? What if time runs out and there is no more tomorrow? What is it about us that we think that we will live forever? We think that we'll always have tomorrow, another day, another chance. We don't. For some, it's later; for some, G-d forbid, it's sooner. Inevitably, death knocks on our door.

Our sages taught: "R. Eliezer said, 'Repent one day before you die.' His students asked him, 'Does one know when he will die?' He replied, 'All the more so! One should repent today, lest he die tomorrow, so that all days be spent in *teshuvah* (repentance, returning to G-d)'" (*Shabbat* 153a).

~ ~ ~

"Hurry, it's almost *Shabbat*!"

I don't know how this happens. In the summer months, when the days are long and the sun burns bright into the evening hours, I still find myself rushing to get everything ready for *Shabbat*. I thought that I had so much time, but no, there's never enough time. I look up at the clock. Wasn't it just 2:00? Now it's already 4:00?

"Everyone take a bath. Quick. Hurry!" Where did the time go? Where did the day go? Now the holy *Shabbat* is quickly approaching, and we are not even close to being ready...

The summer draws to an end, and the days begin to get shorter. In Israel we change our clocks back this *Shabbat*, the *Shabbat* proceeding *Yom Kippur*. Today I have an appointment with two clients. Knowing that I have much to do and that the day is short, I set my alarm clock for 5:00 in the morning. The *challah*s are rising by 6:00, and by 8:00 delicious smells of *Shabbat* fill our home. The kids are out and ready on time, and while I see my clients, my husband mops the floor. By noon, our home is ready. At 3:00 everyone is bathed and dressed, and even though it's still so early, there is nothing left to do. We sit on the couch and read calmly as we wait for the time of candle-lighting.

Why is it when I know that I have so much to do and so little time to do it, I get it all done, and when I have so much time and so little to do, I find myself rushing?

~ ~ ~

As *Rosh Hashanah* and *Yom Kippur* approach, the days get shorter and shorter. These shorter days are days of reflection, days of prayer, and days of growth. During these days, we blow the *shofar*, say *selichot* (penitential prayers), give more to *tzedakah* (charity), and ask for forgiveness. It's almost as though by making these days of repentance shorter, G-d is giving us a message: Take advantage of your time and plan accordingly. You won't live forever!

In college, I had friends sigh and say to me, "I can't keep *Shabbat* now, but I will when I graduate, when I'm older." "When I get married, I'll keep a kosher home." There are always excuses, always reasons to put things off for the future. What if the future doesn't come?

In our relationships, we are no better. "I'll call her only after she calls me." "I'm willing to apologize, but he has to apologize first." "I'll settle down and have a family after I build up my career." Tomorrow. Later.

Rabbi Eliezer teaches us that you can't live your life thinking that "it can wait until tomorrow." That day that seemed so long and felt like it would never end, that long summer day – it's over. The sun is setting, the day is ending, and you know what? You can't get that precious time back. I hear my dear relative's voice echoing in my head. "*Give me another chance.*"

Yom Kippur is coming. The day is short, and I'm going to set my alarm clock to get up early. I realize that time is precious and there is much to do. And later might be too late.

The Process of Teshuvah

After eight weeks of pregnancy, my second ultrasound confirmed my fears: there was a sac, but no heartbeat or fetus. A blighted ovum, a miscarriage. My heart sank.

Now, I have to explain to you that I am Mrs. Natural. Not only is it my lifestyle, as far as eating healthfully and exercising, it's what I do for a living as a reflexologist, massage therapist and doula. I don't like pills or drugs and am somewhat afraid of hospitals. The thought of getting a medical procedure to remove the sac terrified me. So I tried everything. I tried herbs and castor oil packs. I went to acupuncture and did reflexology. I went running and mopped my floors with vigor. Nothing worked. I just kept feeling more and more nauseous and tired.

By now I was ten weeks into this non-existent pregnancy, so I finally succumbed to the procedure. I told my husband, "I tried everything, and ironically I find myself in the exact place where I didn't want to be. I tried to run away from it, and I'm here." I was fasting, since the procedure would be done under general anesthesia. I was hungry, tired and very frightened. When my turn came, I whispered a prayer as I drifted off to sleep…

A strange thing happened after I woke up. I felt so so much better. Not just because the nausea was gone, but because I felt a sense of acceptance, a sense of "this is truly from G-d." I had tried everything to do it one way, and it was simply not His will. I felt a sense of growth and a sense of true closeness to Him. Part of me also questioned, "Why didn't you just do the procedure two weeks ago and save yourself all this heartache and pain?" But I knew that I had to go through that process. I needed the clear revelation that this was G-d's will. I needed to transform and learn acceptance.

When we left the hospital, I told my husband, "*Mazel tov*! We had a baby. We don't get to take home the body, but we were partners in creating a soul, and after 120 years when we are up in the Heavens, that soul will be dancing with us."

And now, six months later, I am fasting once again. But this time the circumstances are totally different. This time it's *Yom Kippur*, the holiest day of the year, and I am not fasting alone. I am fasting with my entire nation. Dressed in our finest, we make our way to the synagogue to pray. The prayer of *Kol Nidre* starts. I hear the cantor, see the people dressed in white. The synagogue is packed, and there is an energetic buzz in the room. With emotion, everyone begins the evening service of *Maariv*. The silent *Amidah* prayer is said along with a confession. You would think that with all the energy and emotion, all the initial desire to change and improve, that this would be enough. But no, this same prayer and confession is repeated the next morning during *Shacharit*, after the Torah reading during *Musaf*, and again in the afternoon service of *Mincha*. And on *Yom Kippur*, there is also a fifth service, *Neilah*.

As the day goes on, people start to feel more and more light-headed. By the afternoon, it's harder to concentrate, and you don't feel the same buzz as you did the evening before when *Yom Kippur* started. And then something very, very special happens as *Neilah* (which means "closing gate") begins. The entire congregation is rejuvenated. The energy comes back, and people straighten up. They pray with such emotion and fervor. It's the fifth and final service, and the gates are closing. You say the same words, the same confession, but after a whole day of fasting, after a whole day of praying and reflecting, and G-d-willing connecting, you are not the same person. And this is what "*teshuvah*," (repentance or returning to G-d) is about. It's about a process. You can't skip a stage or an experience. Each step brings you closer and has the potential to make you into a better person.

This process of *Yom Kippur*, highlighted by the *Neilah* service, is a process of a lifetime. It's a journey that we go through with each test and challenge that we face. It's not about looking to find an answer to "Why did this happen to me?" or "Why are You doing this to me?" But rather, "What can I learn from this? How can I grow from this? How can I use this to change?" It's a process of acceptance of that which is beyond our control because it comes from a Higher Source. And no matter what we could have done or should have done, it doesn't really matter. Because in the end, you have to see where you are standing at that moment and know that whatever you had to go through, it got you to where you are. Now just ask yourself, "What should I do now that I am standing here? Do I change? Do I reach out? Do I seize the opportunity of *Neilah*? Do I become a stronger person? A more thoughtful person? A person who can accept, and forgive and go on?" It's powerful, the process of change. It would be such a waste not to open your eyes to it...

Sukkot & Simchat Torah

As a little girl, I used to travel a lot with my mother. Before each journey, there was always that moment when we stood by the opening of the door, and I watched as my mother placed her hand on the *mezuzah* and prayed for a safe trip and a safe return. "Elana, kiss the *mezuzah*," she would tell me. I would reach up on my tippy toes, touch the *mezuzah*, and then kiss my hand.

I went to college, and the *mezuzah* came with me. I got married, and the *mezuzah* came with me. My husband and I moved, and we moved again and again and again. But no matter where the location, no matter what type of apartment we moved into, one thing stayed the same – the *mezuzah* we affixed to our door. The *mezuzah* gave our place of residence an identity; the *mezuzah* told everyone who passed by, "This is a Jewish home."

When I enter my home, I reach up to kiss the *mezuzah*. I leave it, I do the same. I tell my children as they leave for school, "The *mezuzah*!" They reach up on their tippy toes to touch and kiss the *mezuzah*. The *mezuzah* connects us to our faith. The words written on the parchment contained inside the *mezuzah* case declare the oneness of G-d; they are the words of the "*Shema*" that we lovingly say every day.

However, for one week of the year, the entrance of my home doesn't have a *mezuzah*. For a week, I eat and I drink, I sit and I chat, I sing and I read in a place where there is no *mezuzah*. When? During the holiday of *Sukkot*, my *sukkah* doesn't have a *mezuzah*. Why?

A *mezuzah* symbolizes permanence. However, the word *mezuzah* contains the word *zaz* (move). When you look around your home and you see all your possessions, what do you think? "These are my things. This is my home. I live here." This is fixed, here to stay. But really, we are wrong, and the *mezuzah* on our door teaches us that this world is only temporary. Our sages teach us that this world is merely a corridor to the next, an illusion of stability. But when we die, we take **nothing** with us. The only things that we keep forever are our good deeds, our *mitzvot*, our acts of faith and belief in G-d.

During the holiday of *Sukkot*, we are commanded to leave our homes and our worldly possessions, and go live in the *sukkah*. For seven days, we dwell in this temporary residence that cannot have a permanent roof. The *sukkah* represents the clouds of glory, the Divine Presence which protected us for forty years in the desert. It teaches us that the only thing we need is G-d. The *sukkah* is so powerful and so holy that we don't need a *mezuzah* to remind us that everything in this world is really temporary. We are merely passersby in this journey of life, as the wise King Solomon teaches us in his book, *Kohelet* (Ecclesiastes), which we traditionally read during *Sukkot*:

> **Vanity of vanities, all is vanity...** I accumulated for myself also silver and gold, and the treasures of the kings and the provinces; I acquired for myself various types of musical instruments, the delight of the sons of men, [and] wagons and coaches. So I became great, and I increased more than all who were before me in Jerusalem; also my wisdom remained with me. And [of] all that my eyes desired I did not deprive them; I did not deprive my heart of any joy, but my heart rejoiced with all my toil, and this was my portion from all my toil. Then I turned [to look] at all my deeds that my hands had wrought and upon the toil that I had toiled to do, and behold everything is vanity and frustration, and there is no profit under the sun... **All go to one place; all came from the dust, and all return to the dust... And I saw that there is nothing better than that man rejoice in his deeds, for that is his portion, for who will bring him to see what will be after him?** (*Kohelet* 1:1; 2:8-11; 2:20; 3:22).

And this is why, for a week, I enter and leave my holy *sukkah*, and my hand doesn't reach up to touch and kiss the *mezuzah*. I sit in my *sukkah*, and my eyes glance up at the bamboo which is my temporary ceiling. I close my eyes and take a deep breath. I am surrounded by the clouds of glory. I'm protected and safe. I enjoy the moment and know that this I will always take with me.

I had met Yael in an anatomy class years ago. We lived in the same neighborhood, and used to occasionally walk home together. On our walks, I found out that Yael had a younger sister with a heart condition. Well after our anatomy course ended, I ran into Yael and her sister on *Simchat Torah*.

Simchat Torah is the culmination of an extremely joyous period. In Israel it is the day after *Sukkot* (and outside Israel it is a two-day holiday), which the Torah refers to as the "joyous holiday." "You shall rejoice on your festival [Sukkot] – you, your son, your daughter, your slave, your maidservant, the Levite, the proselyte, the orphan and the widow who are in your cities" (Deuteronomy 16:14).

On *Simchat Torah* there is a custom to dance and do circles with the *sefer Torah*. As I watched my husband and children dance with the Torah, I looked over at Yael and her mother holding her sister, who was a pale and weak-looking child, and I started to pray for them. My heart felt for them, as I knew that the future looked bleak for Yael's sister. Every day after that, I prayed for Yael's sister.

Last year I walked into the synagogue on *Simchat Torah*, and received a wonderful surprise. I stopped in my tracks as I saw Yael's sister jumping up and down, her color robust, her cheeks a beautiful pink, and her eyes glowing. Could it be? Was this the same girl who had appeared so sick and weak a year before?

I started to cry from joy. I went up to her and hugged both Yael's mother and her sister. "I'm so happy!" Yael's mother hugged me back tightly, which is amazing considering that, aside from taking anatomy with Yael and seeing her once a year in this synagogue, I really don't know her, her mother or her sister. I had never even had a conversation with Yael's mother, and yet my joy was so real and so sincere that she felt it. (I found out later that Yael's sister had had a very complicated but successful surgery that year. It would take time and much recuperation, but – thank G-d – she fully recovered.)

Later, when I told my husband the wonderful news, I tried to figure out just what about it made me so happy. Like I said, I really don't know this family, especially not Yael's mother or sister. So how could I feel such happiness, and feel as though their joy was my joy? I know that in part it's because I prayed for it. When you pray for another person, it brings you closer to him. One Jew's joy is all of Israel's joy; one Jew's pain is all of Israel's pain.

Every day during *Sukkot* we fulfill the *mitzvah* of *lulav* and *etrog*. In order to perform this commandment, you take four species: the palm branch, the willow, the myrtle and the *etrog* (a citrus fruit). These four species are held together and shaken in a specific way. If you are missing one, the *mitzvah* is not complete. The sages say that the four species, with their different characteristics of either having or not having taste and smell, represent four different types of Jews. Each person is represented by one of these categories. Only when they are held together can you perform the *mitzvah*, symbolizing the importance of every single Jew. Without the unity of the Jewish people, we can't do anything.

In the times of the Holy Temple, not only did everyone come to the Temple to celebrate and wave the *lulav* and *etrog*, but they also came to bring offerings to G-d. Each day a number of animals were brought, including bulls. On the first day thirteen bulls were brought, and each day one less bull was brought, totaling seventy bulls. These seventy bulls represent the seventy nations of the world. On *Shemini Atzeret*, however, only one bull was brought, representing Israel. As I mentioned before, in Israel the single day of *Shemini Atzeret* is also *Simchat Torah*.

The *Midrash* writes that on this culminating day of all the holidays G-d told us, "Every day all the nations of the world come to celebrate with Me, but today I want just you [Israel]. Come alone, and bring me just one bull offering." Why only one? Because there is one G-d, one Torah, and the Jewish people are one.

Whoever has the opportunity to see the dancing with the Torah on *Simchat Torah* can see this. Joy is peace and unity, which is the gift that G-d gave when He gave us the Torah. The Torah tells us to rejoice, you and your entire family, alongside the poor person, orphan, widow, etc., pointing out to us that only if people less fortunate than you are rejoicing can you rejoice too. There are situations where you feel helpless. You don't see anything that you can do to help another person, but that's not true. You can pray for him; you can feel for him. By praying for him you connect to him, and this is truly a help.

Cheshvan: Fall / Winter

Why Do Leaves Fall?

can't help wondering as I see the beautiful transformation from green to yellow, to orange, red, and brown, "Why do leaves fall? Why do they change their color?" On one hand, the transformation is beautiful, but on the other hand it leaves the trees barren and lifeless. It appears the tree is dying in the fall and dead by the winter, but I know that the tree isn't really dead, it's only sleeping.

Leaves are the food factory of plants. Water soaks in through the roots, gases are absorbed through the air and sunlight is used within the leaf to turn water and gas into food. Chlorophyll, a chemical which gives leaves its vivid green color, makes all of this happen. When the trees notice the days becoming shorter and the nights getting longer, their ability to synthesize chlorophyll reduces.

Thus the green disappears and yellow and orange carotenoids and xanthophylls, which were always present, but hidden within the leaf, shine forth their colors. Other chemicals are produced that make the leaves appear red and purple. Any water and nutrients that were in the leaves go down to the stems as the tree prepares for the winter. When no food is left in the leaf, it falls, leaving behind a scar and a bud for the next year's growth. The tree appears dead, but really it's sleeping, waiting for the spring to arrive when buds will blossom and it will be green and lively once again. So actually, the very falling of the leaves is a sign that the tree is still alive.

~ ~ ~

The *Midrash* relates that there were three advisors to the Egyptian Pharaoh, Balaam, Job, and Jethro. Balaam encouraged Pharaoh to kill the Jewish males and devised a plan on how to do it. Job kept silent. Jethro refused to take part in the slaughter and couldn't bear to watch it happen, so he ran away. Each man was paid back for his actions measure for measure. Balaam was killed by the sword. Job experienced terrible sufferings – the worst kind imaginable – losing his family, fortune, and health. And Jethro merited having descendants that served as High Priests in the Holy Temple.

The *Midrash* asks, "Why was Job punished with terrible suffering for remaining silent, while Balaam, who actively contributed to the murder of Jewish babies, was punished with only a quick death?" The *Midrash* tells us that we can learn that life, even with suffering, is greater than death. Job's sufferings demonstrated that he was still alive and when you are alive, there's always hope, and always the possibility of change.

~ ~ ~

Challenges are how one grows and develops. If the leaves always remained green, we would never have the opportunity to see the breathtaking colors that are within, the vivid oranges and yellows. With the shedding of the leaves we see the tree's strength and are awed by its capacity to rejuvenate, growing even taller and bringing forth more fruits and beautiful flowers.

When leaves fall off trees it may appear as though the trees are dying. When they lie barren, it may seem like they're dead. But when leaves fall, they leave behind a scar and a bud proving that they are still alive. They sit patiently waiting for the days to grow longer and the nights to become shorter, for the day when they will blossom again.

It's been over ten years since I had the conversation, but I still remember it clearly. At the time we were going through an infertility treatment, and it was my sixteenth day of hormone injections. I was visiting a friend who was just getting over a bad cough, and for about twenty minutes she was going on and on about her one penicillin shot. There I sat, sore from sixteen shots. Of course, she didn't have any idea that I was undergoing an infertility treatment, let alone the fact that I had to be injected with hormones every day. And yet it took so much strength not to scream out, "Enough with your complaining already. I have it much worse!" But despite the screaming going on in my head, I kept silent. I thought to myself, "Maybe her one shot is equal to my sixteen. You never know where the other person stands. Maybe my tolerance to pain is greater than hers. Remember Rachel, our mother…."

You know those days when you are beyond exhausted? It could be that you were up all night long with your crying baby. You feel tired and worn out. The telephone rings, and it's a friend; she phoned you so that she could complain to you about how tired she is. She tells you how she went to a wedding last night, and instead of eight hours of sleep, she got seven. You feel like screaming out, "Seven hours!! It's been seven *years* since I got seven hours of sleep. I didn't even get two hours of sleep last night, due to my crying baby. You think you're tired? You don't know what tired really is!" But instead, you bite your tongue and you keep quiet. Maybe G-d gave you more strength than her. Maybe you need less sleep than her. Who knows who is more tired than the other? She's calling you for empathy, not for reproach or for a lecture on how good she really has it. You remember Rachel, and you keep silent.

You just finished cleaning up your home. You swept and mopped the floor. Your son comes home, and he drops his bag on the floor, as his dirty sneakers make a trail from the doorway to the kitchen. You glare at him. You want to scream, "I just spent an hour cleaning, and look at the mess you made! How many times do I have to tell you: when you come home, hang your bag up and take off your shoes by the entrance? Don't you see how hard Mommy works? How can you be so inconsiderate?" Before the words spill out, before you glare at him, take a deep breath and remember Rachel. Remember her immense motherly love, and how she was always able to focus on the importance of her relationships. Keep silent! Maybe he was excited to come home, and didn't notice the freshly mopped floor? Maybe he was absentminded, and didn't even realize that he placed the bag on the floor. If you want to punish him, punish him for not listening to Mommy's rules, but don't punish him for being a child. Don't think he did it on purpose, because he didn't. Bite your tongue. As hard as it is, keep quiet and think of Rachel.

~ ~ ~

The *Midrash* tells us that when the Patriarchs and Matriarchs went to intercede with G-d, Who was angered by the idol that King Menashe placed in the Holy Temple, G-d was not reconciled. Rachel then entered and said, "Master of the Universe! Whose mercy is more abundant – Yours, or that of man? Surely, Your mercy is greater. Yet I brought a rival (Leah) into my home, even though all the work that Yaakov did for my father was only for me! And when I came to the wedding canopy, my sister was brought in my place! Not only did I remain silent, but I even gave her my signs, the secret signs which Yaakov and I had for recognizing each other, so that she would not be put to shame. Though Your children have brought a rival into Your home, be silent and do not punish them." G-d answered her, "You have defended them well. This is the reward for your efforts and for your righteousness in having given your signs to your sister."

Not only did Rachel keep silent during the wedding of her sister, but even during all those years when she was barren and Leah bore child after child, Rachel never said a word to her. She never taunted her by saying, "Yaakov really only loves me." When Reuben brought *dudaim* flowers (fertility herbs) to his mother, Rachel asked her, "Please give me some of your son's *dudaim*." Leah responded, "Was your taking my husband insignificant? And to take even my son's *dudaim*!" Here again Rachel kept silent. She could have rightfully retorted, "Who took him from whom? It is you who took him from me first!" But instead she kept silent.

This is Rachel, our mother. Rachel taught us the great importance of keeping silent in the heat of the moment. And yet she also taught us the importance of speaking up at the right time. Rachel made peace and prevented arguments. We do see her expressing herself in the Torah, we hear her pain and frustration, but we see how she judges favorably and thinks about another's pain without comparing it to her own. This is Rachel, our mother. Because of her merit, her silent tears and her powerful words, her children returned from exile, and will do so again.

~ ~ ~

I ask my husband to go buy some plums from the market, so that I can make a plum torte for *Shabbat*. I tell him three times, and even write it down for him. He comes home with red apples.

"Where are the plums?"

"Plums? I thought you wanted apples!"

"Where's the paper I gave you?"

"I lost it."

I bite my tongue. I don't tell him, "Every time I ask you to pick something up, you bring me the wrong item." It's not true. Nothing is true "every time." And he was trying to do me a favor.

There's always a solution. Instead of a plum torte, I'll make an apple cake.

As I put the ingredients into the bowl, I pray for the strength of Rachel. With my silence, I will have peace in my home.

Shabbat

Just Coffee

I went to the supermarket to buy my husband a bottle of Nescafe coffee. I went there *just* for the coffee. My first mistake was to take a shopping cart. After all, who needs a shopping cart for a jar of coffee? I've bought coffee before in this supermarket and I know which aisle it is located in – aisle four. My shopping cart and I started off in aisle one. Why? I remembered that I wanted to buy mushrooms. Aisle one, two, three, four. I finally got to aisle four via the first three aisles. My shopping cart was now full. There was no Nescafe in the store. I went to the checkout aisle. I left the supermarket with eight bags of groceries, not one containing a jar of coffee.

~ ~ ~

It wasn't so long ago that all I had was a telephone. You know, a standard telephone that didn't light up and wasn't digital. Now I have a digital landline, a cell phone, internet, and a VOIP DSL telephone that allows me to have a US number while living in Israel. I can be connected to everyone, anywhere, anytime. However, with all this communication going on all week-long the only one whom I'm not connected to or communicating with is myself. Then Friday afternoon rolls around and I unplug my phones, shut down my computer and as I light the *Shabbat* candles and welcome the holy day of rest, I suddenly find myself connected. Even though I make it a point to sit down to talk with my husband each night when he comes home, our time together is brief and often interrupted. However, on *Shabbat* there are no interruptions; there is only us, talking and singing and enjoying. It's the only day where we can sit down with our children and observe how much they've grown and learned during the week.

"Six days you shall do your work and on the seventh day you shall rest" (Exodus 31:16). The language that the Torah uses to describe the rest or cessation that is commanded on *Shabbat* is "*Shabbat Vayinafash*," literally translated as "your *nefesh* (bodily soul) will cease.' On *Shabbat*, we gain a *neshama yetera*, an additional soul. While so much of *Shabbat* is about physical pleasures such as eating, wearing fine clothing, and sleeping, the pleasure and "rest" that one derives from *Shabbat* is deeper than these things, for you could take part in them during the weekday and yet you wouldn't be observing *Shabbat*.

In the midst of all this physical enjoyment, we disconnect from the outer world and reconnect to our spiritual inner selves. It's the one day where you don't get distracted in your journey on this planet, and instead of walking out of the store with eight bags of unnecessary groceries, you walk out with the one item that you needed and sought. It's the day where you reconnect with your family and friends. Just as important, it's the day when you reconnect with yourself.

~ ~ ~

I remember that when I was a student in university, I spent many *Shabbat* days alone. There was either nowhere to go or nowhere that I wanted to go for a meal. It wasn't ideal. *Shabbat* is a beautiful day that is best shared and not passed alone, but at the time I didn't have many options. I'll never forget how those moments alone of reflection made me incredibly in tune with myself, my goals, and my direction.

Now as a wife and mother, I bask in the beauty of quality family time that *Shabbat* gives us, and while I recharge physically from *Shabbat* to *Shabbat*, it also remains the only time when I can unplug the phones and plug into Elana.

Experiencing Shabbat

I have a weekly ritual that I share with my children. Quiet descends upon our home as I light the *Shabbat* candles and usher in the *Shabbat* Queen. I finish the blessing on the *Shabbat* lights and the prayers that pour forth from my heart and then I turn to my children and cry out in an excited voice, "Good *Shabbos*!" This is their cue. One grabs my hand, the other tugs at my skirt and we begin to dance and sing as we welcome the Holy *Shabbat*.

"Lecha dodi likrat kalla, penai Shabbat nekabelah."
"Come, my beloved, to meet the bride, let us welcome the *Shabbat*."

"Likrat Shabbat, lechu v'nelcha, kee hee mekor habracha."
"To meet the *Shabbat*, come, let us go, for she is the source of blessing."

It's magical – the dancing, the singing, the way we welcome in *Shabbat*. It's magical, the way only a moment before the day was like any other day with a million and one things to do and to get done, and now time is suddenly different. No more of the hustle and bustle of life's activities, now I have time to sing and dance with my children.

~ ~ ~

Now it's dinner time. We're all sitting at the table. My son to my right and my daughter to my left. My five-year-old son has a book in his hand. He's slowly reading out the words; he's reading us a story. I stare at my husband, smiling. We both can't believe it. Last week he still stumbled over certain vowel sounds and now he's reading us a story.

Look at what happened in a week!

"Mommy," my two-and-a-half-year-old daughter says to me. "Toilet!" I jump up, I grab her and off we go. I look to my husband, our eyes meet. Last *Shabbat* she was not yet toilet trained and had constant accidents and now she's telling us beforehand.

Look at what happened in a week!

According to the *Midrash* (*Midrash Rabbah*, Exodus 29:9), when G-d gave the Torah, no bird squawked. No winged creature flew. No cow mooed. The *ofanim* didn't soar. The *seraphim* didn't say, "Holy, Holy." The sea didn't sway. People didn't speak. Rather the world was completely silent, and a voice rang out: "I am the L-rd, your G-d."

Rabbi Shimshon Dovid Pincus, of blessed memory, explains this with the following parable. Imagine a great and powerful king. One of his sub-jects goes to see him in the royal palace. On the way to the king the subject stops to hear musicians (who are playing for the king) playing beautiful music. He can hardly pull himself away when his ear picks up a fascinating discourse given by one of the king's ministers. He becomes so caught up in the lecture, the music, the beautiful palace, that he almost forgets about the king. The king stands up and cries, "*Quiet!*" Suddenly silence fills the room and the beauty and splendor of the king fill the palace.

Six days a week I have an incredibly hectic schedule. There are so many things going on that six days of my week can pass and I won't even notice how much my children have grown. I won't have time to talk to my hus-band, not about my work or the grocery shopping, but about us, life, our dreams, our goals. Six days a week I have distraction after distraction and then...*Shabbat! Shabbat Kodesh*, the Holy *Shabbat*.

The world around me stops. Like a radar I am able to focus in on my family, on myself. I see things that I missed all week long. This is one of the things I love most about *Shabbat* and this, I imagine, must be one of the reasons why *Shabbat* is the source of blessing. Because *Shabbat* gives me the time, the attention that I need to see the blessing and that in itself is a blessing.

"*Lecha dodi likrat kalla, penai Shabbat nekabelah.*"
"Come, my beloved, to meet the bride, let us welcome the *Shabbat*."

"*Likrat Shabbat, lechu v'nelcha, kee hee mekor habracha.*"
"To meet the *Shabbat*, come, let us go, for she is the source of blessing."

Staying on Track

"Asher Yisrael, come on, *bubbaleh*. Let's go. The park." The distance from my home to the park is about three minutes, but when walking with my toddler, it can easily take at least thirty minutes to get there. We take a step forward. He stops. He looks around. The birds distract him. He chases after them and screams, "*Kishta!*" Every item on the ground is interesting and needs to be picked up, examined, and occasionally tasted, if I'm not quick enough.

"Asher Yisrael, put it down. It's *yichsa*! It's garbage, *bubbaleh*. Let's go. Keep walking."

Getting to the park is always an adventure, and actually, I never know how long it could take. For example, if there happens to be a cat in the way (and here in Jerusalem, that is definitely a common occurrence), the journey from my home to the park could even take thirty-five minutes. And if by chance we see a dog... wow, a dog could mean forty-five minutes, at least.

This is what toddlers do. They wander and stray from the path, and our job as parents is to get them back on track. We need to gently remind them of the "destination."

~ ~ ~

The bills pile up. A child is having a hard time in school this week. We have a leak in our ceiling, and my husband tells me there are problems with work. Life is stressful. There are so many distractions throughout the week, and I'm having a hard time focusing. Remind me again, what am I doing? What are our goals? Where am I going?

Friday arrives. I stand before the *Shabbat* candles and I take a deep breath. The phones are disconnected. My computer is put away. My children surround me and watch me as I light the candles. Peace descends on my home. The *Shabbat* Bride enters. The *Shechina* (Divine Presence), the feminine manifestation of G-d, is welcomed with song: "Come, Bride… Come, Sabbath Queen." She does Her job, like a mother, to put me back on track. Life's distractions try to sway me from arriving at my destination, but She comes every week to remind me where I need to go.

We sit and eat together as a family. We talk and we sing. I connect to them, they connect to me. I connect to the Shechina, She connects to me.

My children sing a *Shabbat* song:

Because I guard *Shabbat*, G-d guards me.
It is a sign for eternity between Him and me.

In our daily life, we have obstacles that prevent us or stall us from getting to where we need to be. But each week, we receive a gift, *Shabbat*. Every week, *Shabbat* comes, bringing abundant blessing and clarity. Like a mother, She gently guides us, putting us back on track to help us reach our destination.

Because I guard *Shabbat*, G-d guards me.
It is a sign for eternity between Him and me.

"Will you just relax?"

Don't you just love it when people tell you to *relax?* I find it the most un-relaxing thing in the world.

I have a friend who has been searching for her soul mate for years. *"Relax,"* they tell her. "Just relax and you'll find someone." To the woman suffering for years with infertility treatments: "If you would only *relax,* you would become pregnant." To the woman in labor: *"Relax,"* the doctor tells her, "and the baby will go down." To the one who just lost her job and needs to pay the rent by the first of the month: *"Relax,* you'll find another one."

I'm not saying that these things are false; in fact, they have a lot of truth to them. If you relax, it can help you to find a spouse, a job, a baby, health – you name it. Relaxation is great. But I never saw anyone relax (and I am a both a massage therapist and a doula) from someone telling her to relax.

So how does one relax? Relaxation comes when you let go and let G-d do the job.

~ ~ ~

Last night a woman came to me for a massage. She wanted me to help her sleep better. She had no physical problems. Her insomnia comes from anxiety and fear. She is in her eighth month of pregnancy, and she is petrified. Not of the birth, but of after the birth. After her first child was born, she suffered terribly from post-partum depression. For four months she didn't live; she barely functioned, as thoughts of suicide, darkness and despair overwhelmed her. At last, with lots of support and medication, there was a light at the end of the dark tunnel. She made it. Now, even taking preventative medicine, she fears the return of that darkness.

"Will you teach me to relax?" she asked me. As much as I kneaded, massaged and soothed her muscles, I knew that there was nothing my hands could do to take away the tension. The only lesson that I could offer her was one of faith.

~ ~ ~

Six days a week I can't take a nap. I've tried. I lie in bed, close the curtains. I'm exhausted and I know that I need a nap, but I can't. I can't relax. As soon as my head hits the pillow, I start to think about…the laundry, what to make for dinner, letters that need to be written and phone calls that need to be made, lists and lists of things "to do." There went my nap.

Saturday comes – *Shabbat*. We finish our morning meal. I leave snacks on the table for my kids and wish them "Good *Shabbos*" (and good luck!). I close my bedroom door. My head hits the pillow, and in less than a minute I am asleep and am taking the most delightful nap. If no one were to wake me, I would sleep for three hours. No work to do, no errands to run. It's *Shabbat*, and everything that needed to get done is done. For six days I made my effort; I did my part. I bought groceries, cleaned the home, cooked the food and laundered the clothing; now the seventh day comes, and with the lighting of the candles I completely relinquish control to G-d. This is His day, the day that we meet Him face to face. We invite the Divine Presence to our dining table as we sing and sanctify the day with wine. I am completely and totally relaxed.

The Talmud tells the story of a vineyard owner. One *Shabbat* morning he took a walk and noticed that there was a hole in his fence. "Oh no," he thought. "I will have to fix that as soon as *Shabbat* ends, so that animals don't come into my fields and eat the grapes." He immediately felt bad. "Why am I worrying about my fields and planning on what I will do later tonight, when it is now *Shabbat*?" He felt so bad that he decided that he would not fix the fence – ever. G-d performed a miracle for him, and a tree began to grow in that exact spot, covering the hole.

In Hebrew there are no names for the weekdays. Sunday is the "first day"; Monday, the "second";…Friday, the "sixth." Each day receives its name from its distance from the past *Shabbat*, and we count towards the next *Shabbat*. The entire week of work and activities is centered around the holy *Shabbat*. We await "her" presence like a groom awaits his bride on their wedding night. As we go through the week, we make preparations. We make our effort, we do our part, but ultimately we know that G-d is in control. With this in mind, we don't have to worry. We can relax.

~ ~ ~

I looked my client in the eyes and took her hand. "You are taking preventative medication. You have a team of family and friends lined up for support. Pray that it is not going to happen again, and leave it up to G-d." Her face softened; the muscles went limp. "That's something that I will have to work on."

"We all do," I admitted.

She took a deep breath, smiled, and left a bit more *relaxed*.

Chanukah

I'm one of those women who can't sit still. I like to be busy – doing things, going places, making things with my hands. I enjoy creating. I enjoy doing.

This past spring my mother in-law became very ill, and like always, I shifted into my "doing" gear: sending e-mails to friends asking them to pray, getting my husband a ticket to see his mother, calling experts and doctors, arranging for this, taking care of that. The whole spring and summer long, as my husband flew back and forth to be with her, as I tossed and turned in an anguished sleep, as I cried in despair, I kept doing.

"What can I do for you?" I kept asking my husband.

One day he answered me, "I don't want you to do anything. I don't need you to do anything. I just need you to be present. I want you to be with me, and not do."

His words knocked me off my feet.

"What do you mean? I'm always here. I'm with you in everything."

"You're here physically, but you're not present. You're always busy doing something."

I had to think about his words. They were hard to listen to, but the more that I thought about it, the more I knew that he was right. It's easy for me to cook and clean, arrange for things and do the shopping, make phone calls and give baths, but it's not so easy for me to be present while I'm doing these things. I'm serving lunch, but I'm thinking about the laundry. I'm playing a game with my children, and I'm thinking about the client that I need to call or the class that I want to teach. I'm always worrying about this person or that person. My hands are engaged in a thousand activities at any given time, and my head is occupied with a thousand and one different thoughts. He's right. I'm here, but I'm not here.

There's really only one time of the year that I'm truly present. It's *Chanukah* time. It's the time after we've lit our candles, when I spend a few minutes just gazing into the flames.

On the surface, *Chanukah* appears to be a very simple holiday. There's no spring cleaning (yay!), no big meals to cook for, and no major expenses or preparations involved. All you need are some wicks, oil (or candles) and a holder. There are customs to eat oily and dairy foods, and it's wonderful to play *dreidel* and sing songs and dance, but really, the only commandment of *Chanukah* is to light the candles and watch them burn. Pretty simple, right?

~ ~ ~

The *Chanukah* story is well known. Many years ago, the Greeks took over the land of Israel. They prohibited the Jews from learning Torah, keeping the Sabbath, performing circumcisions and sanctifying the new month. One man, Mattathias ben Johanan the Priest, stood up against the tyranny and the evil decrees and cried, "Whoever is for G-d, come with me!" A small group of Jews joined him, and they waged war against the numerous Greeks. Miraculously, they won the war. They then went back to the Holy Temple and tried to make order from all the havoc and destruction that the Greeks had caused. They searched and searched for pure, untouched olive oil to light the golden *menorah*. They found one small flask, a day's worth of oil. The oil miraculously lasted eight days, and hence we light our *menorah*s today for eight days in commemoration of the miracle of the oil. But what about the miracle of the war? The weak fighting against the mighty, the few defeating the many?

The miracle of the war is actually also memorialized through the candles that we light.

How is it that the Jews won the war? It was obviously not a logical defeat; their victory would not have been possible if not for G-d's hand. So, what was their role? What did they do? They were present. Their battle cry was, "Whoever is for G-d, come with me!" They were saying, in effect, "G-d, I'm here. I'm present. I'm with You. No person, no one thing, can distract me or take me away from serving You."

What does G-d ask of us when we light our *menorah*s? A simple thing that's really not so simple. He wants us to be with Him. He wants us to gaze into the flames. No plans, no worries, no distractions. It's just Him and us. This is *Chanukah*. This is the light in the darkness. This is the type of relationship that enhances marriages and brings children closer to their parents. It's simple and it's profound. It's being present.

Pregnant with Hope

I remember the first time I met Sima, her belly was beautifully full. It stuck out, and she waddled. She came to me for a prenatal massage.

She told me her story. She was thirty-eight and pregnant with her first child. She was so worried. Every time she went to her doctor, he scared her. They wanted to perform all kinds of exams and tests. They thought that they had found something in one of her ultrasounds that could mean that something was wrong with the baby, and they wanted to do more exams. She and her husband refused. The doctor told her, "Prepare yourself for the worst."

I listened. I searched deep within myself for the right wisdom to tell her. My nature is to say, "Everything will be fine. Don't worry." But I couldn't say that; it was neither the place nor the time to tell her such words. What did I say? Nothing. There is an expression, "Sit and don't do." I massaged, and I listened.

Sima came back a few weeks later. She felt different. Her shoulders were not so tense, and her forehead was more relaxed. "Sima, what is going on?" I asked her. She explained. Between our two meetings, she had gone to her rabbi. She cried her heart out to him and asked him for a blessing. She wanted him to tell her how to brace herself for the worst. She wanted him to give her advice on she should deal with the situation once the child was born. She wanted him to bless her with strength. He didn't. You know what he told her instead? He told her that a person should not ask to be able to pass a test that they don't even have. "How do you know that there is even anything wrong with the baby? For now, all you need to do is pray that the baby is healthy and continues to be healthy. You need to take each step as it comes, and deal only with what is right in front of you. As of now we don't know anything, so there is no reason to worry about something that might not even be. Just pray for a healthy baby."

Sima told me that she felt calm. His words comforted, and all she did now was pray and pray for the health of the baby.

A few weeks later the baby was born – a healthy, full-term, vibrant baby.

~ ~ ~

I want you to picture the scene: Men returned home from winning a miraculous battle against the mighty Greeks, and found our Holy Temple desecrated. They started to clean and make order. The *kohanim*, the priests, wanted nothing more than to perform their holy service and to light the golden *menorah*. They searched and searched for an unbroken flask of olive oil to light the *menorah*. All the flasks were broken. And then they found a flask, but only one flask, which is enough to burn for only one day. It takes eight days to make more oil; what good was just one flask?

I always wonder. When the Chashmonaim found the oil, what was their first thought? Did they jump up and down for joy that they found enough oil to light for that day, or did they feel disappointed and begin to worry about the lack of oil for the next seven days? History tells us that they must have seen what they had in their hands, at that moment, and couldn't worry about what would be the next day.

They lit the *menorah*, and guess what happened? (I know you know your history…) The next day – the oil in the *menorah*, it kept burning. Each day, for the next seven days, there was exactly enough oil needed for the *menorah*.

Each day, all eight days, they had to live in the moment and deal only with the test that was right in front of them, not the one that could be, or might possibly be, tomorrow.

This is one of the messages of *Chanukah*. Today I found oil to light for today – I don't have enough for tomorrow…live in the present, and light the *menorah*. The same G-d who takes care of you now can take care of you tomorrow. Take each moment as it comes, pray for the best, and there is no reason to expect the worst. Open your eyes and see the miracles that G-d does for you today. Tomorrow is tomorrow.

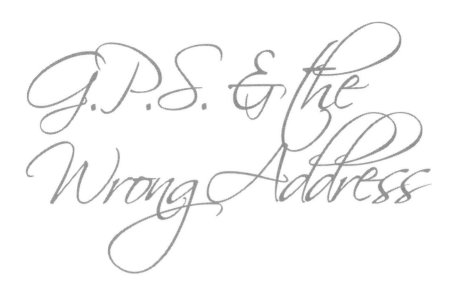

G.P.S. & the Wrong Address

This was the third time that this happened to me-where I received a last minute call from a woman asking me to be her doula. It was five o'clock in the morning when the phone rang. "Elana, I think that I'm in labor. I know that I didn't think that I wanted a doula for this birth, but can you come? Here, I'm putting my husband on the phone; he'll tell you how to get to us."

"This is an exciting way to start my day," I thought to myself.

The husband came on the phone. "It's really easy to get to. All the taxi drivers know the way and if not, they all have a GPS in their car."

I quickly got dressed and called the cab company. I settled into the taxi and told the driver the address. He had no idea where it was, but not to worry – the taxi had a GPS.

First it took Mr. Taxi Driver at least fifteen minutes to figure out how to enter data into the GPS. "Not to worry Lady, give me one more minute and it will all be okay." Press button, press button, press button. At last the GPS showed the city that we were going to.

"What's the name of the street?"

I told him again.

Press button, press button, press button. "It's not in here."

"What do you mean?"

"The street's not in the GPS."

I tried calling the laboring couple. No answer.

"Let's just go to the neighborhood that they said and we'll ask when we get there."

At each red light Mr. Taxi Driver fiddled with the GPS and pressed buttons. It was the blind leading the blind. Neither of us knew where we were going and the GPS certainly didn't know where we were going. As we got closer to the neighborhood the husband at last answered the phone. It turns out in all the excitement I had heard the address incorrectly.

"Lady," Mr. Taxi Driver explained to me, "With a GPS you need the exact address otherwise it doesn't show up. That's why it didn't work." Without the correct name of the street, your destination doesn't exist.

A beautiful baby girl was born that morning and I learned a very valuable lesson taught to me by Mr. Taxi Driver and the GPS.

Alexander the Great conquered many lands including Israel. When he lived Israel lived in tranquility, but when he died the Seleucides (Syrian-Greeks) took over and began to oppress the Jews. The conflict between Israel and Greece was not a power struggle. There was no question that Israel was subservient to the Greeks. Instead, the conflict was based on diverse spiritual values. The rulers of Greece were willing to accept most of the Torah, but there were three mitzvot which they sought to annul: *Shabbat, Rosh Chodesh* (the sanctification of the months), and *Brit Milah* (circumcision). By outlawing these three mitzvot they wanted to teach that the world has no Creator (*Shabbat*), that the year is devoid of sanctity (*Rosh Chodesh* – which determines when the Jewish holidays are celebrated), and that the body and soul are not hewn from one Source – that the body lacks restraint (*Brit Milah*). Essentially what they were trying to say by prohibiting the Jews from keeping these *mitzvot* is that you can do what you want, when you want and that there isn't Anything spiritual above you, holding you accountable for your actions.

The Greeks had no problem with eating *matzah* ball soup and gefilte fish. They were willing to put kugels on their menu and they allowed you to wear a long skirt, a scarf, or a wig. They were willing to let you be "culturally Jewish" and observe Judaism as long as it was kept on a superficial level. The Greeks were trying to convince the Jews that they could still use their GPS even if the destination was missing, that they could still be Jewish without G-d.

The Kohen Gadol, Mattiahus Maccabee, stood up with his sons and declared, "Whoever is for G-d, come with me!" His cry was a declaration that the Torah wasn't just a nice book and that Judaism wasn't a superficial cultural connection. Judaism, the Torah, encompasses all – it is everything. Every action, every thought, from the most mundane to the most spiritual can and should be made Holy. Judaism allows the traveler to travel on many different paths and each person has his or her own journey, but the ultimate destination requires that G-d is the final address. If not, you simply can't arrive.

~ ~ ~

Chanukah is celebrated in the middle of the winter and we are commanded to light the *menorah* at night, when it's dark outside. In Hebrew the word for darkness (*choshech*) and the word for forget (*shachach*) share the same letters. We therefore light the *menorah* at night to illuminate us and remind us that in Judaism we are not allowed to forget – who our Creator is, why we are here, or what we are doing. We light the *menorah* and we are reminded that everything, every *mitzvah* that we do, is important and brings us closer and closer to our Destination.

Planting a Seed

Right outside my window are three tall, majestic trees. As I watch their leaves blow in the wind, I feel so grateful for their presence. Looking at these trees takes me to a different place, a different state of mind. My intense city life, which never seems to stop for a second, comes to a halt as I look at those beautiful trees. I feel calmer, more at peace. I wonder to myself, "Who planted these trees?"

Thirty years ago, my neighborhood didn't even exist. Then someone with a vision came and built. They built building after building. Someone with a different vision came with a few seeds. They planted the seeds. And now, thirty years later, in front of me are three gigantic trees.

The world of a good friend of mine was recently turned upside down. She found out that many children in her neighborhood had been abused by one of her neighbors. She sent an e-mail asking for help to raise money for psychological support for the victims and their families. She took a chance, and with a pure heart, planted a seed. Within a very short amount of time her seed grew into a tree, as many women wrote back, donating thousands of dollars for assistance.

The other day, I took my children outside with big garbage bags and a box of ice pops. I couldn't take the sight of the litter that I encounter every time I step out of my apartment building. I was also tired of complaining to my husband about it. We opened the bags and bent over, starting to pick up the trash. Curious kids and neighbors came to see what we were doing.

With a big smile I called out, "Anyone who wants to help us, please do so, and take an ice pop for the effort!" Within a short time, I had quite a few volunteers. I planted a seed, and in a few hours the seed grew into a tree, as we threw out eight big bags full of garbage.

Over two thousand years ago, a battle raged in Israel between the Greeks and the Jews. The Jews miraculously won the war and, upon returning, went to clean up and rededicate the Holy Temple. They wanted to light the *menorah*, but there were no unbroken flasks of olive oil with which to light it. All of sudden, someone found a flask of untouched, pure olive oil. The flask contained enough oil for just one day, and it took eight days in order to make more oil. They lit the *menorah*. With a pure heart, they took a chance and planted a seed. G-d performed a miracle, and the little amount of oil lasted for eight days.

Chanukah, the festival of lights, is all about taking chances and planting seeds. We live in a world of a lot of darkness, of concealed light, but it doesn't take much to reveal the light that is within and about. In fact, you need only a little bit of light to illuminate an entire room of darkness. You have an idea, you want to help someone. Take a chance, plant a seed. Whether the seed turns into a tree or not is not in our control; but the effort of planting, that's up to all of us. I can't tell you how many volunteer organizations, how many schools and classes, how much goodness in this world is revealed from the effort of one person who had one idea and took a chance to plant a seed. You might not see the results now, but maybe in thirty years, someone will benefit and be grateful for the trees that you planted.

Celebrating Being Different

In my senior year of high school I saw an advertisement for a Junior Miss Pageant. The reward for winning was a $10,000 college scholarship, and when I saw that grades were a factor in selecting the contestants I thought to myself: "Why not give it a try?"

Really, it was a little bit far-fetched, a 5'1" girl winning a pageant, but I decided to give it a shot. I spent an entire Sunday competing. I danced before the judges, gave a speech, handed them my report card, and did a lot of smiling. And then we waited for the results. To the utter shock of my parents and myself, I won the regional contest.

The next stage was the state competition. I was off for three days to a small town in California. I *really* felt out of place. I had always stuck out in one way or another. I was used to being different and certainly used to being a distinct, brunette Jew in my small school full of blond-haired, blue-eyed Protestants. But this time I couldn't help feeling estranged as I noticed that I was the *only* Jew. And I wasn't the only one to notice. All the contestants noticed, too. I had never felt so isolated or scrutinized as I did when everyone held hands in prayer circles and started to talk about a belief that was completely foreign to me. "You're one of those swindling Hebrews?" I was asked as I declined to join them.

What had I gotten myself into? I kept to myself, and ignored their comments.

Then came the moment of truth. The auditorium was full of people. As I stood on the stage looking out into the audience, the judges asked me:

"Where is your favorite place, and why?"

Should I give them an answer that they want to hear, one that won't separate me from the group and will increase my chances of winning, or do I tell them what is really in my heart? I thought back to the trip that I had taken two years before, to the land that I had vowed that I would return to and to the place that I now call home.

"Mi la'Hashem eilai" – "Whoever is for G-d come to me," a voice within my soul cried out. I opened my mouth and with the biggest smile I could muster I said with confidence, "Israel" as I began to explain my love of the Holy Land and my ancestral heritage.

Needless to say, I lost the pageant.

~ ~ ~

Over three thousand years ago the Nation of Israel left Egypt. Before they entered Israel they were faced with tests, one of which was patience. Moses went up Mount Sinai to receive the commandments from G-d and the people started to panic as they thought that he delayed too much in coming down. They jumped to the conclusion that something fateful had happened to Moses and they started to complain to Aaron. The result was disastrous.

The men donated all their gold and jewelry to make a Golden Calf. The women however refused to participate in the building of the Calf and the idolatrous festivities that followed. When Moses came down with the two tablets of the Ten Commandments he was so shocked and angry by what he saw that he broke them. He then called out, *"Mi la'Hashem eilai!"* – "Whoever is for G-d come to me!"

Only a small group of Levites joined him. The Levites were later rewarded with the honor as serving G-d in the Temple. They took the privileges of the first born and became the Nation's priests and teachers. And according to the *Midrash*, G-d gave the holiday of *Rosh Chodesh* (the festival of the New Moon/Month) to the women as their reward for not sinning with the Golden Calf. Therefore it is an accepted practice in many communities that women refrain from certain mundane work on *Rosh Chodesh*.

Rosh Chodesh is a special, festive day. An extra prayer service is added to the morning service. Some people have the custom to wear a white shirt on *Rosh Chodesh* and eat a special meal, and there are prohibitions against eulogies and fasting. However, for the most part, work is permitted on *Rosh Chodesh*. On a superficial level, *Rosh Chodesh* looks like any other day. It is not like *Shabbat* or holidays on which work is prohibited. We also don't have to sanctify *Rosh Chodesh* with a blessing on wine like we do *Shabbat*, *Pesach*, *Sukkot*, or *Shavuot*.

Chanukah is also a holiday on which mundane work is permitted. During *Chanukah*, we are not required to have a special meal or keep the laws and customs reserved for other holidays. But what we do which is unique to *Chanukah*, is light the *menorah*.

The Rambam (Maimonides) writes that the commandment of lighting the *Chanukah* candles is very precious. All the commandments are precious and loved by G-d, but the Rambam singles out this one in particular.

The rulers of Greece were willing to accept most of the Torah and have it "incorporated" into Greek beliefs, but there were three Torah commandments which they sought to annul: *Shabbat, Rosh Chodesh* (the sanctification of the months), and *Brit Milah* (circumcision). They tried to persuade the Jews to join them and be like them. It was a very difficult time and the Greek offer to be like "everyone else" was very tempting.

However, just like in the incident with the Golden Calf, one man (in this case, Mattityahu), stood up and cried out, *"Mi La'Hashem Eilai!"* A small group of men joined him, as well as, of course, the holy Jewish women – who defied the Greeks in their own way.

The women did everything in their power to defy the harsh decree that had been issued by the Greeks. The Greeks ordained that every single girl had to be first brought to the Greek leader before she could be wed. One woman, Yehudit, the daughter of Yochanan the High Priest was exceptionally beautiful and the Greek General, Eliphorni, desired her. She pretended to acquiesce, came to his tent and fed him cheese and gave him wine. He became intoxicated and fell asleep. Praying to G-d for strength she fearlessly beheaded him with his own sword and brought his head to Jerusalem. When the enemy commanders saw what had happened they fled. As a reminder of their bravery and loyalty to G-d, there is a custom that as long as the *Chanukah* lights are burning women refrain from doing work. (The Maharil writes that this is a tradition for both men and women.)

In the winter months when the day is short and the night is long we are commanded to light the *menorah* at nightfall, illuminating the darkness. The flickering lights contrast against the black of the night. A small amount of light amidst a lot of darkness makes a great distinction. The miracle of *Chanukah* is not the winning of battles. We did that before and we have done that since. The miracle of *Chanukah* is in the light; it is in the miracle that G-d performed for us by making the small amount of pure oil last for eight days and the message that comes with this miracle. The message that we were created separate and distinct. And the message that we were created to be a light in the darkness.

Lighting Souls

I was sitting on a park bench talking with another mother as we watched our toddlers play. The two boys were enjoying each other's company, and so were we. The other mother turned to me and said, "My son is so difficult. I have a really difficult child." I know this mother and I know her son. I don't see her everyday and we share no living spaces together, but I've spoken with her frequently.

"Hmmmm," I sighed. "You *really* think that?" My heart weighed heavy in my chest. I'm sure every mother, at one time or another, has these thoughts. What is so sad is that we feel this way over healthy, "normal" children who do what healthy, normal children do – cry and throw tantrums and act defiantly. I wanted to empathize with her, I wanted to be tactful, but I also wanted to express my disagreement with her. "I know it's difficult, but the situation is difficult, the age is difficult. Your child *isn't* difficult." I held my breath, not knowing how she would respond.

"You mean your son throws tantrums too?"

"Almost every day," I smiled.

I've recently started attending a parenting class, and in the past three weeks, I've noticed incredible differences in my son's behavior and in our relationship. While I give much credit to the strategies I'm learning, the one point I've learned most is that I'm not alone! Everyone has difficult moments. I'm not a failure as a mother if my son misbehaves, and he's also not a failure when he misbehaves. He's just a child and I'm just a parent. With this in mind, my whole attitude has changed. I find myself more patient and able to take things in strides. He mirrors my behavior and cooperates with joy. Instead of feeling relief when he falls asleep at night, I feel fulfillment for the beautiful day we spent together.

~ ~ ~

A great man in history, Noah, lived in a generation when the population rebelled against G-d. He was given a task to influence the people to change their ways, but couldn't. Noah prophesized the flood, warning the people of their doom. No one listened.

One explanation given for his failure is that it was in his tactic: He told the people that they were doomed, and the people fulfilled these words, living up to his expectations. Perhaps, if instead of telling the people of their wickedness, he would have told them of their great potential, his words would have brought about a positive change. I was once told, "Never tell your children that they are going to fall, because they will. Instead tell them, 'Careful, you *could* fall.'" Our words, just as much as our actions, have the power to make things happen.

~ ~ ~

When the High Priest would light the *menorah*, he had to place the fire by the wick until it was alight on its own. He didn't just light it and step back to see if the flame would catch, but made sure it would light. During *Chanukah*, we do the same. We stay with the wick until we see that it ignites and then we step back holding the candle that lit the flame. Not only that, but on *Chanukah*, we're required to provide enough oil or wax for the candle to burn for at least a half an hour. The flames have to be in a straight line, and no two flames can touch.

In Jewish literature, the soul is often referred to as a candle. When my husband and I light the *menorah*, we imagine ourselves lighting our child's soul. The measurements are difficult. First there needs to be sufficient oil or wax to feed the flame. If we don't encourage our children, and give them enough physical and spiritual nourishment, even if lit, their wicks will quickly burn out. Secondly, we need to stay with the wick, making sure it catches, but once it does catch, we need to stand back. This is comparable to giving our children space to stand on their own and illuminate the world with *their* light, not ours. Lastly, too much fire is dangerous. If we pour oil on the actual flame with our negative prophesies, the fire will rage and burn uncontrollably.

Every night after we light the *menorah*, we stay with the flickering flames for at least a half hour and sing and dance by its light. I whisper petitions to G-d by the *menorah*'s glowing light, praying for my family, asking Him to guide me as a mother and illuminate me with the wisdom I so need to be a good mommy.

It's hard to be a parent. It's more than a profession or occupation; it's all-encompassing and never-ending. But it's easier to find the goodness when you see it through joyous eyes. You also have a better chance for positive results when you predict positive outcomes. The foundation of the self-esteem and self-confidence of our children lies in our hands. If we perceive them as good and beautiful beings, then we are giving them the basis to not only believe in themselves, but to fulfill these constructive prophesies of goodness.

True Beauty

There I was, sitting on the park bench. My children were playing on the swings. They climbed on monkey bars and slid down slides. My eyes wandered between watching them and observing all the other people around me. I saw one woman in particular. Her beauty made an impression on me. She had a certain glow to her. She was gorgeous. But if I were to tell you how she looked, I'm not sure that you would believe me. So let me first describe her, and then give me just a minute of your time to explain.

I couldn't tell her weight as there was not a single item of clothing that clung to her body. Her neat attire was elegant and tailored. It was far from tight or snugly fitted and it certainly wasn't baggy. I'm assuming that she was average weight; I can't remember but I think average height. Her clothes were far from trendy but at the same time they didn't look old-fashioned. They were simple, clean. She looked timeless, classic, incredibly feminine. The colors of her skirt, shirt and sweater were neither too dark, nor too bright. Lastly, the hair of this married mother was perfectly covered, her head-covering tucked neatly into place. So what exactly was it about her that made her so beautiful?

Her face shone with light. She flashed me a radiating smile. She waived to her children just like I did, giving them encouragement and attention, and then she took out a book of Psalms and began to say their words. This woman, in her modesty and simplicity, struck me with her confident presence. She didn't stand out and yet you knew that she was there. "This," I thought to myself, "is the beauty I want people to describe when they see me or my daughter." This was the beauty that King David described when he said, "All the glory of the princess is within" (Psalms 45:13).

~ ~ ~

In Jerusalem, where I live, the dark winter streets come alive during the eight days of *Chanukah*. Everywhere you look, you see candles or glass flasks of olive oil lit alight. It always strikes me, the beauty of the light, the beauty of the *menorah*s, the beauty of *Chanukah*. It's the same beauty that struck me with the woman in the park. What is this beauty? It's an internal beauty that radiates outward.

Over two thousand years ago, there was a war between the Greeks and the Jews. This was not a war over physical matters. It had nothing to do with territory or monetary issues. It was a war over the concept of beauty. The Greeks tried to convince the world that the body and the external presence define beauty. They defiled the Holy Temple, attempting to convert it into an ordinary building where the Divine Presence would not rest. They wanted to convert the body into an empty vessel that has no soul. The Jews, few in number, stood fast to their beliefs. The Holy Temple was not just a building, but a Sacred place to connect to the Creator; the body was not just an object, but a holy container to house the soul. Real beauty, they countered the Greeks, stems from within. In the end G-d helped the Jews win the war and the Truth was revealed for all. "All the glory of the princess is within."

After the Jews returned from winning the battle, they cleaned and re-dedicated the Temple. They wanted to light the *menorah*, which is a symbol of wisdom and spiritual splendor. All the oil flasks had been broken and opened. At last they found a single untouched flask, a tiny bit of oil which lasted for the eight days needed to press more. The *menorah* was lit. How did the *menorah* burn? There were three cups to the left, three cups to the right and one cup in the middle. The three flames to the left burned in the direction of the middle flame, the three to the right did the same. All light was focused to the center, inward. Why? Because Torah, Wisdom, the Soul, real beauty, do not need any externalities to improve their appearance or make them beautiful. They are the true definition of beauty. Beauty stems from an internal source that in turn radiates outward.

Being thin, having curves, wearing the most stylish clothes and having the trendiest accessories don't define a person or make her beautiful. The Greeks of today – the media, movie stars, models and pop singers – try to convince us that the body is just an object and beauty is only superficial. However as you light your *Chanukah menorah* and bask in its light, remind yourself of the truth which you already know, "All the glory of princess is within."

The Value of a Smile

After seven years of living in Israel without one...we finally bought a car! No more *shlepping* a stroller and two kids to the grocery store. No more changing buses and traveling for an hour to get to work. Finally, a car.

And it is a wonder we were able to get one as we didn't have the money for it and knew nothing about where to look or what to buy. But amazingly friends and the bank loaned us money and somehow, someway, my husband left one day in the morning and came back a few hours later with a car.

And then my friend called: "What's going on with the car?"

"We bought one! Salomon is bringing it home now."

"What kind?"

"I'm not really sure."

"Did you get it checked out first?"

"Um, I don't think so, I'm not really sure, he told me that he just bought it. "

"How could you by a car without checking it out first? "

All I could hear was bad. I wanted to cry. My cell phone rang, it was my husband telling me to come down to see our new car. I hung up the other phone with the "friend" and all I could think about was, "How could he have done this? How could he have bought the car without me? Without checking it out first" etc. etc. etc.

My children and I went down to see the car. They were jumping up and down with excitement. For them, a car is like a trip to Disneyland. I saw the car, but I didn't see the car. All I saw were the dents and the scratches. "This is the car?" I growled at him. My husband's face fell.

"Come let's go for a ride."

We drove around our neighborhood. My children singing and clapping, myself sulking. Then all of a sudden by the grace of G-d I snapped out of it. "Elana, you have a car! Your husband tries so hard to please you. Be appreciative, be happy!" I apologized to my husband and started to notice that the car was comfortable and it worked, we were driving!

When we came back home I promised myself to never allow a person to damper my happiness or to influence me in such a way that it would lower my opinion of my husband or family ever again. I also learned an incredible lesson about the importance of giving someone a compliment, of either saying only good things or of keeping my mouth shut and not saying anything at all. Once a deed is done, it's done. Once the item is bought, compliment it.

~ ~ ~

In the Talmud the Sages discuss whether or not a person can lie at a wedding and tell the groom that his wife is beautiful, even if the person thinks that she is ugly. The Sages conclude that not only is it permissible, but one should tell the groom his wife is beautiful because it's not a lie, since to the groom she surely is beautiful. Additionally it is praiseworthy to elevate her in his eyes.

One of my teachers pointed out to me that the *menorah* is in the same shape as a smile on a person's face. When you walk the streets of Jerusalem during *Chanukah*, you not only see *menorah*s alit, burning bright from every window, but you see them on the street in front of homes and apartment buildings.

I'll never forget the gigantic *menorah* of my youth in the middle of Union Square, SF. The Chabad rabbi used a crane in order to be able to reach it to light it with his big blow torch. On *Chanukah*, the bigger the *menorah*, the better. The more people can see it the better. Why? Because part of the *mitzvah* of lighting the *menorah* is to publicize the miracle that occurred thousands of years ago involving a small flask of oil and the Holy Temple's *menorah*.

When the few Jews returned from winning the battle against the mighty Greeks they came back to find the Temple in ruins. They started to clean up, and wanted to rededicate the Temple and light the *menorah*. They found only a small flask of the pure olive oil. They decided to light the *menorah* even though it wouldn't be enough to last for the eight days that was needed to make more oil. A miracle happened and the oil burned and lasted for the entire eight days.

When I see the *menorah* burning so brightly, telling me that yes, "miracles" really do happen, that yes even in the darkness, there are always sparks of light I can't help but smile. The light of the *menorah* is beautiful and its shape reminds me, "Elana, smile!!!! Even if you don't feel like it on the inside, smile on the outside. Publicize your smile and by doing this you will shine light and make people happy." You don't like your friend's new dress? You don't have to express your opinion about it – smile, compliment her on her shoes instead. You think the drawing that your child brought home is a scribble and he thinks it's a masterpiece. Smile. Don't ruin it for him, compliment him on his effort. Your husband made you a surprise dinner that tastes burnt. Smile. Appreciate his thoughtfulness; it will actually make the food taste better. Whatever you do, don't forget to smile!

A Time to Light Your Child's Way

I sat down to say some psalms and pray as my toddler pulled on my skirt. His pulling and pleading became more insistent and I ignored him. I knew his cries were a result of being tired and cranky and I had thought that he could wait. "Mommy needs to pray."

Being ignored only made him more frustrated and he ran over to the bookshelf, a look of anger on his little round face. Looking straight at me, he took a book and slammed it to the floor, hoping to provoke me. I didn't flinch, which was not the reaction that he wanted. He sat down to cry and I quickly finished praying.

I realized as I put my book down that my prayers had essentially been in vain. Mommy didn't *need* to pray, Mommy *wanted* to pray, and there's a big difference. What Mommy needed to be doing, her only obligation, was to pay attention to the needs of her toddler.

~ ~ ~

A friend of mine came to me one day exasperated. She was having a very frustrating day. At the end of her tale she shared with me that she wanted nothing more than to call and talk to her mother, but she said that she couldn't. I asked her why not. She told me that her mother never had time for her, never listened to her. Even as a child her mother had always been "too busy" to pay attention to her. As a result she simply shut down and stopped confiding in her. She told me that she wouldn't tell her mother about her day because she couldn't stand the thought of being ignored – again.

~ ~ ~

From early spring until the fall the Jewish people get caught up in a whirlwind of holidays: *Purim, Pesach, Shavuot*, the fasts of the Seventeenth of *Tammuz* and the Ninth of Av and then of course *Rosh Hashanah, Yom Kippur, Sukkot*, and *Simchat Torah*. When you are in the middle of festivities, planning, cooking, shopping, cleaning, and building, you can more easily reach a feeling of closeness to G-d and His Torah. But then comes the cold winter months of nothingness, and perhaps, distance. However, in the middle of this very darkness, G-d gave us the festival of lights, *Chanukah*.

Chanukah has two very important aspects: publicizing and educating. It's one of the only holidays when we are commanded to actually go out and "publicize" the miracle. I'll never forget seeing the large *menorah* proudly standing in the middle of Union Square in my native San Francisco. I continue to be captivated by the lights as my husband and I walk the streets of Jerusalem, admiring the wicks of the many *menorah*'s flickering from the windows and doorposts of every home.

Publicizing is an easy component of *Chanukah* to understand, but what does it have to do with education? The word "*Chanukah*" means inauguration, but it also has the same root as the word "*Chinuch*" education. In the middle of the dark winter months, G-d performed miracles for us. He enabled a few Jews to win a war of survival against the huge Greek army and he enabled the amount of one day's worth of oil to burn for eight. Of the two miracles, we publicize the one of the burning oil.

What happens when you light a candle in the dark? It illuminates everything and grabs your attention. This is *Chanukah*, and this is the lesson of education. Before your child acts out and misbehaves to get your attention and before, G-d forbid, your child shuts down and distances himself from you, ignite a spark, captivate, and get his attention.

This is the festival of *Chanukah*. It's the holiday when G-d tells us, "Hey I'm here, don't turn away from Me. Even in your most obscure moment, I'm the flame that illuminates your way." With the miracle of a burning light G-d taught us this key on how to raise and educate our children. Be their light and grab their attention.

Every Word Counts

My husband and son danced as I cried and stared into the glowing flames of the *Chanukah menorah*. I was told that *Chanukah* is the end of a long journey that begins with *Rosh Hashanah*. On *Chanukah* the gates of Heaven are wide open to receive prayer, and one's judgment for the year is finally sealed. Salty tears wet my cheeks as I prayed my heart out. Why so much? Why such emotion? After all, I had a son, a healthy child. My prayers had been answered with a gracious "yes!" before; why then the longing and the feeling of rejection? Because my husband and I had just celebrated six years of marriage, and in four more months my son would be two-years-old, and my womb was once again empty. Maybe the yes had been a merciful, one time occurrence and I would never know again what it would be like to bring another child into the world? I finished my weeping and brought myself back to my husband and son and joined them in their dancing.

A week or so later I was looking through some papers when I came across my *ketubah*, my Jewish wedding contract. I looked at it and my eyes fell upon my name, Elana. Elana? Where was my other name? I generally only go by my first name, but my parents gave me two names: Elana Mira. I quickly showed it to my husband. Why hadn't we noticed this before? Did it really matter? I insisted that he take it to a rabbi the next day to ask. I wanted to make sure that we were doing things right. We were told that we should have a new marriage contract drafted. The following week on the eighteenth day (which is the numerical value of *chai*, life) of the Jewish month of *Tevet*, we had a little ceremony with a new *ketubah*.

About a month and a half later, I went back to my infertility specialist doctor. I sat in his office with my son. He wrote out a set of prescriptions for hormone injections and a plan for me to follow. I don't know why, but I suddenly told him that I wanted to wait until after *Pesach* when my son would already have turned two. He didn't pressure me, but told me, "No problem, everything is all written out and ready to go. When you want to start, come back, and we'll start."

I left knowing that I wouldn't be back. I came home and explained to my husband that I just couldn't do this again. I would take herbs, I would follow a strictly healthy diet, but I couldn't start with the treatments again, with the running around like a madwoman, the ups and downs, and the anxiety. I just wanted to be happy with what I had and be thankful that I had a son. My husband fully supported me. Two weeks later, I conceived; but it wasn't until two months later that I found out that I was pregnant. I went to have an ultrasound to determine the due date of my baby because I had no idea when I conceived. They told me that the due date was the first day of *Chanukah*. My daughter was born eight days early on the eighteenth day of the Jewish month of *Kislev*, eleven months to the day after we changed our *ketubah*.

What's the deal with the *ketubah*? Did it make a difference? Did it change something in the Heavens? I don't know. What I do know is that the prayer I had offered as I stared into the flickering flames of the *Chanukah* lights changed something above, and changed something within. And when I saw my *ketubah* with part of my name missing, I knew that something wasn't right.

~ ~ ~

A long time ago, a really great miracle happened. A tiny Jewish army fought against the biggest army of the time, the Greeks, and they won! But that wasn't the only miracle. On *Chanukah*, we celebrate the tiny bit of oil that lasted eight days. Hmmm. Which sounds like a bigger miracle? And really, what's the big deal with the oil?

The Jewish fighters came back from the war and started cleaning up the Holy Temple. They wanted to rededicate it by kindling the *menorah*, but all the pure oil, the oil sealed by the High Priest, had been spoiled by the Greeks; the seals had been broken. And then they found one tiny flask of this special oil. It would take eight days to make new oil, and they didn't have enough to last that long. They had a choice: to use oil that wasn't so fine and pure, but know that the *menorah* would be lit during the time that it took to make new oil, or to go ahead and use the purest and finest oil that they had, even if it would only last a short while. In thankfulness and praise to G-d for winning the war, they took a chance; they decided to only light with the pure oil. They gave the best that they could give, and G-d performed a miracle. It was as if G-d told them, "You give Me the best that you can, and I will take care of the rest."

~ ~ ~

My daughter turned one-year-old, thank G-d, and once again, we are getting ready to light the *Chanukah menorah*. My husband carefully pours the oil, and I kiss my daughter's cheeks as I offer thanks. I pour my heart out once again as I watch the majestic flames and I say my name aloud: Elana Mira.

Tu B'Shvat

My Little Tree

The other day I was in the park with my son when I met another mother. When I told her that my name was Elana, which comes from the Hebrew word *elan* (tree), she asked me if I had been born on *Tu B'Shvat*, the fifteenth day of the Hebrew month of *Shvat* which is the *Rosh Hashanah* (beginning of the year) for the trees. While my birthday is not *Tu B'Shvat*, my name does encompass my essence, as I have a love for nature, trees, and fruit.

~ ~ ~

In the month of Nissan, which always marks the beginning of Spring, a special blessing is recited in appreciation for the pleasure we get from trees. But it is in the month of *Shvat* that we have *Tu B'Shvat* – the "birthday" so to speak of the trees. The day has *halachic* (Jewish law) implications with respect to agricultural tithes and the laws of *orlah*. There is also a custom to eat many fruits, especially the fruits of the Land of Israel (dates, olives, grapes, pomegranates, and figs, and grains – barley, and wheat) in recognition of the bounty and goodness of the Land.

For the first three years of a fruit tree's life we are not allowed to eat its fruits. During these three years the tree is called "*orlah*." There is a custom widely practiced amongst Chassidic and Sephardic Jews not to cut boys' hair until they are three years old. This custom is partly derived from the idea of *orlah:* for the first three years you let the child's hair grow – he remains untouched.

The Torah likens man to a tree (Deuteronomy 20:19) and the word for man, *adam*, comes from the word *adama* (ground/earth) because G-d created man from the ground. The Maharal asks: why is only man called *adam* if all creatures were also created from the ground? He answers that only man has the potential to grow with work. He is just like the ground in that if you cultivate, irrigate, and plant it so to you actualize the potential within.

~ ~ ~

On the way home from the park I gave my son a box of raisins. After he finished eating his raisins he took the box, with his little ponytail bobbing in the air, he ran up to the garbage bin and threw the box away. I started to clap and smile, "Bravo Avraham Nissim!!!" I told him. "Great job, I'm so proud of you. You're so thoughtful and caring." I was so proud of my son, who was still more than three months shy of his second birthday.

I was also amazed at how I never told him to throw it out, and yet after seeing me always throwing away my garbage, picking up litter as we go, and making sure to never drop litter myself, the seeds of his education in consideration for the public had sprouted. My son is my little tree and my job as a mother is to water him, shower him with sunshine and happiness, and set a good example for him to follow. Our children are the seedlings that grow into great trees.

Is it Worth it?

Is it worth it? It's a question I as a mother find myself asking all the time. Is it worth it?

Yesterday there wasn't a rain cloud in sight; the sky was clear and sunny. My toddler insisted on wearing his rain boots to preschool. He insisted. I thought he looked so silly, but I asked myself, "Is it worth it? It is worth the tantrum or for him to go to school in a bad mood over rain boots?"

There are days when right after I just made the beds, my children will grab the pillows and blankets. They start hanging and tying sheets, the bedroom turns into jungle and a tent. "I just made the beds. You are making a mess!" I catch myself and ask myself as the words come tumbling out of my mouth, "Is it really worth it?" Can I just let go, let them play, and ignore the disarray? Now, at this moment, is this worth a fight? Is it worth it?"

There are days when they ask me for a treat. They can ask and ask and ask and in the end I give in. At that moment I don't feel like saying "No" is worth it. But these same children who know how to ask and ask, once asked me to buy a candy from a store when we were traveling. "No, it's not kosher," I replied. They didn't ask again, because they knew that on this Mommy wouldn't budge. This was worth it.

A few weeks ago my son asked me to buy him a Game-Boy. I don't like Game-Boys. I don't like any computer or electrical games. I love that my children play ball outside, ride their bikes, hang on bars and use toilet paper rolls to make worlds that are filled with imagination. I like that they cut and tape paper and build with blocks and clicks. I love to watch them read and play with puppets. I don't like them to stare at a screen and sit for hours and hours. I don't like that when a child (or an adult for that matter!) is playing with an electrical device you can call his name twenty times and he won't hear what you said. The time can pass and in the end when she finally puts the game down or closes the computer you realize that all that she did was nothing. So when my son asked me, "Mommy will you buy me a game boy," you don't have to be a mind reader to figure out my answer: "No."

His reply: "Do you want to think about it?"

"No, I am so sure that I don't want you to have one and I feel so strongly that it's not good for you that I don't need to think about it."

He didn't ask me again. Why? Because he understood that for me, it's worth it.

I'm home alone with one of my children. I see them take out a toy that belongs to one of their siblings. I tell them to put it back and that they are not allowed to take or use something that doesn't belong to them without asking permission first. "But they won't know and I'm sure that they wouldn't care anyways."

"No! You need to put it back." For me this is a battle in which, yes – it's worth it. I can't have my children feeling unsafe in their homes, feeling that their property and space are not respected. The Torah doesn't allow me to raise my children to think that they can take things which are not theirs without asking, or that the fact that "no one will know" makes it okay. G-d runs the world and He sees and knows everything.

~ ~ ~

Many years ago a friend and mentor of mine told me, "Elana when your children do something that you don't like or don't want, first ask yourself if this is something that they will still be doing when they get older. Look at the long term consequences and try to base your reaction on that.

The Torah likens man to a tree for "man is the tree of the field." I think what my friend was trying to tell me was, "See what actions your children do which will actually bear fruit." What seeds do you want to plant in your children? What water do you want them to drink from and from where are they getting their sunshine? Is wearing rain boots on a sunny day, an act that will be outgrown and bear no fruit, really worth the bad mood and argument? And on the other hand, what things do we need to stop before they take root? What is really worth it?

I look at my children, the fruit of my life. I pray that they grow and blossom into beautiful trees. That their roots be firmly planted in our ancestors, that their bodies grow strong and that they are stable like the trunk of a tree, that their limbs are busy in doing good deeds and learning Torah and that their actions bear beautiful fruit for the future. And so, before I open my mouth to reprimand I ask myself, "Is it worth it?"

Purim

Revealing Your Mission

"*How* did you get into this?" "Why did you get into this?" I get these questions all the time. How did a Stanford graduate in international relations get into helping women who are trying to conceive with the assistance of (a lot of prayer! and) alternative medicine? The "how" is answered by the "why," and the "why" is answered by my story.

My husband and I were married nearly four years, and had gone through numerous fertility treatments. Nothing seemed to work, as we ran from doctor to doctor.

I went through ups and downs – moments of hope and moments of disappointment. My husband and I had each other, of course, and we grew so close due to the experience, but I still felt so alone. Could anyone understand what I was going through? I felt like a pincushion, as each shot of hormone was injected into my body. I lost my always-present smile, as I was on an emotional and physical roller coaster. I wanted to give up, and yet I knew that I couldn't. There were times of despair and of asking, *Why?* There were times when I said, *Enough. Stop waiting, stop wanting, live your life.*

After nearly four years, a friend suggested giving alternative medicine a try. We looked into it, and went to a recommended religious practitioner. I walked out from his office sobbing. It was the first time that anyone had ever looked at me and asked me how I am. I wasn't just a name on a record. I wasn't just an ultrasound or x-ray; I wasn't just a blood test. I was a person. The practitioner was humble. He didn't make promises, and yet he gave me hope. He was thorough, he was professional, and he made me feel like a human being instead of an object. Later I found out that he himself had been married for years without children.

We gave it a try and, thank G-d, had a healthy boy less than a year later. I had a beautiful pregnancy, a beautiful birth, and I told my husband, "I want to learn, and I want to help other women." That was almost eight years ago, and now, thank G-d, I have a list of women in whose process to conceiving or birthing a child into this world I have merited to have a part.

~ ~ ~

The king of Persia, Achashverosh, was in search of a wife after having sentenced his queen, Vashti, to death. The search dragged on for four years. Thousands of prospects passed through the imperial agencies, but none even came close to finding favor in the eyes of the king.

One woman, a Jewish orphan named Esther (related to the word *seter*, which means "hidden") was hidden by her devoted uncle, Mordechai, who was prepared to risk his life to prevent her from being taken to the palace. She was spotted, and taken – against her will – to the palace. The search came to an end as Esther was chosen as queen.

Can you image what she was thinking? I know what I would be thinking: *Why? Why me? Why this?* The reason was hidden from her, but not knowing the "why" didn't shake her. By order of her uncle she concealed her true identity, and continued to stay connected to Mordechai and to her faith.

In the meantime a wicked man, Haman, rose to power. He devised a plan to kill the Jewish people, and with the consent of the king, a decree was sent throughout the Persian empire that in eleven months, in the month of Adar, all the king's subjects should attack and kill all the Jews.

Soon after the terrible decree went public, the hidden became revealed, the mysterious "why" answered. Why had Esther been chosen as the queen? Mordechai informed her: "Esther, Providence brought you to this unlikely station for a purpose, and you must fulfill it. Now is the time for you to speak up on behalf of our people. There is no time to waste."

Esther – Queen Esther – understood with these words that she had been chosen as queen and put into her situation so that she could be the messenger to save her people.

Queen Esther was a messenger. It is within all of our powers to be a messenger.

~ ~ ~

Now, thank G-d, three children later, my perspective is obviously so different than what it was when I felt that longing, that wanting, those irrational feelings of guilt. But when a woman comes to me for a treatment, I always make myself remember. I look at her in the eyes. I see the person before me, and I try to see the whole picture. And as much as anyone could possibly understand the pain of another, to some extent, I do. I am called all the time for medical advice, support, a listening ear. I look back now at my journey and I know that the challenges in the beginning got me to where I am now. I do what I do because I love it, and because I realize that all those treatments – they weren't for nothing. It feel as though G-d told me, "I am putting you in this situation so that you will have more understanding, that you will use this to help other people."

~ ~ ~

G-d's name is not mentioned in the entire book of Esther. The sages teach that the path a person wishes to take is the path towards which he'll be directed. You could look at your life and all the challenges and say to yourself, *For what? Why? What a hardship, what a waste.* Or you could look at those very same challenges and say, *What a hardship! Let me use what I learned from this experience to help others. Let me use my position, skills, knowledge, money, power, etc., that I have, to help others.*

The story of *Purim* teaches us that everything is for a reason. We have a choice to see and reveal the reason, or to keep it hidden.

A Single Act

I was in my ninth month of pregnancy, it was early the morning, and I was taking a walk. In rain or sunshine, pregnant or not, you'll always find me walking or running in the early morning hours when the sun is just beginning to rise and you can still hear the chirping of the birds.

I walked past a bus stop just as a bus pulled over and opened its doors for me. I assumed he opened the doors because he thought I wanted a ride. "No, thank you," I shouted to the driver, "I'm just walking. I don't want to get on the bus."

"I know," he replied, "I see you every morning. *Kol hakavod* (a Hebrew expression of congratulations), I just wanted to let you know that you've inspired me. Because of you, I started walking too, and I've already lost six kilo (thirteen pounds)." Now it was my turn to tell him "*kol hakavod*." I wished him a good day and we both went on our way. Maybe this man would have lost the weight even if he hadn't seen me walking. But I was the catalyst which set it into motion. Unbeknownst to me (until that morning) my simple act of exercise made a difference in another person's life.

~ ~ ~

The very existence of the Jewish nation is in jeopardy. There is one woman, Esther, who is in a position to save the nation. Her uncle, Mordechai, tells her to take action. Esther replies that she can't, because if she does, her life will be in danger. He responds to her, "Do not imagine in your soul that you will be able to escape in the king's palace any more than the rest of the Jews. For if you persist in keeping silent at a time like this, **relief and deliverance will come to the Jews from another place**, while you and your father's house will perish..." (Esther 4:12–14). Mordechai is telling Esther that if she doesn't do her part to save the Jewish people, someone else will.

We are familiar with the expression, "It's all in G-d's hands." But if everything is all in G-d's hands, does it really make a difference what I do? Can a small act, a smile, a kind word, or standing up for your convictions, really make a difference?

~ ~ ~

Everything is in G-d's hands, but He gives us a choice. He allows us to choose whether we will be the ones through whom He reveals Himself. Esther could have easily kept quiet and ignored Mordechai's orders. No one would have known, and even if they did, who would have blamed her? After all, she would be putting her life in danger by approaching the king without first being summoned. Esther heard Mordechai's words: salvation would come, if not through her, then through another. She could have easily replayed this message in her heart and not worried about her brethren. Someone else would come to the rescue. She was an orphan without any siblings. She could have just saved herself and her uncle, and let someone else worry about the rest of the Jews. But she decided to take the risk, to be the one to save her nation, including people whom she didn't even know.

Moses was also put in a position to act. G-d came to him and told him that he would be the one to lead His people out of Egypt. Moses, in his humility, questioned G-d. "Who am I to lead Israel? Choose another person who is better; it should be my brother Aaron." But G-d insisted. He didn't want someone else, He wanted Moses. And Moses thus became the greatest leader of the Jewish people. However, the commentators explain that because Moses doubted his own capability and was hesitant to perform the job, the priesthood was taken away from his descendants and given to Aaron's.

~ ~ ~

Imagine the influence of all the little acts we do that we don't even realize. How much more so is the influence of the acts that we *do* perform with the consciousness to elevate ourselves and help those around us, especially the ones for which we don't receive any credit.

On *Purim*, we read the Book of Esther. In the entire book of Esther, the name of G-d is never explicitly mentioned. Unlike *Pesach*, where we see G-d's involvement and open miracles, on *Purim* His involvement and miracles are merely alluded to, His greatness is hidden. He receives no glory or praise for the kindness that He does.

So too did Esther act behind the scenes. No one, except for Mordechai, knew of her incredible self–sacrifice, and yet she did it. While *Purim* celebrates the triumph of the Jewish nation over an enemy, we also celebrate the act of a single Jewish woman who cared enough to risk her own life for her people. Before Esther courageously confronted King Achashverosh and Haman, she asked the nation to join her in a three-day fast. The entire people fasted with her in unity. Their fast has become our fast. Her example to act serves as an inspiration for us to act. One can never get discouraged and refrain from action due to the fear that it "wouldn't matter anyway." We have to always remember the lesson Esther taught us. It's not "Can I make a difference?" but rather, "Will I be the one to make a difference?"

Behind the Mask

I'm trying to decide how to dress up my two year old for *Purim*. He's our first child and I remember last year I almost didn't make him a costume because it seemed silly to dress up a baby. But in the end, with the excitement of everyone getting dressed up, I did make him a costume. I cut a piece of felt and made it into a tunic and glued fish all over it. He was the "splitting of the red sea." My son, Avraham Nissim, who was born on the last day of *Pesach* and whose second name means "miracles," is our little miracle child. I became pregnant with him after a three and a half year journey of fertility treatments. The miracle of the splitting of the red sea was thus a perfect costume.

This year once again I had the dilemma as to which costume to choose for him. I remember hearing a learned woman say that one should never disguise their children on *Purim* in a costume that represents something negative. "Don't put them in costumes as monsters or gangsters," she warned. The costume is an element of the essence of the person; it leaves an impression on the soul. How we dress influences us and our actions.

~ ~ ~

The whole idea of dressing up and wearing masks on *Purim* is interesting. The name of G-d is never mentioned in the story of *Purim*. G-d is alluded to when the story speaks of "the King," but you will not find His name written anywhere in the *megilla* (the scroll on which the story is written). One of the reasons we dress up is to "hide" ourselves just as G-d was hidden from us. When you hide, you know that, of course, you exist. On *Purim* this "hiding" is an act of faith as we demonstrate that even when the presence of G-d is hidden from us, He's always present.

Not just on *Purim*, but everyday we use our dress as a means of hiding and revealing. I remember how I used to dress ten years ago. Nothing was hidden, I let the world see my body. Everything was revealed, but "me," as a person, was certainly hidden. Now, while I still care about being presentable and attractive, my goal is no longer to attract. My dress hides the exterior and the interior, "me," is allowed to shine.

I've always been very much an individual. I took great care in trying to form my own style and portray myself as "unique" with my clothing. However, I realized the more eccentric I tried to be with my exterior, ironically, the more I looked like everyone else who was also trying to be trendy and different. Before I became observant I remember seeing "religious" people and thinking to myself, "They all dress the same, they're so boring." As I got to know them more and more I began to discover the uniqueness of each individual. The seeming similarity in their outward appearance forced me to look inside and see each as unique person, to see them for who they really were. In contrast, my former fashionable garb acted as a barrier to who I really was. People saw the outside and didn't look any further.

~ ~ ~

When the Torah speaks of our matriarchs, it mentions how they were all beautiful women. While the Torah is, of course, speaking of the spiritual beauty of these women, it is also talking about their physical beauty. Sarah was even abducted by the kings Avimelech and Pharaoh for her great beauty. The Torah also describes how Abraham was completely unaware of Sarah's beauty due to her modesty and the modesty of their relationship. As I read this I thought to myself, "It's possible to be so beautiful and not need to expose it?"

I remember once being in a class of over seventy Jewish women. The teacher was lecturing and all of sudden she stopped and commented, "Wow, look at you! *B'not Yisrael*, daughters of Israel, you are truly beautiful." I'll never forget that comment as I looked around the room and saw that yes, each was truly attractive in her own way.

In the story of *Purim* the main character is Esther, another Jewish beauty. Esther's name is similar to the Hebrew word, *hester*, meaning "hidden." Esther was chosen as queen for her physical beauty and also because she remained mysterious and covered up. The Sages describe how even when living in the Royal Palace, Esther took great care to eat only kosher food, honor the Sabbath, and dress modestly. She did this all while never revealing her true identity. Esther was able to be the savior of the Jewish people by keeping what was important, totally hidden. In the end, Esther did reveal her Jewish identity, but it was at the right time and under the right circumstances.

~ ~ ~

When I started to think about my son and his costume I had a number of ideas, but the one that my husband and I chose was to dress him up as Avraham, our patriarch. Again, I'm using his name (Avraham), and again I hope that the costume captures his essence. I plan to make a brown tunic this time in the shape of a tent and put welcome signs, "*Bienvenido*, *Bienvenue*, Welcome, *Beruchim haba'im*" all over it. Abraham and Sarah's tent was always open to guests; they were famous for receiving people and making them feel at home. My little Avraham Nissim already gets excited as he greets the guests that grace our home. He shows them his toys and books and brings everything to them.

As I look at my son and prepare the materials, I recognize the miracles in my life, both revealed and hidden, and pray to myself, "Let this *Purim* costume capture his essence and let this be his beauty."

Prevailing Whispers

The brown-haired girl stood out amongst the heads of blond hair. You could tell that she was not like the rest of her classmates. The physical differences were obvious, but there was something else that marked the difference, something that you couldn't quite put your finger on, but you knew was there. She was different.

For example, at the beginning of the school year her classmates noted her absence. First she was gone for two days, and then a week later she missed another day. "Why did she get to miss so much school?" they wondered. What were all these "holidays" anyways? The little girl herself didn't want to miss those first days—the excitement of a new teacher, a new year in school. But she accepted.

There was also that week in spring when she brought *matzah* and cream cheese sandwiches to school while her peers munched on Wonder Bread with peanut butter and jelly. That special week, when on Pizza Day she didn't touch a slice as everyone else gobbled down seconds. She was different, all right, and everyone knew it.

They called her names. They wanted her to believe that the thing which made her different from them was terrible. They told her that she was "weird." They called her ugly. It would be a lie to say that the words didn't hurt. Those words did have some power over her. It would have been impossible for them not to have affected her self-esteem to some extent. But her mother whispered other words into her ears. Her mother told her that yes, she was different, but this difference made her special. She whispered to her that she was beautiful, graceful. Her mother told her over and over to be proud of who she was and never to run away from it. In the end, the internal whispers prevailed over the external shouts.

The girl grew up; she excelled and blossomed in everything that she did. She held on to the whispers of her mother. She discovered that time expanded for her and bowed to her whim. Her peers asked her how she could manage and do so well, how she could work, have to time to hang out and still get good grades, while taking every Saturday off – for what? To rest, to eat, to pray?

She grew more and went on a journey. Wherever she went she managed to prepare or arrange for kosher food, because after all, "she was different, she was special," the whispers reminded her. She was the daughter of the King, and princesses don't just eat "anything," they don't just wear "anything."

~ ~ ~

The orphan Esther grew up under Mordechai's care. He was like a father to her. Then one day came a knock on the door. The king's ministers took the graceful Esther away from her home, away from Mordechai. Before she left he whispered into her ear, "Don't forget to keep the Jewish commandments and customs."

Esther found herself in the royal palace surrounded by luxuries and delicacies beyond anything she could have ever imagined. They anointed her queen over the Persian Empire, wife to the ruler of 127 provinces. Despite the opulence and temptations, the *Midrash* tells us that Esther ate only vegetables and garbanzo beans. Not once did she eat non-kosher food, and she kept the holy *Shabbat*. How did she manage? How did she find the means to keep the commandments in the palace? I always wondered: from where did she get the strength to not succumb to those loud voices?

Haman told King Achashverosh, "There is one nation in your realm. They have strange and different laws…They are a blight to your empire, and there is no reason you should tolerate them!" The king handed over his signet ring and the decree was sealed. Death to the Jews! Now the external voice was very loud, very powerful. How could she resist it?

She had whispers.

Mordechai told her, "You must do it. You must try to save your nation. You are a Jew. You are special, the daughter of the King."

The whispers prevailed. She didn't succumb. Esther fasted and prayed for three days. On the third day she donned her royal gown and approached the king. In the end she revealed her identity and helped save her nation. She was a Jew. This is what made her different, this is what made her was special.

~ ~ ~

Yesterday my son came home from school. I was in the middle of mopping the floor, surrounded by soapy water. The door burst open. "Mommy, I don't want to go back to class!" I dropped the mop, left the water. I walked over to him and hugged him. "What happened?" "David called me terrible names! I don't want to go back. He makes fun of me..."

"That must hurt so much. Let's try to think of a solution."

We talk. I make some suggestions. I tell him to look at me in the eyes and I whisper in his ears. "You are the best. I love you. You're special."

Every night I whisper in his ear. "You're wonderful. I love you, Papi loves you. Most importantly, know that G-d loves you."

I pray that with the right whispers, he'll grow to have self-love and confidence. I pray that the whispers always prevail.

Sharing the Credit

Believe it or not, my kids love salads. They also love eating whole-grain cookies and cakes. Why salad, and how do I get them to eat healthy, whole-wheat goodies? I have them make it! Okay, so I wash the vegetables, I cut them open and check to make sure that they don't have any bugs. I put them in a bowl in front of them. I give them a chopper. They then put the veggies on the chopper, press down, and voila! "They made" the salad.

While they are doing this, a pepper goes into one child's mouth, a tomato in the other's. As they chop, they eat the veggies along the way, and at dinnertime they all want to eat the salad that "they made." Am I happy to give them all the credit? Absolutely! Would I have been able to make the salad without their help? Absolutely! Would I then have told them to eat salad at dinner? Yes. But would they then eat it so happily? I don't think so.

It's the same with the dessert. I arrange all the ingredients. I tell them the measurements, and sometimes, depending on the age of the child making the cake, I even have to measure the ingredients out. But they put them into the bowl. They mix it. I pop it into the oven, and voila! "They made" a cake! The flour happened to be whole wheat, the sweetener was dried fruits or juice and not white sugar, but do they still eat it – and even like it? Of course! – because *they* made it!

We were eating dinner, and my eldest was a bit surprised when I told him that when Mashiach comes, all the Jewish holidays (*Pesach, Shavuot, Sukkot,*

Rosh Hashanah, etc.) will pale in comparison to the miracles of Mashiach, except for *Purim*. What? How can that be, that our most important days, the ones when we eat *matzah*, stay up all night to study Torah, and shake a *lulav* and *etrog*, won't seem like such a big deal any more compared to *Purim*? The holidays that have lengthy prayer services, including the Days of Awe, or that commemorate the Exodus – the formation of our nation – aren't going to seem as important as that really fun day where you get dressed up, give out gifts of food, eat a yummy meal, listen to a cool story and give money to the poor? How can it be that only *Purim* is on the same level as our final redemption and the coming of Mashiach?

Before I could answer, my son took a bite of his salad – you know, the one that "he made" – and answered his own question for me.

"Ohhhhh, I know! It's because in *Purim* and *Chanukah*, *we* battled, but when we left Egypt, G-d did everything."

Hmmm. I had to think about that for a moment.

First things first, let's get this straight. G-d does everything all the time – whether "we fight" or not, He's the One going into battle and winning the war for us. But my son definitely had a point. In both *Purim* and *Chanukah*, *we* battled against the enemy. *We* fought with weapons and with our hands, with prayers and supplications. *We* fought with whatever we had, and *we*, the few against the many, miraculously won the wars. In other words, G-d did all the work to prepare the salad, and He let us press down on the chopper. He gave us the ingredients, and let us mix the cake. He let us be "partners" with Him in our redemption, so that when Mashiach comes, we are going to say, "This holiday is ours!" This one is precious to us because we made it happen.

When confronted with physical persecution, we continue to pray, to cling to the truth, and to fight to live! *Purim* is a beautiful treasure that teaches us that even when we think that what we do doesn't make a difference, it really does. It also teaches us that when a person puts his energy into something and gets involved in it, he takes ownership of it.

"This is an amazing insight," I tell my son. "Can you pass me the salad you made? It's delicious! By the way, I thought that we could get started on cleaning *your* room for *Pesach*. I know that *you'll* do a terrific job making sure that there is no *chametz*."

"Aba," I call to my husband, "don't you remember how *the children* prepared our home for *Pesach* last year...."

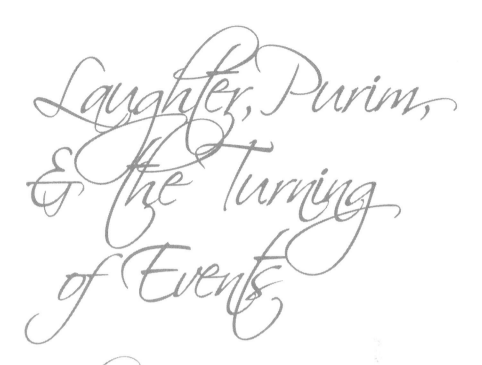

Laughter, Purim, & the Turning of Events

The other night my toddler was up all night long with a stomach virus. In the morning we kept him home from his preschool, but I decided he was well enough for me to take him out for a walk. I wanted to change him into clothing. He wanted to stay in his pajamas. "Okay, not a big deal," I thought. But there was more to it. Picture the scene of an adorable pudgy two-and-a-half year-old with long curly hair wearing pajama pants, his sister's pink socks, shiny black *Shabbat* shoes (which he insisted on), a coat, and to top it all off, the hood of his coat on his head (again he insisted).

I stepped outside my door and couldn't help noticing the raised eye brows and smiles on people's faces. He looked hysterical. He looked cute. The sight of him caused laughter.

Laughter. What is it?

I read in my anatomy book that research shows that laughter is good medicine. Laughter increases blood levels of important immunity components which helps fight infections in the upper respiratory and gastrointestinal tracts, and may increase levels of disease-fighting T-cells and natural killer cells. It helps protect the immune system and decreases stress.

What else is laughter?

Laughter is a recognition of something new, something different, something unexpected. A little boy with pink socks, pajama pants, fancy shoes and hooded jacked is certainly out-of-the-ordinary (or at least in some neighborhoods here in Jerusalem it is!).

You are walking down the street and someone tall and elegant slips on a banana peel. This is certainly not funny, but you laugh. Why? Because it was so unexpected – this turn of events, this occurrence that turned this person upside and changed his situation, surprised you. The response is laughter.

~ ~ ~

The Sages relate the number of years that our Foremother Sarah lived – 127 – to the number of provinces over which Queen Esther ruled, the same 127. Sarah was the first Mother of the Jewish people and Queen Esther, through her heroic acts to save the Jewish people was also a mother to the Jewish people. My zeidy z"l (grandfather, may his memory be blessed) escaped alive from the grave that he was shot into by the Nazis. He was found and taken in by a woman who hid him. He always said that he had two mothers, the one who gave him life and the one who saved his life. The same similarity exists between Sarah and Esther: Sarah gave us life, and Esther saved our lives.

Sarah and Esther also share another quality: laughter.

The Sages relate that not only was Sarah barren, but she didn't have a womb! There wasn't even a possibility that she could have children. For her, and for us – her descendents, G-d turned the situation upside down. He created something new, something from nothing. She had her name changed: Sarai, Sarah's given name, was no longer Sarai, but Sarah. She became a new person. The barren woman without a womb became fertile, bore a son, Issac (from the Hebrew word that means "he will laugh") and became the mother of the Jewish people. This occurrence caused laughter.

The Persian king was in cahoots with his evil Prime Minister Haman to kill the Jewish people. Haman built gallows to kill the righteous Jewish Sage, Mordechai. The Jewish people fasted, they prayed, and G-d created a "laughable" situation. He reversed everything. The Persian king's beloved queen, Esther, turned out not only to be Jewish, but Mordechai's niece. Instead of destroying the Jewish people, they grew stronger. Haman was hung on his own gallows, Mordechai became the new Prime Minister and the king's own son then allowed the building of the Second Temple.

Laughter is a recognition that in a split second our situation can change.

The Sages tell us that when the month of Adar (the month when we celebrate *Purim*) begins, we must increase our happiness, but they don't tell us to increase our laughter. Why is this so? Laughter is an expression of happiness, but it is happiness in its fully revealed state. We cannot really laugh until Mashiach comes, bringing with him a full revelation of the truth, a time when we will say "aahhh, so that's why that happened" and "that's why I had to go through that" and "now I understand how that hardship was for the best."

We cannot truly laugh now, but we can increase our happiness and know that as descendents of Sarah and Esther, we will, as the verse states in Proverbs when speaking of the Woman of Valor, "laugh at the end of days." We can be joyous and smile in faith knowing that the down will be up and the difficulties will be sources of pleasure

Pesach

Mirror, Mirror on the Wall

"Mirror, mirror, on the wall. Who is the fairest of them all?" I gaze into the mirror. For once, it's spotless. My *Pesach* cleaning has done away with any smudges or finger prints. I look at my reflection and give a heavy sigh. It's the first year that I don't have my mother-in-law to call for advice about *Pesach* cleaning or making the family charoset. I see a sad face in the mirror. A tear falls from my eye. I wipe it away and look again. "Smile, Elana. Do what she would do. Do what she would want. Be beautiful and smile."

My mother-in-law, Mrs. Frida Mizrahi, always had a twinkle in her eye and a smile on her face. She was always dressed up and elegant, her home always neat and welcoming. Everything she made was delicious, and looked it, too. Every word she spoke to us, her children, was encouraging and positive. Mrs. Frida Mizrahi was, if I can be so bold as to describe her in a mere word, beautiful.

I clean the mirror one more time and ask it, "Mirror, mirror, on the wall. Am I, too, beautiful?"

The Sages tell us that due to the merit of the righteous women, G-d redeemed the nation of Israel from Egypt, and through the merit of the righteous women, we will be redeemed again. What was the merit of the women in Egypt?

The *Midrash* describes how these women, who lived a life of slavery and torture, beautified themselves. After working a very long, hard day of back-breaking labor, the women would catch and cook some fish. They then put on makeup and made themselves attractive. They proceeded to serve the fish to their husbands, who had returned from torturous labor, and entice them with the mirrors. "Look how beautiful I am!" a woman would say to her husband. She would tease him, "I'm more attractive then you!" He would look into the mirror and see his wife. He would see himself. With the mirrors, all the pain dissolved and they lovingly came together.

With the mirrors, there was faith and there was desire. Faith and desire led to redemption.

I always wondered about this *Midrash*. Why the mirrors? Yes, these women of faith knew that G-d would redeem them, and therefore, they continued having children. Yes, they brought the redemption with their faith and belief in the future. But why did they have to use mirrors?

Why? Because it's not enough to look and be beautiful. You have to see your own beauty. Beauty, real beauty, is not superficial. True beauty is internal, and if you can't see it and don't reflect it, then there isn't any beauty to see. The women of Egypt had the power to not only make things beautiful, even amongst the most difficult circumstances, but they had the power to help their spouses see that beauty within themselves, as well.

Those encouraging words, those smiles and twinkling eyes. The optimism and positivity. The power to reflect goodness and help others see their own goodness and beauty. This was the merit of the Jewish woman in Egypt. She gave hope. She had faith. She had desire. This is the legacy of my mother-in-law, a Jewish woman who poured her heart out in prayer for her family, who fed and took care of everyone with such joy, who made everything and everyone beautiful – this is what she taught me.

Her precious soul returned to her Maker just a short time ago, but as I gaze into the mirror, I smile and I see her smile back at me. I'll set my table this *Pesach*, and I'll do what a Jewish woman is empowered to do – I'll bring the redemption closer. And I'll make it beautiful.

Knowing the Goal

What is the difference between *Pesach* cleaning and Spring cleaning? Both involve a lot of soap, water, and rags. Both require hard work, energy, and time. So what is the difference? I could ask you the same question about a lot of things. What is the difference between cooking and *Shabbat* cooking? Both involve ingredients, time and energy. So what is the difference?

Ten years ago as I felt waves of pain rushing over my body and I rocked and swayed to this pain I came to realize the difference. You see, ten years ago, on the last day of *Pesach*, I gave birth to my son – my first-born, my long awaited child – and my thought process during his birth changed everything.

As I fell to the floor like I cat I repeated to myself, "With each contraction I am opening up for my baby." I didn't just breathe, I "breathed my baby down." My pain was labor pain, good pain. Its purpose was so crystal clear to me. Through this pain my body became a vessel to release my child into the world. As the intensity increased, the pain brought me closer and closer to my goal. I kept telling myself, "Soon, soon, I don't know exactly when, but this pain will eventually end."

And it did.

As I imagined the Nation of Israel crossing through the Red Sea my body opened up and Avraham Nissim entered into the world with a cry and a shriek.

When Pharaoh's horse came with his chariots and horsemen into the sea and G-d turned back the waters of the sea upon them, the Children of Israel walked on the dry land amid the sea. Miriam the prophetess, the sister of Aaron, took the tambourine in her hand and all the women went forth after her with tambourines and with dances. Miriam called out to them, "Sing to G-d for He is exalted above the arrogant, having hurled horse with its rider into the sea" (Exodus 15:19-21).

How did Miriam and the women know to bring tambourines? They were forced to leave Egypt so quickly, there wasn't even enough time for their bread to rise (and thus the reason behind us eating flat unleavened bread – *matzah*) and yet they took time to bring musical instruments including tambourines. The commentaries explain, "The righteous women of the generation were certain that the Holy One Blessed is He (G-d) would perform miracles for them, so they took tambourines out of Egypt."

These were the women who, after an excruciatingly long day of back-breaking labor in the fields, would go home, dress beautifully and seduce their husbands with warm smiles and open arms ensuring the proliferation and survival of the Jewish nation. They were the same women who never gave up hope and this hope manifested itself in tambourines and dancing. The leader of the women was a woman named Miriam. Miriam's parents gave her the name Miriam from the word *mar* (bitter) because she was born during a time of great suffering.

When Miriam was a child, Pharaoh made a decree that all the Jewish male babies born would be murdered. Upon hearing the decree her parents separated, reasoning that it was better not to bring any children into the world if Pharaoh was going to kill the males. Miriam confronted her parents and told them that what they were doing was worse than what Pharaoh intended to do: by separating they automatically prevented both males and females from entering the world, whereas Pharaoh threatened to "only" kill the males.

Miriam also prophesized about the birth of the future redeemer, Moses. Her parents remarried and her prophesy was fulfilled. Eighty years later Moses led the Nation out of Egypt and Miriam, with her steadfast faith and eyes which always looked ahead at the goal and the bigger picture danced and sang in praise to G-d for His salvation open miracles. She took the bitterness out of her name and concentrated on the *yam* (sea), an allusion to the splitting of the Red Sea.

~ ~ ~

This year as I sit against a comfortable pillow at my *Pesach* table, my home sparkling clean, my closets neatly organized and my home in order (at least for twenty-four hours) the smile that I sport on my face is genuine.

Reaching this moment was not easy, but the whole time I told myself, "Stay focused on the goal."

With each drawer that I cleaned, I sang, and with this singing I know that I brought holiness down into the world. And this, my dear friends, is the difference between *Pesach* cleaning and Spring cleaning, between cooking and *Shabbat* cooking. It's about focusing on the end goal and knowing that with each action that you do you can raise it up and make it holy. Sounds far-fetched and just a theory? Just try saying "in honor of *Pesach*" the next time you mop and let me know what happens.

Breaking the Speed Limit

$\mathcal{I}$ drove home from a class the other night, when all of a sudden a car sped up behind me. The driver honked and flashed his bright lights, signaling for me to speed up. I kept my pace – the speed limit. Impatient and frustrated by my lack of response, the driver switched lanes and zoomed past, leaving me what I thought was far behind. Well, it wasn't so far behind, because less than a mile later we were side by side at the same red light. With all his speeding, bright lights, honking and going over the speed limit, the other car ended up exactly where he would have been had he continued to go at the speed limit and had stayed, if not behind me, at least to the side of me.

This incident happened in the same week when my daughter's kindergarten teacher told me that she would be staying back and repeating kindergarten next year. Why? Protocol. My daughter is young. She's the youngest in her class, and all the girls in our school district born during the month of *Kislev* (the Hebrew month usually corresponding to November/December time) have to repeat the year. It doesn't matter that intellectually and emotionally my daughter is very mature, or that she – thank G-d – is very bright; she's doing kindergarten again. But so is at least twenty percent of her class.

I have to tell you, when I first heard that she had to repeat the year I was, well, upset. Or maybe the emotion I felt was disappointment? I can't put my finger on it – I wasn't thrilled, to say the least. Where I grew up, in the States, everything was about getting ahead and getting ahead quickly. If you could skip a grade or two, it was all the better: "Go, get ahead, and get there fast." In my daughter's school, the system is different. Instead of "go, go, go," the motto is, "Have confidence, feel capable, be ready." It's a different approach. The more I think about it, the more I appreciate it and the more I like it.

~ ~ ~

On the seventh day after leaving Egypt, the Jewish nation arrived at the Red Sea. Pharaoh and his army rode their chariots towards them. G-d performed a miracle: the sea split open, and the Jews walked through on dry land. Pharaoh charged forward. As the Jews safely reached the other side, the waters came gushing back together, and the nation witnessed their oppressors drown. It was a huge miracle. The Children of Israel raised up their voices, and with joy and gratitude they sang praise to G-d. The Torah describes this outburst of song: "*Then* Moshe and the Children of Israel sang..." (Exodus 15:1).

Why the word "then"?

"Then" means at that precise moment, not before and not after.

Can you imagine the scene? There were 600,000 men, at least the same amount of women, and well over a million children crossing the sea. The sages explain that the sea split into twelve different pathways, corresponding to the twelve different tribes. Over two million people crossed the sea, and yet there was no pushing or shoving. Some were obviously in front, some in the back, and some of course in the middle – and yet, as the Torah tells us, "Then Moses and the Children of Israel sang." *Then*, at that time, all together, not before and not after. They all got to the other side, and they all arrived at the same time to sing.

In life there is a speed limit. A person can push and push and push, but you know what? You are not going to get to your destination any quicker that way.

I even see this in my own home. It's early in the morning, and I want everyone up and ready for school. Breakfast and lunch need to be made. I need everyone dressed, fed, and ready by 8 AM, or else... I'm tense and I'm nervous. I myself have to start working, and the clock is ticking and ticking. My blood pressure is rising. "*Nu*, let's go. Hurry up. Come quick." Speed up, flash the lights, push and push ahead. "If they're late, I'm late." "Let's go, let's go, let's go."

You know what happens during those mornings? My children's feet move slower. The milk spills quicker. Everyone is in a bad mood, and we are always at least fifteen minutes later going out the door. I think that I'm in control of the situation, and try to hasten and make everyone go at my speed. Instead, my children slow down and show me that I am far from being in control.

I've learned to use other tactics instead. "Elana, go at the normal speed limit. You'll get to where you need to end up anyways, and arriving at that destination will be so much nicer. Everyone will get to where they need to be, when they need to be there."

I open the curtains with a song. I tickle and joke with the little ones to put their clothes on. The one who needs more time getting dressed – I wake her up first. Nothing spills, and if it does, we quickly clean it up. We're ready and out by 7:55. What changed? A small, simple thing: I try not to rush. By rushing, we don't get ahead.

There's an order in life, and when you try to shake it up, you end up with nothing. You push, they'll pull. You speed up, you'll be stopped. And this is one of the lessons of *Pesach*, because *Pesach* is all about the *Seder*. In Hebrew, *seder* means "order." *Pesach* tells us, "Stop trying to trample! Just go at the normal speed limit. You'll still get there!" When the Jews left Egypt and crossed the Red Sea, they taught us that in life each and every one of us will get to where we are supposed to, and it will be at the precise moment, not before and not after.

"Then Elana and her children sang…!"

Birthing Ourselves

Shira called me from the delivery room. We had been through so much together. She came over almost every other day during her ninth month to receive encouragement, emotional support and a massage. She knew that I couldn't physically be at the birth with her, but I prayed for her during her labor, and certainly felt like my soul and heart were with her.

I was honored when she called me within minutes of giving birth to tell me the news. *Mazel tov*, she had a baby boy! She proceeded to tell me her entire birth experience. We hung up. A few hours later, she called me again and retold me the entire story. Again the phone rang a little while later. Shira talked and talked. She called me about seven times over the next few days, retelling me the story, reliving the experience. I wasn't physically at the birth, but by the third day of listening to her, I knew the story so well that I could have been.

I admit that after each one of my births I did the same. I talked about it. Over and over, I replayed the birth to all my close family and friends. I relived it: the experience of it, the pain of it, the miracle of it, the feeling of desperation of it as one calls out to G-d, turning to Him, instinctively knowing that He is the only one who can get you through it, and the beauty of it as at last your baby makes its way into our world.

Shira and I are not alone. I hear it all the time. Women talk about birth. They talk about it, and they relive it each and every time they tell the story. Why? Because they didn't just give birth to a new life; they gave birth to themselves. They also didn't do it alone. They couldn't. Each and every woman realizes this as she approaches transition and tries to push the baby out. There is no angel with her, no messenger, no one to turn to, just G-d. This is certainly something to talk about!

~ ~ ~

Pesach. The *Seder* Night. What are we doing on this special night? Yeah, I know what you are going to say. We do a lot of eating, but really, what are we doing the entire night? We are talking. The Rambam writes that it is a positive commandment of the Torah on *Pesach* night to relate the miracles and wonders that were done for our fathers in Egypt. We have an obligation to tell our children. If we don't have children, we tell our spouses; if we don't have a spouse, we ask the people sitting around the table. And even if you are alone, you still have an obligation to ask yourself and to talk about it.

The main purpose of the *Seder* Night is to tell the story of the Exodus from Egypt. On this night we are supposed to ask questions, recount the story, and talk and talk. The entire night is set up to provoke questions. We eat bitter herbs. We recline. We drink four cups of wine, and eat *matzah* (unleavened bread). The children sing. "Why is this night different than all other nights?"

Pesach: if you break up the word you get *peh* (mouth) and *sach* (discussion/talking). Why are we talking and talking? Why, every year, do we retell the story? Because we gave birth! It didn't just happen to our ancestors thousands of years ago. It happened to us, and we have to talk about it. "You shall tell your son on this day, saying, 'Because of this G-d acted on *my* behalf when *I* left Egypt."

We have to re-experience it: the pain of it, the miracle of it, the way we hit rock bottom and realized that we had no one to turn to except for G-d. We relive how He and He alone, not an angel and not a messenger, took us out of our slavery, our misery, and helped us give birth to ourselves, as a free nation and as individuals. And how does the *Seder* Night end? We finish the evening, like a new mother with her baby in her arms, singing praise and giving thanks to G-d.

Every year on the *Seder* Night, we relive our birth experience. We are new. We are free. We are reborn. This certainly is something to talk about!

Free Yourself

I looked over each garment carefully. Our new home would have less closet space, and that meant I had to make a selection. There were a few items that I spent more time on. The grey pleated skirt, for instance. I hadn't worn it in years and yet this skirt has always managed to come with me, from home to home and move to move. I hadn't been able to give it away in the past. It represented the size that I used to be, the size that I tell myself I'll be again. I gave it a hard look and then my husband encouraged me, "Yeah, let go and give it away." I did it. I threw the size-two skirt in the big bag for clothes to donate. I felt a tremendous sense of relief.

When I was in college, I spent hours exercising. The majority of my diet consisted of fruits and vegetables, and I had to make a conscious effort not to get thinner than size two. When I was newly married, the two was steady until I realized that I needed to add more to my diet. The two became a four and when I, at last, had children, the four became a six. I'm not sure what size I am now, but I'm always trying to get back down to that two. And I can't. It's like I'm enslaved to that size, a size which is, and probably always was, unhealthy for me. I'm very active and I exercise, but, thank G-d, I no longer have hours to spend perfecting my body. As a woman who has spent the past three-and-a-half years pregnant or nursing, I realize that I can't survive unless I also eat a variety of proteins, carbs and even some fats.

~ ~ ~

When G-d chose a leader to take the nation of Israel out of Egypt, He didn't choose an ordinary Israelite, He didn't even choose a leader or elder from among the enslaved Hebrew nation. He chose a free man who had grown up in the palace of the Egyptian king. The commentators explain that He did this because a slave will always see himself as a slave, and a person raised among royalty will always see himself as a royal leader. Only a free man could bring a nation to freedom.

In preparation for the lamb offering that was to be eaten on the night preceding the Exodus (*Seder* Night), G-d commanded the Jews to tie lambs to their front doorposts. The Jews complied. This was a very courageous act that demonstrated their complete trust in G-d. The lamb was one of the divinities of the Egyptians. To tie lambs and prepare them for slaughter was a great provocation for the Egyptians. The Jews had no idea how the Egyptians would react and could only expect the worst, and yet they did it. Here was their first act of freedom, of throwing off the chains of their slave mentality. The way a person perceives himself is how others perceive him as well. They waited to see what would happen. But there was nothing; the Egyptians didn't react. Even though the Jews were still in Egypt, the Egyptian masters no longer had power over them because the Jews didn't give them that power.

~ ~ ~

Pesach cleaning is more than just getting rid of any leavened foods. It's also more than spring cleaning. The mystics explain that when you physically clean your home for *Pesach* you are symbolically doing a spiritual cleaning, as well. As one cleans out the cupboards, one simultaneously cleans out one's mind, one's heart, and one's thoughts. As one cleans, one removes the shackles – chain by chain – of those self-destructive images that hold us back and keep us enslaved. All the preparations before *Pesach* enable one to arrive at *Pesach* as a free person.

On *Seder* Night, we sit like royalty and celebrate our freedom. Jews did this even in the darkest times when they were forced to do *Seder*s in secrecy, or behind prison gates, or in concentration camps. Physically, they were enslaved and yet, they celebrated their freedom. They celebrated the freedom that comes when you perceive yourself as free, and when you don't allow anyone to enslave your soul or your heart.

~ ~ ~

When I let go of that skirt, is was as though I was letting go of the past and accepting myself as I am in the present. It allowed me to be happy with the way I am, and not as a slave to what society dictates I need to be. For me, it was an act of bravery, and really, I feel free.

The Kind Road to Redemption

It was one of those moments when you wish that you had the magical power to turn back the clock and change the situation. In one split second my toddler had climbed onto the counter and then jumped down, bringing the tea kettle with him. Hot tea fell onto his delicate baby face. He screamed hysterically and uncontrollably. How I would give anything to be able to redo that life-changing minute.

I quickly snatched him in my arms and tried to soothe him as I put cold water onto his face. He continued to cry and sob in pain and I was helpless to comfort him. I had no idea what to do as I held him, rocked him, nursed him. I didn't realize the seriousness of the situation until a few minutes passed and blisters began to appear on his forehead. My heart leapt out of my body and I grabbed my phone to call my husband and ran with him in my arms to my neighbor.

Within minutes one neighbor called an ambulance as another helped to try to bathe him with cold water. Their children ran to my side to distract my son's attention. From the time I sought help with my neighbor until today, more than a week later, I have had one person after another trying to help me and my son: There was the ambulance medic who blew balloons out of the sterile plastic gloves, the people who gave me advice at the hospital, the strangers who came up to me in every random location from the supermarket to the Western Wall asking me, "What happened?" "What's the child's name so that we can pray for him?"

We were told about an organization that refers people to experts in emergency situations. At 11:00 on a Saturday night we brought my son to a woman who not only received us at this late hour into her home but welcomed us with a kind face and warm smile. One would think that a person who treats burns and wounds everyday would become desensitized, but that was clearly not the case as she kissed my son and offered him sweets and toys to play with.

~ ~ ~

There is a debate recorded in the Talmud between Rabbi Akiva and the Roman Nobleman. The Roman asked Rabbi Akiva, "If your G-d is so powerful and mighty, why are there poor people in the world? Why can't He provide for them?" Rabbi Akiva answered the Roman, "There are poor people in the world so that others have an opportunity to be able to give to them and perform acts of kindness for them."

I have to be honest with you – I never understood this answer. Now I do.

Upon returning from the hospital one of my neighbors gave me a pamphlet for an organization that provides food to thousands of poor families. She suggested that I call them. I immediately did and gave a donation knowing that cures are not just found in medicine. People reached out to us and we had to use this horrible situation to reach out to others.

Living in Israel, in Jerusalem, is a blessing all of its own. But this incident revealed to me another side, and showed me that there is something very unique about Israel and about the Jewish people. I've done an extensive amount of traveling and I've come across a lot of incredible, interesting people, but nowhere I've traveled or been have I encountered people who actually care about me so deeply as I have in Israel.

At first, I found it somewhat intrusive as I would sit on the bus with my baby and the person next to me, a complete stranger, would tell me to bundle him up because surely he's cold, or to do this or that to take care of my child. If I were in my native California no one would dare tell me what to do. There just simply isn't that comfort level that you would interject your personal opinion unless asked. But this is not the case among the nation of Israel, for we are taught and raised to worry and care for the other. We are not strangers, we are family, whether or not we have formally met before.

I'll never forget as I stood outside the market in Jerusalem and witnessed one beggar take money out of his cup to give it to another beggar. Can you imagine such a thing?

But this is not something new; it's inherent in Jewish values and an integral part of the Torah. And we learn these very lessons and qualities from Israel's greatest leader.

The Jewish people had been enslaved for 210 years when Moses took them out of Egypt. There is a beautiful *midrash* describing why G-d chose

Moshe as Israel's leader. Moshe was a shepherd who cared for his father-in-law's sheep. One day a lamb wandered off and Moshe went after it. Moshe realized that the lamb was thirsty and tired and that's why it wandered off. He took the lamb and carried it upon his shoulders. A voice from Heaven called out that this person, who was so kind and sensitive to an animal, would be the one to lead the Jewish people.

Moshe was born in the palace of the king and had the choice to be oblivious to anyone else's problems. He could have lived his life in luxurious comfort and no one would have thought badly of him or blamed him for minding his own business. But he didn't; the Torah writes that Moshe "went out" to see the pain and suffering of his brethren. He shared in their agony and put himself in their position. This was the beginning of the redemption.

We live in a world of statistics and numbers where people are dehumanized and desensitized. This amount of people were killed, this amount live in poverty. They're all numbers, and we hear them so often that we forget to care. There was a psychological study about an incident that happened in New York where a woman was attacked and dozens of people witnessed the event. Not one helped her or even called the police.

My son, whose face was distorted by swelling, blisters, and burned skin, and who now is nearly completely healed and everyday is getting better, is the proof that this isn't always the case. It isn't the way among the Jewish people. *Pesach* is the time of redemption and the time when G-d performed open miracles. It's the time when Israel became a nation under a kind and caring leader. It's also the time when we open our doors and cry out, "Whoever is hungry, come eat at my table." This is the key to redemption.

Just One More

My husband and I had been married for three-and-a-half years, and we desperately wanted children. We were living in Jerusalem at the time. *Pesach* was coming to an end, and although we had had a wonderful holiday, there was a sadness that clouded our joy. It had been another *Seder* without a baby, another week of *Chol HaMoed* without a child to take around to parks and festive events, another year of asking, "When will our personal redemption come?"

On the seventh day of *Pesach* we ate what I thought was going to be the last holiday meal in the mid-morning, and I settled down to read and enjoy the last hours of *Pesach*. (In Israel, *Pesach* is celebrated for seven days; outside of Israel, an eighth day is observed as well.) All of a sudden, I heard a knock on my door. Two friends had come to visit. One of them was single, and the other newly married.

"Elana, come. We're taking you to my mother-in-law's cousin. She's married to a great *tzaddik* (righteous man)." Here was an opportunity for me to receive a blessing for children.

We wound our way through the twisted alleyways of a very religious neighborhood in Jerusalem, until we arrived at the *tzaddik's* home. The *Rebbetzin* (rabbi's wife) opened the door. She greeted us as though we were old friends, although she didn't even know who I was or why I was coming to meet her and her husband. She rushed us to the dining room table, which was laid out with salads and delicacies. Before I knew it, I was sitting at the table, surrounded by this incredible family and being served tons of food.

Now, just as a side note, by this point in the week, I had already had my fill of meat and chicken and potatoes. I definitely was *not* hungry and had no idea that I was going to be eating yet another (mind you, delicious) *Pesach* meal. I thought that I was done. But no, the *Rebbetzin* informed me that we were taking part in the *Seudat Mashiach* (Meal of the Messiah). I had no idea what she was talking about. She then turned to me and said, "I'm not trying to be nosy, but do you want a blessing from my husband for children?"

I nodded yes. I had already received various blessings, undergone many, many treatments and tried dozens of things to become pregnant. How could one more blessing hurt?

And, a year later to the day, I gave birth to my son. A few months after his birth, my single friend got married, and five years later, she gave birth to her second son, also on the last day of *Pesach*.

So what is the *Seudat Mashiach*? What is its power?

G-d took the Jewish people out of Egypt, and seven days later they stood before the Red Sea. The Egyptians were almost upon them, and there was nowhere to go. They felt desperation. Should they go back to Egypt? Should they fight? What now? Moses stretched out his arm and raised his staff to the sea. Nothing happened. Then one man – Nachshon, the son of Aminadav – jumped into the sea. Nothing happened. He kept walking until the water was up to his chest, then up to his neck, then his nose. And then it happened: the sea split, and the Nation of Israel passed through. Once they reached the other side, their enemy came chasing after them, and the wall of water crashed down, drowning the Egyptian soldiers in the stormy sea.

What would have happened if Nachshon hadn't jumped in? What would have happened if he hadn't kept walking into the waters? Would G-d have split the sea open? I don't know. Maybe, maybe not.

What would have happened if you decided you couldn't meet "one more" person? What if you had turned down that opportunity to go on "one more date," the one where you met your husband? Would you be married now? I don't know. Maybe, maybe not.

What would have happened if you decided that you had already had enough and you were done trying to conceive? What if you decided this when you had only one more chance to ovulate? Would you have a baby now? I don't know. Maybe, maybe not.

And what if you were tired of dealing with rejection and sending out resumes? If you hadn't sent out that last one, would you be working now? Maybe, maybe not.

The last day of *Pesach*, when we have the *Seudat Mashiach*, is about the "one more." The one more meal, the one more blessing, the one more date, the one more try. It's about the one more good deed that will tip the scales and bring the redemption.

And for me, it will always be about the blessing I received on the last day of *Pesach*, and the precious baby I was given on that day – my Avraham Nissim, for "*nissim*" means "miracles."

Shavuot

Alone with
G-d

Do you know that type of person, the one who doesn't fit in anywhere? That's me. That is the way I always was, that's the way I am, and that is the way I will most likely always be. I just don't fit in, anywhere.

There are times when I am sitting in the park, and all the mothers are dressed in chic black skirts and elegant black sweaters, and I silently sit alone with a plain green sweater and simple brown skirt. And there are times, in a different park, when all the mothers are dressed in flowing flower skirts and funky sweaters, and I silently sit alone with a plain green sweater and simple brown skirt. I sit alone and I watch my children. I sit alone, in silence, and I feel alone. I think to myself, "Wow, I really don't fit it in."

The ironic thing about my not fitting in is that I have an eclectic group of friends from all over the world who, even though they do fit in somewhere, also find themselves not really fitting in, in one way or another. I have hippie friends and yuppie friends. I have friends who are ten years younger than me, and friends who are forty years older. I have friends who are vegans, and friends who eat meat and potatoes (the potato being the only vegetable that they will eat). And you know what, I love them all, and I know that they love me.

My husband is the same way, and we found each other, and thank G-d we have each other. So I ask you, why at times does the loneliness overcome me? And what do I do when it does? I take out my book of Psalms and I begin to read the words of King David: "I am always with You; You grasped my right hand. In Your counsel may You guide me, and afterwards You will take my soul unto You. Whom else do I have in Heaven? And when I am with You I do not desire anything on earth..." or I open my mouth and in a soft whisper I pour my heart out to G-d.

~ ~ ~

An incredible thing happened when G-d gave us the Ten Commandments. The entire nation of Israel – men, women, children – everyone was there, waiting, eager, excited to receive the Torah. Can you imagine the scene? Can you picture the noise and commotion – the babies crying, children whining, women chattering and men talking? And what happened next? There was silence! Not a word was spoken, not a cry was heard.

The sages tell us that not a bird chirped, nor did a cow moo. Even the angels were silent. Silence. Every Jew stood at Mount Sinai, they stood united as one nation, and yet each one stood alone in silence to hear the words, "I am the L-rd, your G-d. The One who took you from the land of Egypt, from the house of slavery."

The great sage Rabbi Yochanan explained that the voice split into seven voices, so that each one could hear it according to his or her capacity. Moses heard it according to his level, the men according to theirs, the women according to theirs, and adolescents according to their capacity. The children heard it according to their level, and the elders according to theirs. And these seven voices were further divided into seventy languages, so that the seventy nations of the world could hear and understand these ten phrases, which begin with "I am the L-rd your G-d."

On the holiday of *Shavuot* there is a custom to read the entire book of Psalms, which was compiled by King David. Before he was anointed as king, David was a shepherd who played the harp and herded his father's sheep. David didn't fit in amongst his seven handsome and intelligent brothers. Really, he didn't fit in anywhere, and felt most comfortable alone with his harp and his sheep. He would meditate, learn Torah, and pour his heart out to G-d in song. This sensitive soul, who didn't seem to fit in anywhere, was the one who G-d chose as His anointed king. He was the one who stood alone, and yet who knew that he was never alone because he knew that he could turn to G-d in every moment and in every situation. He was the one selected to lead the nation of Israel.

How powerful that King David died on the day when G-d gave us the Torah and told us in a voice that related to everyone individually that He is our G-d, that no matter where we are, no matter what we are doing or who we are with, "I am the L-rd your G-d." You are with Me, and therefore you are **never** alone.

"Why did you do this?"

I didn't have to *see* what was going on to know what was going on. My husband had walked into the bathroom and stepped into a pool on the bathroom floor. My son had poured bowlfuls of water from his bath onto the floor. My husband asked, "Why?" as though there were actually an answer! Why? I laughed to myself as I headed straight for the mop and rag. How many times had I asked the same question before? "Why did you hit your sister? Why did you just spit out your food? Why did you color on the walls? Why don't you listen? Why?" – the famous why that has no answer. "Why? I don't know, because I'm a child and I wanted to? Or maybe I didn't even want to do it, but I just did it?"

After trial and error I have now discovered the best thing to do when facing the sticky, or in this case, the wet situations in which I find myself with my children. Instead of asking "why" – the question that has no answer – pick up the mop (or if they are old enough, hand them the mop), clean up the mess, tell them that we don't do this sort of thing (and then, of course, *they* ask why), and move on.

~ ~ ~

The realization of how senseless it is to ask "why" dawned on me one day after my children and I had finished cleaning up their room. Three seconds later my son started to throw his toys everywhere and make a huge mess. What was this, a rebellion? "Why are you making a mess after we just cleaned up?"

He looked me squarely in the eyes and said, "Because I want to."

I took a deep breath and thought about the situation. "Elana, as much as you try, you simply have no control. Life is not a neat square box and neither are your children. You ask why, but what you are really saying is: "I am not in control.""

"You know what," I told my son, "it's your room. Go ahead – make a mess, but keep the mess in here and when you are finished, please clean it up."

My son looked at me – at first stunned and bewildered, and then relieved. Was it such a terrible thing that I did, to relinquish control? In the end, he did clean up his mess.

I thought about the birth that I had recently attended as a doula. The woman giving birth labored beautifully. She was focused on the baby within, on the end result, and not on the pain of the contractions. I felt that we were in-sync as we breathed together and swayed together, breathing the baby down and into the world. But then there came a point, the point of transition, the point when the woman starts to feel like she's not in control. And then as the baby is pushing its way out, the woman cries, "I can't do this." It's the moment of truth. The woman calls out, "G-d, *help* me!" The baby is born soon after she relinquishes control.

~ ~ ~

Do you ever wonder, "Why did I do that? What would have happened if I had done something else?"

We ask this senseless "why" all the time – a "why" that has no answer. Would it really matter if we had done something different in the past? Who is in control anyhow? Are we? All we can do is to pick up the mop, try to clean up our mess and learn from our mistakes – going forward and relinquishing that control.

~ ~ ~

Imagine the scene: the Nation of Israel was about to receive the Torah and for the first and only time in history the entire nation stood in union and uttered, "*Na'aseh v'Nishmah* (We will do and we will listen/understand). There were no "whys" because there was no reason to ask why. Everyone understood Who was in control and no one needed to ask, "Why aren't I?" The *Midrash* describes how each person received two crowns at the giving of the Torah, one for *na'aseh* and one for *nishma*. By letting go, they gained royal status as Children of the King.

The next time you find yourself in a sticky or wet situation, do pick up the mop, do grab your rag, but don't forget your two crowns. Why? Why not?

Under the Wedding Canopy

I've tried to stay consistent, but I can't help it; I'm not. I sprinkle Hebrew here, Spanish there, English everywhere, and even a bit of Yiddish gets thrown into the communication pot. My sentences don't always make sense, but they are expressive and full of color. My husband gets it, my kids get it, and most importantly, I get it.

"Mommy, look, the *pajaratos* ('little birds' in Spanish) are dancing in the *chalon* ('window' in Hebrew)." "*Papito, quiero* ("Daddy, I want" in Spanish) to eat *achshav* ('now' in Hebrew). I'm hungry!" These are my children's sentences.

I've been warned not to do it, but it just sort of happened, and all in all, my kids are doing fine. In school, they are consistent and fluent. In the street, they know which language to speak, and to whom. But in our home we sprinkle the language spices freely. *Aqui* (here), *sham* (there)…you get the idea.

How did this happen? An American *Ashkenazi* (of Eastern European Jewish descent) married a Mexican *Sephardi* (of Spanish/Middle Eastern descent), and they live in the capital of the world, in Jerusalem. Everyone always asks, "So, how did you guys meet? Did you already know Spanish?"

"It's a long story that involves a *Shabbat* table. No, not really, but I speak French."

"Did your husband speak English?"

"A little bit."

"So, how did you guys understand each other?"

We just did. We measured our words carefully and got to the point. I told my husband, "I want to grow. I'm looking for someone who wants to grow with me. Relationships require work. Marriage is hard work. Are you willing to work?"

"Yes, I am willing to work," he answered.

We smiled, we laughed. We got to the point. In less than two months we were engaged, and we've been working at a beautiful relationship ever since. I don't think about myself without thinking about him. He doesn't think about himself without thinking about me. We've been married for over eleven years, and thank G-d, my heart still quickens with excitement when I hear his key in the lock.

Why? Because we work at it. Love, respect, harmony and holiness are well worth all the energy, effort and hard work. And for this kind of work, sometimes speaking the same language is not necessary. You listen, you work hard, and that creates a relationship.

With all my talking and communicating, I am naturally inclined to prayer. I love to pray. I talk to G-d all the time; He's with me throughout the day. But it wasn't always like that. When I was a little girl, my prayers were reserved for the nighttime, when it was dark and scary.

But things changed. I changed, and as I got older, something drew me to Him. I wanted a real relationship with Him. But how can a person have a relationship with G-d without knowing His language? How can you communicate with the Infinite?

But to have a relationship, you don't have to speak the same language. You don't have to understand everything. You just have to be willing to work.

~ ~ ~

When the nation of Israel stood at Mount Sinai, it was as though we were standing under the wedding canopy with G-d. "I am the L-rd your G-d, who took you out of Egypt," G-d said. "This is who I am. I want a relationship with you. Do you want one with Me? Are you willing to work?"

The Jews responded, "*Na'aseh v'nishmah* (we will do and then we will understand.) We don't speak the same language. We have yet to learn Your laws, but we want to grow, and we want this marriage. Yes, we're willing to work!"

G-d is not just our Creator. He's not just our "Father" in some distant place that we call heaven. G-d is, as King Solomon describes Him in Song of Songs, our lover. And we are His beloved. G-d created everyone and everything. But only to Israel did He say, "You are *mine*. You are My wife, my love."

As we approach *Shavuot*, the holiday when G-d gave us the Torah, let's listen for the key turning in the lock. Who is on the other side? It's our Husband, our Lover, and we are His beloved, His perfection, His bride. The knob turns; let us stand up quickly, as our heart pounds with excitement, and welcome Him through the door.

Teaching by Example

It was one of those Spring days that appeared more like winter. For twenty-four hours my children and I stayed indoors as the wind howled outside and the rain poured down. I had never played as much Legos, Blocks, and Kapla as I did that day.

At one point I was in the kitchen preparing food while my five-year-old played Kapla. Kapla is a box of wooden sticks that you use for building and creating various things. All of a sudden I heard a pile of sticks fall to the floor – KABOOM, a grunt-like scream come forth from my son's mouth and then my younger daughter crying hysterically. I didn't have to see what happened to know. My toddler had knocked down my son's tower and he hit her.

"Avraham Nissim!" I yelled from the kitchen as I walked towards him. "Why did you hit her? It was an accident. I can't believe you hit her over Kapla!"

"Why did he hit her over such a trivial thing as Kapla?" I thought to myself. "How do I teach him not to get angry, and to show his frustration in a different manner?"

"Come, we'll build it again. I'll help you." I sat down on the floor and started to build. I got really into it. I built an entire house with a fence for a garden. My son handed me the sticks. Then he wanted to help – after all, he is the kid and it's his toy, right? He put a stick on top of my house's roof and KABOOM! The entire project fell to the ground.

The Jewish Woman's Year in a Nutshell   249

I certainly didn't want to smile and say, "No worries, let's do it again." No, that wasn't what I felt like doing. I felt like doing something similar to what he had done a half an hour before to his sister. But thank G-d I didn't. I remembered my thoughts from before and turned to him saying, "That's frustrating. But don't worry, now we have a chance to do it again and make it even better."

We started building again and then came my pudgy-handed enthusiastic toddler. She also wanted to help. My son and I watched as she put a stick on top of our creation. KABOOM! Of course you know what happened, it fell to the floor. "That's okay Mommy. We can always do it again," My son reassured me.

My son taught me two huge lessons. One – what's merely a toy to you just might be a gem to another. In other words, another person's pain or problem should never be taken lightly just because to you it doesn't seem like a big deal. To him it certainly is. We all have our own tailor-made challenges and struggles and we all have our own personal thresholds.

And lesson number two – the most effective way for me to teach my children is by example. By not being afraid to get down to their "level," I bring them up.

~ ~ ~

For seven weeks we count the days from the Exodus of Egypt until the Giving of the Torah. The Sages say that during these seven weeks it is an appropriate time to work on any bad character traits. This is partly because when we left Egypt we were at a very low level of spiritual purity and it took us forty-nine days to work our way up. Really, when we left Egypt we were at the point of no return. If we had stayed there any longer it would have been impossible for us to come out and so with a "mighty Arm G-d took us out."

We crossed the Red Sea, saw open miracles, and wandered around for seven weeks until the time came to receive the Torah. We merited it at this point because, as the Torah describes, we were "united like one man with one heart" (not a simple feat, by the way).

We purified ourselves over a three-day period. Why? Because as the Torah tells us, G-d says, "I am Holy, so you must be holy." Follow My example, do what I do.

Then the day came. Thunder, lighting. Not a bird chirped, not a wave crashed. The first Commandment roared forth in the voice of G-d Himself. What would you expect it to be? "I am the L-rd you G-d." Yes, this I would expect and can understand. "The One who took you out of Egypt." Now this second piece is the tricky part. Why do we need to hear from G-d that He is the One who took us out of Egypt? Duh. It was only seven weeks ago. How could we forget?

Let me tell you something. The second part, that is my favorite, most comforting part. He's my G-d and He personally took me out of Egypt. In any situation in which I find myself, in my personal or national Exile, He will always be my G-d and even He, in all of His greatness, will never abandon me. If G-d Himself is willing to get down to my level to help me bring myself up, how much more so should I be willing to lower myself to another one's level to help bring him up.

There we were at Mount Sinai: my neighbors' problems were my problems, their joy was my joy. One man with one heart, we mimicked our Creator. At that moment we were like kings and queens, like royalty with crowns upon our heads. We had been at the lowest of the low and now we were at the highest of the high. KABOOM, the Kapla falls. "Don't worry Mommy, when you get down to the floor to sit and play with me, I learn from you. We can always build it again."

"I am the L-rd, your G-d. I took you out of Egypt...not another..."

The Staircase

I'll never forget the look on my father-in-law's face two years ago when we stood him before the very big staircase located in the mystical city of Tzfat. He gave us such a look of skepticism. A look that said, "You have got to be kidding me if you think I'm going to climb up."

"You can do it." We reassured him. "Slowly, slowly, you can do it."

I ran ahead leaping the steps two at a time to show him that it really wasn't as bad as he thought. Up I ran and then back down. "You see, they're not so bad." He laughed at me and shook his head no. But slowly, slowly he made his way up.

When we arrived at the top he looked at us with pride and said with a hint of disbelief, "I did it!"

Ten years ago, I left for college and I started to keep *Shabbat*. There was no pressure, no influential momentum making me do it. I just wanted to. I found myself at a turning point, at the bottom of the mountain, and I felt that I needed to go up. At times it was slowly, slowly taking one step at a time; other times I felt like running and leapt many steps at once.

~ ~ ~

Ten years ago I had no idea what *Shavuot* was, let alone that it was a Jewish holiday. *Rosh Hashanah, Yom Kippur, Chanukah, Pesach, Purim, Sukkot,* even *Tu B'Shvat* and *Simchat Torah* I knew and had celebrated in my childhood in one form or another, but not *Shavuot* and *Tisha B'Av*. You might ask why, and the answer is simple: they were the two holidays on the Jewish calendar that always fell during summer vacation. I didn't celebrate them in my home and I didn't have a chance to learn about them in Hebrew school either.

I remember how I stayed up studying all night long with a friend for the first time in my life, six years ago. Before the first rays of light burst into the sky I left her and congregated with the throngs of people flocking to the *Kotel* to recite the morning prayers. The scene was too intense for me, the *Kotel* too crowded and I quickly left the area and said my prayers at a distance on the street.

This past year I broke my ritual of studying all night as I nursed my six-week-old son instead. My role, my life changed and I found myself at a different mountain, the mountain of motherhood, with new stairs to climb and challenges to overcome.

~ ~ ~

For me *Shavuot* is a very special holiday. It's a holiday about personal growth and discovery; about coming closer to our Creator and surpassing mountains of obstacles and steps to climb. It's also a holiday about unity and solitude. Because as much as the encouragement of people around you helps, in the end, what gets you up the stairs is your own two feet. The question that's put before us this *Shavuot* and every *Shavuot* is, "Can you find the strength and confidence in yourself to climb?"

The "I Can" Crown

"Elana, I can't."

"Yes, you can. Repeat after me: 'I can.'"

"I can't."

Our eyes met. There was so much to her story, so many times along the way when she could have given up, but she didn't. I reminded her of a few of those times. "Laura!"

"I mean, I can. I can."

"That's right. With G-d's help, you **can!**"

Three hours later, Laura gave birth to her miracle baby. She lifted her healthy son in her arms and smiled at the irony of giving birth in the same hospital where she had been told roughly a year earlier that due to her age, it would be nearly impossible to have her own biological child. "You can't," the doctors told her. But her faith in G-d told her otherwise – "I can!"

The *Midrash* explains that before giving the Torah to the Nation of Israel, G-d asked all the nations of the world if they wanted the Torah. "What's inside?" they asked. Upon hearing some of the laws, they flat-out refused. "We can't do that!" One by one, each nation refused to receive the Torah. G-d then asked the Jews. In a unified voice, without batting an eyelash, Israel answered, *"Na'aseh v'nishmah!"* ("We will **do** and we will **listen/understand**.") In other words, "We can!" The *Midrash* continues: suddenly, the angels came down and placed two crowns upon every Jew's head, one for *"na'aseh"* and one for *"nishmah."* In that instant of answering "yes" we became royalty. We understood that we are the children of G-d – the King. And when you are the child of the King, as long as the King wills it, there is nothing beyond your reach. This is the privilege of answering, "I can do it" – the privilege of being a Jew.

~ ~ ~

On Shavuot, there is a custom to read the Book of Ruth. Ruth was born a Moabite princess. She married the son of Elimelech (a prominent man from Bethlehem). Her husband died ten years after they wed, and she was left a destitute widow. Her mother-in-law, Naomi, told her and her sister (who had been married to Noami's other son) to go back to their parents' home. Naomi had nothing to give to them, and she herself, now penniless and old, wanted to go back to her homeland, Israel. Ruth's sister went back, but Ruth clung to Noami. Noami urged her to leave her, and Ruth answered, "Do not urge me to leave you, to turn back and not follow you. For wherever you go, I will go; where you lodge, I will lodge; your people are my people, and your G-d is my G-d" (Ruth 1:16).

In that moment, Ruth was like the Nation of Israel standing before G-d when He offered the Torah. And therefore, she merited kingship; she married Boaz and became the great-grandmother of King David, the king of Israel. Ruth made a decision. She made a choice. She chose to leave her life behind and become the daughter of the King.

Every day, we each have a choice. The choice to say "I can." With G-d's help, anything is possible, because we are the children of the King.

Shavuot is about receiving the Torah and receiving the crown of royalty. It's about faith and belief. Shavuot is the holiday where each one of us has the ability to acknowledge our potential and, with G-d's help, actualize it. It's the day when we affirm, "I can. With G-d's help, I can!"

Tisha B'Av

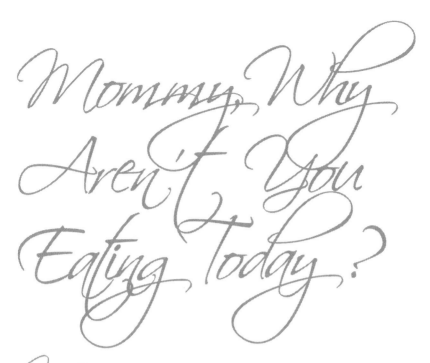

Mommy, Why Aren't You Eating Today?

Mommy, *why are you and Pappy sitting on the floor? Why are you sitting alone and not together? Mommy, why aren't you eating today? Mommy, where is your smile? Mommy, why are you crying?*

The questions roll forth from my little one's lips. Questions. And I need to supply the answers.

Mommy, why is this night different from all the other nights? Mah nishtanah halailah hazeh...

I'm struck by this last question. The question that my children ask me on this night of destruction is the same question that they ask me on the night of the *Seder*, the night of redemption.

Why on this night of *Tisha B'Av* are we sitting alone on the floor? Why on the night of the *Pesach Seder* do we all sit together, reclining like royalty? Tonight we sob; on *Pesach* we sing. Tonight we fast; on *Pesach* we feast.

The Jewish calendar was set in such a way that no matter the year, *Tisha B'Av* will always fall on the same night of the week as the first night of *Pesach*. Why are these two nights so different and yet so similar? Why does the destruction come about on the same night as the redemption?

Why is this night different from all other nights?

My littlest one, my two-year-old, is adorable and sweet — and rambunctious. I watch him. I listen to him. What is he putting into his mouth? What does he eat? It is dangerous? Is it healthy? I watch him. I listen to him. Now he's started to babble, and with delight I listen to his first words: "Mommyyyy! Pappyyyy!"

I say a word and he watches my mouth. I say it again and he repeats after me. "Eye, eye, nose, nose, bye, bye…" I ask him questions. He gives me answers. What is he saying? What words come out? He looks at me with those big eyes, full of curiosity, and asks over and over again, "Waz dis?" ("What's this?") Words, questions. What do I want him to hear? What do I want him to repeat? Am I as careful with what comes out of his mouth as I am with what goes in?

Mommy, why is this night different from all the other nights? Why do I hear your cheerful voice sobbing?

Only four months earlier, on the night of our redemption, we engaged our children in conversation. We provoked them to ask questions. The Hebrew word *pesach* can be split into two words: *peh* (mouth) and *sach* (conversation). *Pesach* is the night to open our mouths and engage in conversation. What kind of conversation? Conversation of redemption, conversation of thanks and praise. *Pesach* is the night when we recount what happened to our forefathers in Egypt. We describe the slavery that we, the nation of Israel, experienced under the rule of Pharaoh.

Who was Pharaoh, the Egyptian king? Pharaoh, the sages explain, was a small man who measured about a foot and a half tall. This small man had enormous power. His name, Pharaoh, can be divided into two words, *peh* and *rah*. "Mouth" and "bad." From Pharaoh's very name we learn that belittling words, evil speech and slander have tremendous power. When we diminish ourselves or diminish others, we become enslaved by the negative images or feelings that our words create. This in turn can lead to self-destruction or the destruction of others.

My little one, why is Mommy crying? I am crying because of the disharmony among Israel, because of our belittling words and because of our negative speech. I am crying, my love, because we sit in exile, a divided nation, like a Mommy sitting alone without a Pappy. My precious son, our Temple was destroyed almost two thousand years ago, and the redemption has still not come, but we can help bring it if we are careful with our speech. My dear child, as you learn to speak, let me teach you sweet words of praise, prayer and song. Know that what comes forth from your mouth is just as important as what enters. Know that words are so powerful that they can cure like medicine or destroy like poison. Don't despair, my child – with our words we can bring the ultimate redemption, and your Mommy will sob no more.

Mah nishtanah halailah hazeh…

Mourning What is Missing

I was sixteen years old when I became enchanted with Israel as I trekked throughout the Holy Land with a group of sunburned teen-agers on a summer youth group trip. I called home to my mother, proclaiming that I wanted to live in Israel and marry a handsome Israeli soldier. The trip wasn't religiously oriented and the mission was more to expose young American Jews to the land than to expose us to Judaism. But when a land and a people are so inherently connected, that sole mission was impossible to achieve. As we went to the holy sites, I thought to myself how I didn't really know what to do there. But when I came upon the Western Wall, my body swayed, my eyes welled with tears, and my lips couldn't stop themselves from whispering petitions. I thought I didn't know what to do, but I did.

Before our journey ended, I remember a certain night that stood out from all the others. It was a dark night and the air continued to hang heavy from the boiling August sun. Our counselors explained to us that the night was *Tisha B'Av*, the ninth day of the Hebrew month of Av, and that it was a tragic day in Jewish history. They didn't go into too many details, but we were told that it was the night of the destruction of the First and Second Temples. We then did a reenactment of an escape from Roman soldiers. At the end we were also told that it was a fast day for the Jewish people.

I fasted through the night and the next day – my first time fasting for *Tisha B'Av*. At the time I didn't fast for the destruction of the Temples. This had little or no significance to me and was something too removed for me to comprehend. I fasted because I found out that it was a fast day for the Jewish people, and as a Jew, I wanted to share in this experience with my people.

Two years later I went to synagogue on the night of *Tisha B'Av*. I found myself sitting on the floor in cloth shoes like a mourner. In a weeping voice, the Rabbi led the congregation in the reading of the book of Lamentations and for the first time in my life I had a sensation of what it meant to mourn and feel a connection to the loss of the Holy Temple.

~ ~ ~

There is a famous story told about Napoleon Bonaparte. He was walking in the streets of Paris when he heard wailings and the sounds of people lamenting, coming from a synagogue. He turned to the person he was with and asked, "Why are they crying?"

The other answered, "They're mourning over the destruction of their Temple."

"When was it destroyed?"

"Almost two thousand years ago."

Napoleon then declared, "A nation still mourning after so long will be eternal. They will return to their land and rebuild their Temple."

Why would Napoleon make such an assertion? Maybe because he understood that people don't mourn thousands of years over broken bricks and stones. *Tisha B'Av* isn't about the destruction of a building. *Tisha B'Av* is about the exile of a people from their homeland, an estrangement of a nation from G-d, and a separation of the spiritual from the physical. *Tisha B'Av* is about national tragedy and about personal suffering. Each one of us has individual struggles and all of us, in one form or another, await redemption from them and await the day when *Tisha B'Av* will no longer be a day of mourning, but a day of celebration.

But why do the Jewish people continue to mourn and weep year after year? Isn't there such a thing as "let go and let live"? Be happy with the moment and forget the past?

The Torah describes how grief-stricken Jacob was when informed that his son, Joseph, was attacked and killed by an animal. For twenty-two years Jacob was inconsolable, unable to get over the death of his beloved Joseph. Rashi (a post-Talmudic commentator) explains that Jacob's mourning was beyond the mourning of a parent for the loss of his child. This is because Joseph was actually still alive. Jacob's wounds could not heal because they weren't closed, Joseph was still alive and Jacob continued to bleed.

Mourning a death is very different than mourning something or someone that is missing. Even if a person is missing and presumed dead, the search for that person, or even the person's body, is never forgotten. We need proof. We need closure. For until there is closure, we cannot begin to move on. This is what *Tisha B'Av* is showing us: we are not mourning a death, we are mourning what is missing. The Temples were destroyed, but not forever, for the Third Temple will be rebuilt. And until it is, *Tisha B'Av* is that reminder of what we have temporarily lost.

This is why in the Talmud (*Shabbat* 31), there is a discussion about which questions are asked by the Heavenly Court for admittance into Heaven after a person dies. One of the questions listed is, "Did you expect (wait for) the Redemption?" The author of the *Melech b'Piv* (a Torah commentary) notes that the word used by the Sages is *tzepita* (expect/wait for). It doesn't use "hope for" or "want," but a word which describes a looking-out-for – with certainty.

This is like the family with a missing child. Years may have gone by, but that family waits every single day for a phone call that their child has been found. Every day they grieve that the child is missing, yet simultaneously, every day they pray and hope. This is the crying and mourning we do on *Tisha B'Av*. We realize how hard it is to live in exile without our Temple, so we wait every single day for it to be returned to us and pray that immediately we will be redeemed.

The Temple Within

I opened my e-mails. One was from Jenny. I always hesitate a moment before opening any e-mail from her, before answering any call from her. I have a love-hate relationship with my childhood friend Jenny. I love Jenny, but I hate what she does – most of all, what she does to herself.

For the past fifteen or so years, Jenny has been in and out of rehabilitation centers, in and out of jail, in and out of trouble. Throughout it all, I have felt totally and completely helpless as I watch her harm herself over and over again. I never let go of her, no matter how painful it was to hold on. I always hoped, always told her parents, "You are going to see. She's going to get better. She's going to change."

However this time when I opened her letter I told myself, "I just can't. I have to let Jenny go." I confided in my husband, "I thought that this time she had really stopped, but from her e-mail I see that she didn't. I can't have her in my life anymore. She won't change."

The entire week I felt defeated, depressed.

~ ~ ~

There was once a little boy named Naftali Tzvi. He was mischievous. He didn't like to study, and was always finding ways to get out of going to school. One night Naftali Tzvi tiptoed into the kitchen. He heard his mother crying, sobbing. "What will be? What will be? What will become of Naftali Tzvi?" The crying pierced his heart.

Naftali Tzvi, who was not the most intelligent child, decided right then and there that he would at least make an effort and apply himself. He studied, he learned. Naftali Tzvi Yehudah Berlin, also known as "the Netziv," became the *rosh yeshivah* (head dean) of the world-famous Volozhin Yeshivah. What would be, what would be of Naftali Tzvi if his mother hadn't cried and prayed over him?

~ ~ ~

There is a custom to remember ten things every day, and to say the Thirteen Principles of the Torah that were composed by Maimonides. One of the ten things is to remember Jerusalem, may it be rebuilt quickly in our days, and one of the thirteen principles of Jewish faith is to believe in the coming of Mashiach. I say these every day. I believe, with complete and total faith, that the Mashiach will come and the Holy Temple will be rebuilt.

I believe. I have to believe. If I don't believe, I am left with nothing. I believe, because how can I not? For nearly two thousand years the nation of Israel has been persecuted and attacked. And yet we live on. They have tried over and over to destroy us, and they can't. Why? Because we believe.

~ ~ ~

In the Torah, G-d commands the nation of Israel to build the *Mishkan* (Tabernacle) in the desert "so that I [G-d] can dwell inside you." The phrase used in the Torah is to dwell, not "among you," but "inside of you." The commentators understand from this that every Jew is a dwelling place for the divine presence. We are all Tabernacles that house the soul, a spark of divinity.

I keep thinking about Jenny. "Oh Jenny, if only you could see you the way I can see you."

When the Temple was destroyed, the sages write, all the gates of the heavens were closed except for one gate, the gate of tears. With a sincere prayer and a face of tears, any decree can be nullified. Our tears rise to the skies and pierce through the gates of heaven.

I remember the story of Rav Naftali Tzvi and the tears that his mother shed. I realize that I can't give up on Jenny. Jenny is like a Tabernacle: her body houses her soul. I cry and I pray, with the same hope and belief that the Temple will be rebuilt and that the Mashiach will come, that Jenny too will rebuild her life and reconnect to her beautiful soul.

Speaking Before Seeing

*I*t was a long summer Shabbat afternoon, and the kids had been playing so nicely together. For at least two hours, their imaginations took them to faraway lands and familiar locales. They played *Abba* and *Ima* (Daddy and Mommy), they made a pizza shop and cooked. The youngest had a birthday party, and the oldest built a city. They ate their Shabbat treats happily, and you could hear laughter and giggling.

All of a sudden, something happened. I don't even know what. Maybe it was now his turn to be Abba? Maybe she now wanted to put the pizza in the "oven"? The peace was shattered. I heard some screaming and crying. Annoyed, I put down the book that I had been reading and barged into their room. "Can't you get along?!" I asked self-righteously. "You guys are always fighting!"

From your objective standpoint, you probably realize how ridiculous I sounded and how mistakenly I acted. (Now, I certainly do!) For two hours, three children of three different ages and maturity levels played wonderfully together, and after one minute of fighting, I had already painted a picture of constant strife. I let the one minute overshadow the two hours, and I let my mouth speak before my eyes could see the real picture.

Doesn't this happen to us so often? You have a wonderful day, and then one person says one thing to you that irritates or insults you, and that's it – your entire day is ruined. You make a delicious meal, full of savory, healthy dishes, and yet you can't get over the one small side dish that had a tad too much salt. Your relationship with a person is ninety-five percent good and pleasant, and yet you focus and focus on that five percent that isn't so good. Why are we like that? Why does that happen?

My answer is...quicksand. Yes, quicksand! At least, that's what I like to call it.

What exactly is quicksand? Quicksand is something that sucks you in, pulls you under, and doesn't let you see anything but dirt.

~ ~ ~

The Nation of Israel was about to enter the Land of Israel. Moses sent twelve delegates to spy out the land. They had a mission: Bring back a report of the Promised Land before we enter. Why was this necessary? It wasn't – G-d had made a promise to them that the land was good and would be good for them (and G-d had been fulfilling miracles for them on a daily basis, including the Ten Plagues and the Splitting of the Sea). But the people asked for it. The commentators explain that Moses was hesitant, but went ahead and fulfilled the nation's request, reasoning, "Let them go and see how good it is; then they will come back and tell of the goodness, and the nation will enter with confidence."

The delegates returned after forty days, on the eighth of the month of Av, bringing with them incredibly large fruits, a sign of blessing and plenty. Two of the men came back with words of encouragement. One of them, Caleb, said, "We shall surely ascend and conquer it, for we can surely do it!" But the majority – ten men – came back and scared the nation. At first, they admitted that indeed it was a land which "flows with milk and honey." They showed the incredible fruits and then continued, "*But*, the people that dwells in the land is powerful...the land through which we have passed, to spy out it out, is a land that devours its inhabitants! All the people that we saw in it were men of measures. ... We were like grasshoppers in our eyes, and so were we in their eyes!" (Numbers 13:27-33).

The nation heard this and nothing else. Night descended and the people became despondent. "And all the congregation lifted up their voice and cried, and the people wept that night. ... And each man said to the other: 'Let us...return to Egypt'" (ibid. 14:1-5).

The Gemara explains: That night was *Tishah B'Av* (the ninth day of the month of Av). G-d said to them, "You wept for no reason, and thus I shall set [this day] for you as a time of weeping throughout the generations" (*Ta'anit* 29b).

Many years later, both the First and Second Temples were destroyed on this day. The city of Beitar was captured. Jerusalem was plowed under. King Ferdinand of Spain enforced the expulsion of Spanish Jewry on *Tisha B'Av*. World War I, which led to World War II and the Holocaust, also began on this day. *Tisha B'Av* is a national day of mourning.

When will the crying stop?

In part, when we start seeing and focusing on the ninety-five percent that is openly good to us and stop crying and talking about the five percent that appears bad. When we jump over the quicksand, instead of allowing ourselves to be drawn into the muck of overreacting and negativity. When we take the time to look and really see the whole picture before judging and jumping to the wrong conclusions.

On *Tisha B'Av*, Jews all over the world sit on the floor and weep, reading the book of *Eichah* (Lamentations). The first chapter of the book is written poetically according to the order of the Hebrew alphabet, from *aleph* to *taf*. But in the subsequent chapters, the letters *ayin* and *peh* are reversed. The letter *ayin* is also the word for "eye," and the letter *peh* means "mouth." With the reversal of the order of the letters, the prophet writes, "All our enemies have opened their mouth wide against us. We had terror and pitfalls, desolation and ruin. My eyes shed torrents of water over the destruction of the daughter of my people. My eye streams and is not silent, without respite…" (Lamentations 3:46-50).

On *Tisha B'Av*, we are reminded that our crying, our yelling, our jumping to conclusions, our saying whatever first comes to our mouth – all this blinds our eyes from seeing the good that we have. And if we are blinded by our words, we can't see the beautiful fruit, the milk and honey. We miss seeing the sparks of light and holiness that exist within each other and in our Holy Land.

~ ~ ~

If I could replay the moment, I would have done it differently. I would have complimented my children on all the time that they spent playing peacefully together. I would have praised them for their ideas and for their creativity. I would have asked them to share with me what they enjoyed most. And I would have told them that I had confidence in their ability to come up with a solution to the problem that provoked the little bit of crying.

This *Tisha B'Av*, let us return the *ayin* and *peh* to their proper order and pray for a day full of happiness instead of suffering.

Mommy, Come Home

"Mommy, I want you home now. I want you here." My youngest demands as he points his hand next to him. "Mommy, are you coming home again?"

The sweet and simple question of my three year old makes my heart ache, "Of course. I will be home in two days."

The answer doesn't appease him, nor does he understand that I already have my return ticket home. Two days, one day, a week, a month. Time means nothing to him. He doesn't know the difference. In addition to this, seeing me on Skype confuses him. We have no television or videos in our home. He doesn't understand where I am or how he can get a glimpse of me and not be with me. He doesn't understand how I am in constant contact with him. My physical presence is not with him , but I am thinking about him and still with him – still very much connected to him, just not in the same tangible way.

It's the first time I left home, left my children. The course, only a week long, gave me a tremendous amount of skills and tools to use in my practice. I felt that the one week separation was worth it, but I was surprised by the reactions of my children, especially the youngest one. I was also surprised by how much I missed them!

I left everything ready: food cooked and frozen, a calendar of events, careful instructions for my husband, and clothes freshly laundered and put away. Knowing how much my children are close with and adore my husband, I didn't even think that, given that all their needs were taken care of, they would even miss me. To my delight I was wrong! There is nothing like the presence, the feminine presence of a mommy.

I wish that I could put into words exactly what that presence is, but I can't. It is something nurturing, but more than that. If I close my eyes I think of an image of warm soft arms, a full belly, a soft shoulder, a sweet smell. I see a woman, doing only what her body is capable of doing, of nursing her baby. It's not that my husband isn't nurturing or soft. I rest assured knowing he gives them loving hugs and kisses, but he's not mommy.

~ ~ ~

When the Holy Temple was destroyed, we didn't just lose our physical place of national worship and service to G-d. We lost that closeness, that physical contact with Mommy (the Divine Presence, which is a feminine attribute of G-d).

We wake up in the morning and breath air, we eat, and everything we need is prepared and provided for us. We do connect and we do learn Torah and pray. We receive hugs and kisses, but in all of our lives in this Exile that we are in, we lack, we miss, we yearn for – "Mommy."

The phone calls and Skype aren't enough. As the years go by we begin to doubt. Will the *Shechina* (Divine Presence) really come home? Will there really be a redemption? Will the lack ever be filled? We will once again have that closeness? The closeness of a baby suckling at its mother breast? The child may doubt it, but I must tell you from the perspective of the mother – it will come. She never forgets. She never stops thinking, stops worrying about her children. Her love is unconditional. In fact, when we went into exile, she insisted on coming with us. She can never really part from us and when the Final Redemption comes she will reveal Herself to us, Her presence will be once again more tangible to us and together with Her we will all return home.

Tu B'Av

Bringing Darkness into Light

When you first meet a person, you see what is in front of you, and you automatically begin to paint a picture of who the person is. You look at the clothes, the facial expressions, and you make judgements and assumptions. The woman sitting in front of me had a pleasant smile and a shoulder-length reddish-brown wig. Her dress was both stylish and elegant. She looked to me like a typical religious woman, a mother of seven. Probably nothing interesting to tell – if anything, maybe boring. But when we started to speak, I saw that she was far from typical! The calm presence and pleasant smile masked an incredibly strong force and a powerful story.

Mina, born, in the former USSR, always knew that she was Jewish, but as a child, had no idea what that meant – except for two things: Her parents told her that being Jewish was very important, and they told her that she could only marry a fellow Jew.

When Mina was eleven, the Iron Curtain fell, and Mina was "free" to be openly "Jewish" – whatever that meant, because she didn't know. At 13, she heard something about *Shabbat* and wanted to keep it. But she had a problem: In the city where she lived, the school week was from Monday to Saturday, and by law she had to go. Her heart cried out to G-d – she wanted to keep *Shabbat*. It was a Wednesday, and *Shabbat* was approaching. All of a sudden, they received a notice from the school. The government was studying the productivity of students who received two days off from school instead of one. They picked one school from the thousands in the city. It was her school. There would be no school on Saturday!

She celebrated that first *Shabbat* in her room, doing nothing. Darkness descended on her, and she didn't reach for a light. Her parents told Mina that she was crazy. (At that point, Mina didn't know that there is no reason to sit in darkness; you can leave on a light that was lit before *Shabbat*.) She told them that she didn't care.

Mina spent her *Shabbat*s alone and in darkness for three years. At sixteen, she had the opportunity to go to Moscow to study in a Jewish school for young women and girls. At the age of seventeen, she came to Israel, and two years later, she married. Now, seventeen years later, Mina's children take for granted that they live in such freedom, that every *Shabbat* there is light and kosher food. They take for granted the Hebrew language that they speak and the Torah that they learn openly. Mina tells me that she doesn't really talk about those times. Her children are eons away and couldn't understand.

When I asked Mina about her time keeping *Shabbat* alone in the darkness, do you know what she told me? She told me that it was amazing. She felt that the Divine Presence was so close. She didn't mind the discomfort; she felt like a queen sitting on a royal throne. She felt important and protected. She was in the presence of the King.

~ ~ ~

There is a certain day of the summer when the sun reaches its peak, when the day is at its longest. There is so much light. From the breaking of the dawn until, at last, the sun sets, so much light. And then, just as the days are getting longer and longer, they begin to get shorter. *Tu B'Av*, the fifteenth day of the month of Av, falls out just as the days begin to shorten. When the Holy Temple stood in Jerusalem, the annual chopping of firewood for the sacrificial altar was concluded on this day. Wood used for the altar was used for the highest purpose – to connect man and G-d through sacrifice. They couldn't collect it after this day because there wasn't enough sunlight to dry it (*Ta'anit* 26b).

The Talmud also discusses how *Tu B'Av* was the matchmaking day. The daughters of Jerusalem would go out in simple white dresses to dance in the vineyards. Men would come, and they would choose a match. No one knew if you were rich or poor, from an important family or from a simple one. There were no beauty contests or competitions. It was a day of connecting. And it all happened on the day that commenced the shortening of days and lengthening of nights. Why?

Because in life we have challenges, and these challenges either bring you closer or further apart. When you get married, you feel like you are at a peak. You look beautiful, your spouse looks beautiful. The future is bright and full of light. And then something pops up, a challenge. It could be financial, it could be related to having or raising children, it could have to do with in-laws or family dynamics. It feels like a dark moment. But if you use that moment to come together and grow from that challenge, it will bring you to heights which you could never have reached before.

On *Tu B'Av*, it was the peak of the summer days, but it was the beginning of the time that leads to the winter. The message was clear: I'm not marrying you for money or beauty or honor. I'm marrying you so that we can grow together. So, too, with our relationship with G-d: We have difficult moments, crises, and challenges. When we use these times to turn to Him and cling to Him, we reach incredible spiritual heights. We are given strength and understanding. It's in those dark moments when the potential for closeness is greatest.

And when it's light? When the year goes through it's cycle and the seasons change once again, when we pass the winter cold and the days grow longer instead of shorter? We need to take that closeness and not forget it. We need to actually bring some of the darkness into the light, because when there is too much light, when you stare directly into the sun, the brightness blinds you, and you close your eyes, turning away from the light instead of towards it.

~ ~ ~

"Mina," I told her. "Don't forget that closeness that you had in Russia! Don't forget that the darkness brought you light and connection. Tell your children about it, and let them hear your stories, even if they don't understand. One day, maybe they will understand. And during their own challenges, they will draw strength from those stories."

Life's
Lessons

Timing is Everything

My son came home with a miserable look on his face. I knew what had happened even before he opened his mouth. I had warned him earlier in the morning when I saw the toy in his hand, "Don't bring your new toy to school. It could easily get broken or lost." Of course, he didn't listen. So when I saw the look on his face, I knew. The toy was either lost or broken.

His story of woe spilled out like a gushing river. I was right. He had lost the toy.

What were the words on the tip of my tongue? What was the phrase I so much wanted to say? "I told you so!" I looked again at the sorrow on his face, at the tears in his eyes, and I kept my mouth shut.

> Rabbi Shimon ben Elazar said: Do not appease your fellow at the time of his anger; do not console him while his dead lies before him; do not question him about his vow at the time he makes it; nor attempt to see him at the time of his degradation (*the Fathers* 4:18).

In this teaching we have the secret to marital harmony, peace in the home, and happy, nurturing relationships. What is the secret? Timing. Timing is everything.

When a person is angry, rebuking him will only make him angrier. When a person is upset, giving her advice will only aggravate her further. With the timing of our words, we have the power to raise our loved ones up, or push them down still lower. As King Solomon teaches, "Everything has its season, and there is a time for everything under the heaven" (Ecclesiastes 3:1). Timing is everything.

Your husband comes home from a terrible day at work. You have all the utility bills in your hand, armed and ready to pounce on him as soon as he walks in the door. You see the defeated look on his face, and put the bills down. They can wait until the morning.

Your teenager comes home with a failed test. She was disorganized and waited until the last minute to study. You fold your arms and give her a glare. "I told you weeks ago that you needed to start studying!" Before the words leave your mouth, before you fold your arms, stop. Think. Is this the right time for discipline? "Do not attempt to see him at the time of his degradation." It is our job as parents to teach, to transmit, and yes, to discipline. But if your child is angry or upset, then it's not the right time. At such a time, nothing will penetrate the heart.

A friend received another rejection. "Cheer up," you want to tell her. "It's not so bad. Another opportunity will come along." Stop. Wait. Is this the right time? There are times when encouragement is not appropriate. "Do not console him while his dead lies before him." Instead of talking, just hold her hand, or maybe leave her alone. Follow her cues, and let her guide you.

Rabbi Shimon ben Elazar is certainly not telling us that we should not appease, not rebuke, not console. In fact, the Torah teaches us that we are obligated to do so, but at the right time and under the right conditions. Timing is everything.

Knowing What is Important

Ten, eleven, twelve. I get to the top of the staircase, say a short prayer and brace myself for the greeting that I am about to receive as I open the door. Every morning it's the same as I arrive at the Eating Disorder clinic where I work. "Elana, either you conquer them, or they will conquer you." I call my work *kadosh* (holy) as I muster all the strength I have to greet my students with a smile and cheerful, "Good morning."

Why does it take so much energy? Well, one reason is because I know that when I walk in, I will meet blank faces, laptop screens, and cell phones that form barriers between me and my students. A lifeless crowd can be more than just a little bit discouraging. Second, it's hard work – to be a teacher – to teach women going through so many struggles and who live in a time of so much confusion. And yet, day after day I continue as I try to shift the distorted focus of these women from their bodies to their beautiful souls. Either I conquer them, or they conquer me. No matter what happened yesterday I remind myself: "today is a new day, walk in with a positive attitude and a smile."

It's eight o'clock at night, my children are asleep. I am sitting down after a long day to work on the computer. I'm in the middle of an important email. I hear the soft knock, the key in the door. I know it's my husband. I force myself to peel my fingers away from the keyboard and stand up. I turn as he enters and find the smile, the cheerful voice, "Hi!" Ten years of marriage and I make an effort to greet my husband the same way as I did the first month we were married. Why? Because I call my marriage "*kadosh.*" That means that for five minutes I can put my work, or the phone call, etc. on hold. Those things can wait; the opportunity for my husband to come home, can't. Either I conquer them, or they conquer me.

~ ~ ~

There is a section in the *Shulchan Aruch*, the main codification of Jewish law compiled by the 16th-century rabbi, Rav Joseph Caro, entitled *Orach Chaim* (The Direction of Life). The *Orach Chaim* deals with everyday matters of Jewish law. The very first *halacha* (law) tells us that one should arise in the morning like a mighty lion to serve one's Creator and that one should wake up the early dawn. I always thought that the wording of the end of this law was a little bit funny and then my husband elucidated it for me, "You wake up the morning, don't let the morning wake you up!" That's right, here we go again, either I conquer the morning, or it conquers me. Either I wake up like a mighty lion ready to serve my Creator and do holy acts; or the lion of despair, discouragement, routine, and lack of appreciation will be the one to wake me up.

I can't begin to count how many times I put this idea into practice throughout my day. It always seems to throw everyone a bit off balance – in my favor. The checkout lady at the cash register who I smile to and greet before I start handing over my groceries, the repair man who comes to fix the faucet (for the third time this month), and of course my children, as they walk through the door or as I pick them up from school. I am able to conquer all these people, bad moods, bills, tantrums – you name it – before they conquer me, with a smile, a cheerful voice, and with a vision that says that by doing this, what I am doing is *kadosh.*

This is also why my favorite prayer of the day is the *mincha* prayer. There are three times in the day set for formalized prayer: morning, afternoon, and evening (The beauty of prayer in general is that you don't need any intermediary between you and G-d, no Skype, no chat, no cell phone, no leader; just you and Him. A Jew can speak and pour his heart out to G-d at any time of the day or night in an informal manner.)

The prayer that is considered the most significant is that afternoon prayer – *mincha. Mincha* is also the shortest of the three; it's in the middle of the day when you are being asked to drop what you are doing to take a few minutes of your time to reconnect and remember what is most important, most holy.

I'll never forget as I was sitting in the barber shop waiting as Asher, the barber, cut my son's hair. The hour was 3:05 PM. A customer walked in the door. Asher told him, I can't help you now. After I finish with the boy I'm going to *mincha*. If you want, you can come back at 3:45 PM. The man was furious and walked out the door. Asher just shrugged his shoulders and looked at his reflection in the mirror. "What does he think? I'm going to miss *mincha*?" At that moment I knew without a doubt that my son's barber was a holy man cutting hair with a holy purpose. Either you conquer them, or they conquer you....

Why Jews Nosh

I sat waiting in the doctor's office with my children. I watched them as they became totally engrossed in the toy trucks and games that were sprawled all over the waiting room. Suddenly, my son got up and started to walk towards the doctor's offices. "Mommy, Mommy?" He had forgotten that I was right there, sitting behind him on the couch. "I'm right here, Avraham Nissim, I'm right here," I reassured him. He flashed me a stunning smile and we both laughed.

Our Patriarch, Jacob, was forced to flee from his father's home to avoid the wrath of his brother Esau. He was scared and alone. Jacob lay down to sleep and had a dream. There was a ladder with angels going up and angels going down. Suddenly, G-d appeared in his dream and reassured him, "Jacob, I am here. I am with you wherever you go."

My baby, she's a *nosher* (snacker). At any time of the day, whether she's hungry or whether she's full, she'll come waddling to me for a *nosh*. If I'm sitting, she pulls herself up on my lap and tugs at my shirt. If I'm standing, she tugs at my skirt. I know what she wants; she wants me to nurse her, she wants me to kiss her and comfort her. Sometimes this snack only lasts a minute. It's like her way of "checking in" to make sure that I'm still there and that I love her.

I have to tell you, I'm also a *nosher* – a prayer *nosher* and a blessing *nosher*, and I can't tell you how much this keeps my sanity and enables me to get up the next morning to face a new day. I go through my routine, day after day, and sometimes I feel like a robot as I check off the activities on my list. "Make breakfast, feed kids, get everyone dressed, pack lunches, get everyone out the door, put baby down to nap, sit down to work, make lunch, iron shirts…" Like a pile of laundry, the list never ends. Then something happens to upset my perfect schedule, something outside of the neat list that I keep handy. A child has a cold, a disagreement with a neighbor, a problem at work, a fight with a friend. I'm sitting in traffic, absolutely stuck and I look up; it's *nosh* time.

"Um, excuse me, G-d are you there? Can You help me out here?" I grab an apple and I say a blessing on it before I take a bite. I nosh and I nosh, I check in and you know what? I feel better. I might be hungry, I might be full. The snack isn't about eating; it's about knowing that I'm not alone and that I'm being watched over.

Jacob awoke from his sleep and said, "Surely G-d is in this place and I did not know" (Genesis 28:16). It was almost as though Jacob realized that he could connect to G-d at any place and at any time, that G-d is truly *everywhere*. Jews have a precious gift: the inherent ability to *nosh* at any time. Why do you think religious people say so many blessings? Why do you think Jews have so many commandments? Before eating and drinking, after eating and drinking, lighting *Shabbat* candles, lighting the *menorah*… the list goes on. Because it gives us a way to connect to G-d to remember that He is here.

The Battle of the Bulge

My skirt feels uncomfortably tight after a week of festive eating. It's the same old story. My tummy starts to bulge ever so slightly and I'm already thinking about going on a diet and what I have to do to take off the weight. It's a battle that feels like it will never end, a classic battle that almost every woman struggles with: The Battle of the Bulge.

It's hard for me to be happy with the way I look. I'm always striving for some unrealistic expectation, some ideal that doesn't exist. I longingly look at pictures of myself ten years ago and remember the flat stomach and the thighs that didn't touch.

Back then I was skinny – too skinny – as I completely obsessed about what I ate and how much I exercised. My life had to be rigid with regards to food and to how much I weighed. I lacked the freedom of flexibility and was a slave to a very sick set of societal standards. I never allowed myself a treat or anything with the three-letter word…FAT.

I had no idea what I was doing to myself until one day I remember my mother crying to me, "*Bubby* and *Zeidy* (Grandmother and Grandfather) were starved in a concentration camp for their granddaughter to starve herself?" The words resonated in my heart as I looked at myself in the mirror and saw a once beautiful young woman turning into a frame of mere skin and bones. What was I doing? How did this happen? I no longer had the body of a woman, but of a skeleton.

I was seventeen years old and applying to colleges when I became anorexic. It caught everyone by surprise, myself included. I was neither heavy nor insecure about my weight or body. However, the pressure of getting into a good school, the pressure to be perfect in every aspect of my life, and the incredible desire to feel in control of the future that I thought other people controlled, drove me to anorexia.

At first everyone told me that I looked fabulous. I loved the attention. Then fabulous turned into dangerously skinny as I dropped below a hundred pounds. Why couldn't I just be happy with my already small frame and why did I always feel that I had to be in such control over every aspect of my life? I tricked myself into thinking that I was healthy. After all, I *was* healthy – I ate lots of fruits and vegetables and exercised, right? And I kept pointing out that I wasn't like the other girls around me, the ones who drank diet coke all day. I wouldn't touch such a chemically filled drink as I drank nothing but water and water and water all day.

What I didn't know is that too much of a good thing isn't good either. I didn't realize that health – for a woman – means a bit of fat, a bit of roundness on her body. Health means eating fats like nuts and avocados; it means eating whole grains and proteins. Health means flexibility and it means loving yourself and allowing yourself to be happy. It also means forgiving yourself if you eat a piece of chocolate and giving your body a break.

And most importantly health means letting go and realizing that you are *not* in control.

So many young women come to me, worried about their lack of menstruation. They come to me for advice. I know that it's hard for them to listen to what I tell them because I tell them the truth: a woman's body can't function unless fed properly and if you want children, you can't live on salads alone.

I know that it's not easy. We're bombarded by advertisements of anorexic women. We're told to be healthy on one hand and yet to eat a deficient diet on the other hand. It's hard to live a balanced life that's truly "healthy."

Maimonides, the great Torah sage and scholar was also a doctor. Maimonides always advised to take the middle path in your life with regards to everything except for two character traits. He said to stay far away from anger and haughtiness and to be extremely humble. Everything else, he advised, one should do in moderation.

I'm always moving. If I have the chance to take the stairs instead of the elevator I choose the stairs. Walking or transportation, I prefer to walk. Every morning I jog past a woman who takes the bus two blocks to drop off her daughter at preschool. She always calls out to me as I jog by, "I admire you; I wish that I could also find the time to exercise." I laugh to myself as she says this because I feel so breathlessly busy at times between taking care of my son, my home, running errands, and work that I couldn't imagine being any more busy. And yet with the fifteen minutes that she spends waiting for the bus, I walk.

But, as we said before life is about moderation. I look at certain women who actually appear perfect in their physical appearance. However when I get to know them and their routines, I actually feel sorry for them. And I remember how I was also like them. I can no longer imagine spending my whole day engrossed in making myself beautiful. Spending hours at the gym, hours clothes-shopping, hours in a beauty salon, and hours worrying about what to eat and what not to eat and reading magazines about the latest miracle diet. How much time of the day can a person waste on such vanities? It's just not for me and it shouldn't be for any sane, "healthy" woman.

I left that life over ten years ago as I started to heal both from within and from without. With the aid of friends who supported me, I quickly sought guidance and went to a nutritionist who helped me gain perspective on my eating habits and who encouraged me to want to live and be healthy. Life is so short and it's so full of meaning. I get so sad when I think about the superficial things that we waste it on. I remember once reading a story by Rabbi Twersky about a person who was crying to his rabbi before *Yom Kippur*. He moaned, "We come from dust and will return to dust." The rabbi answered him, "True, but in between you have a beautiful thing called life."

I know people who are wealthy and never happy with what they have; beautiful and never satisfied with the way they look. Millions of people live malnourished and in poverty yet we live in a world where the wealthiest people actually spend money to look like they're poor! Is that a life to desire or be jealous of?

I know the importance of being beautiful – for yourself, for your husband and for your family. I practice what I preach, as I always make sure to look good when my husband walks in the door and greet him with a beautiful smile. But should the way I look and how much I weigh really be my life's goal? Is this the reason why my husband loves me and wanted to marry me?

I pat my stomach and feel the little bulge. I know that I eat correctly and exercise. I'm active and alive. I realize that I have to accept myself and love myself, and know that my life is more than just my belly.

Two Kinds of Envy

For the past year and a half I have attended a parenting class by a woman who I admire tremendously. Not only is she absolutely-beyond-words-amazing, but I find her very real, very truthful, and very accessible. She's my mentor. I walk away from her class every week feeling inspired to grow, inspired to learn, and inspired to try the wise techniques that she teaches in her class. She pushes me and it's good. I look at her and say, "That is the kind of mother that I want to be." I aspire to have her patience, her wisdom, her clear focus on what is and what isn't a priority. But for the first time since I started the class I came home last week very upset.

Rachel was barren. She looked at her sister Leah, who was having baby after baby, and she was jealous. The Sages explain that Rachel was not jealous of Leah's babies, but she was envious at what she thought was the reason for Leah's fertility. She saw that Leah was an incredibly righteous woman and she wanted to have the same character traits that Leah did. Being envious of a person's good qualities is not a bad thing, in fact, it's great if it is the stimulus for a person's growth and self-improvement. The problem is what happened to me last week…

My mentor described to us a situation and a reality that pertains to her life. She told us how she deals with it and I saw that it was totally inapplicable to my situation in life. I felt crushed. I realized that in this area I just can't be like my mentor. I have a different background than her, a different occupation than her, and a different family situation than her. So why was

I so upset? Because I realized that I had crossed the line between aspiring to acquire the goodness of her and of aspiring to be her! She's a mother of thirteen, as of now, I am a mother of three. She was born into one family and I was born into a totally different family. Her strengths and talents are not mine and mine are not hers. I want to be her, but I can't, because in sum, I'm not her; I'm me!

I wonder if this is why Jacob got so upset with Rachel. She came to him "envious of Leah" demanding that he "give her children." We don't see that she stopped and tried to work on herself in the area for which she envied Leah. Instead she said, "Give me what she has," which is almost like saying, "Make me her." Jacob answered that G-d is the one who made her infertile. In other words: "Your reality is not the same as Leah's. As harsh as it sounds, you are barren and she's not. Being the mother of many children is her fate, but that doesn't mean that it's yours as well."

Rachel then did what she was good at – she acted, and through her maidservant, Bilhaah she had a son. This son Rachel named "Dan," from the hebrew word meaning judgment. The Torah writes, "Rachel said, 'G-d has judged me, He has also heard my voice and has given me a son.'" G-d judged me – who I am, and has heard my voice – as Rachel with my fate and in my situation. The voice that He heard is also the voice of prayer, which was an area of strength in Leah that Rachel didn't have. This was precisely the area that she admired in Leah, and we see by this sentence that she did work on it. Leah's strength pushed Rachel to grow in her ability to pray; but ultimately, Rachel saw that G-d didn't judge her as Leah, He judged her for who she was, and yes, saw her effort and gave her a son. Rachel learned from Leah, she became a mother; but she never was and never could be Leah, nor could Leah ever be Rachel.

We all need mentors and teachers. Everyone needs someone whom she can look up to and aspire to emulate. The Sages say that in an area of self-improvement and spiritual growth, envy is good, it's a positive impetus, but that's where the positive side of it stops. We can't be someone whom we are not, we can't have something that doesn't correspond to us. If it did correspond to us, G-d would have given it to us.

I'm worried. Now that I see that I did this with myself, do I do this with my kids, my husband, my parents, etc? Do I see them, and see someone else and say, "Why can't they be "so and so"? We can only be who we are and work with what G-d gives us. After one hundred and twenty years when a person dies and goes up to the Heavenly Court he is never judged for not being like someone else. The Heavenly Tribunal judges them for who he was, what he did, and for the unused potential that he never developed. A person is not asked, "Why weren't you like so and so?" Instead he is asked, "Why weren't you the best that you could be?"

Ah, I feel better! I'm now looking forward to this week's class. I can continue to grow and take all the good that my teacher transmits to me without the pressure of feeling that I need to be her. I can admire her for who she is and apply what I gain from her, making me the best that I can be, as me.

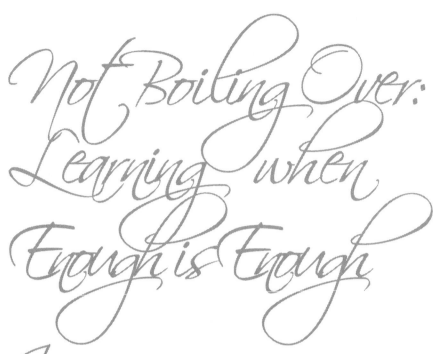

Not Boiling Over: Learning when Enough is Enough

I have a hot water kettle. You put water inside, press the button, and it instantly heats up. The water starts to bubble, steam toots out from the top, and you hear a whistle. The water becomes very, very hot, which is why sometimes before the water boils I click the button off so that the water won't boil so powerfully.

I have a hard time saying no. I have an even harder time asking for help. Even as a child, I would get into fights with my mother, arguing with her not to buy me so much clothing.

I know how to give, but I don't know how to receive.

Part of this is due to my personality. I'm self-motivated and hard working. I don't take "no" as an answer. And part of this is due to how my parents raised me, to the tremendous amount of emotional and physical responsibilities that they gave me turning me into the Mommy of the Mommy.

When I married my husband I learned that if I didn't allow him to give to me, it wouldn't work. In Hebrew the word *natan* (gave) is spelled the same frontwards as it is backwards, to teach us that when you give you inevitably receive and when you receive you automatically give. However, I must admit that even with him, it is so hard for me to ask for anything.

I receive phone calls all the time: "Elana, can you..." before they even finish their request I have already said yes and committed myself to...fill in the blank. I work, I teach, I cook all our meals, clean our home, do all the shopping, receive guests, take care of the children...really I do everything.

I work full time, am a part-time student and am a full time home-maker as well. Why? I ask myself. What is driving me? I'm stubborn, strong-willed. Maybe it's pride or arrogance? Am I afraid of not being loved or accepted? Will everyone still love me if I'm not perfect or superwoman?

I put water in the kettle and turn the button on. The water boils, it gets hotter and hotter. Steam comes out and the kettle starts to whistle.

A year ago I felt incredibly tired, beyond exhausted. I woke up-tired. I went to sleep-tired. My whole day was full of fatigue. I went to a doctor. I did a blood test. My thyroid stimulating hormone levels were very high indicating that my thyroid was sluggish and not working as it should. An ultrasound also showed a cyst on my thyroid. One of the symptoms of hypothyroidism is exhaustion. At the same time our financial situation became more difficult. I pushed myself to work harder and harder. It's no wonder that I was so tired!

To add to the list of things that I do, I am also a healer (I practice reflexology and massage therapy as well as yoga therapy and meditation) and I started to examine my own condition. Holistically, the thyroid is related to faith. The neck (the physical location of the thyroid) is related to one's outlook and stubbornness.

"Elana, if you don't stop this you are going to break," I told myself. "Elana, you need to get help!" I started looking for someone to come help me once a week to clean my home. But all I could do was tell myself we couldn't afford it. Even though I knew we needed it, it is just so hard to change. My husband became annoyed with me. "We need help! It's not a luxury – it's a necessity."

I prayed and turned to the Creator. "Please help me to strengthen my faith. Let me rely only on You and not on myself! Send me the right people to teach me how to receive, because ultimately whatever I take from anyone is accepting and taking that which You give me."

I read Chassidic works on strengthening one's faith in G-d, went to acupuncture to relax me and I eventually accepted help. My TSH levels went back down in less than a month and a half.

When G-d created the world He did it all by Himself. The description recorded in the Torah is in the third-person singular. However, on the sixth day when G-d created man the Torah says, "Let us make man." The commentators explain that G-d was speaking to the angels. Even though He created Man alone, by saying "Let us" He teaches us humility. He also teaches us that there is nothing wrong with asking for or receiving help!

I would hate to think that one day my children will grow up and feel inferior because they can't do something on their own. I would be devastated if they don't turn to me to ask for advice or assistance because I taught them that they had to be perfect and to do everything by themselves.

So once again I put water in my kettle. I turn it on. But before I wear myself thin, before I find myself feeling resentful or overly tired, I press the button off. I stop, I pray, I ask for help. And I feel fortunate that for now I have prevented myself from bubbling over.

I remember, when my husband and I were dating, he called me "*gordita*." *Gordita*, in Spanish, is equivalent to "fatty." I looked at him as I touched my waist and asked him, "How can you say that?" I knew I wasn't fat. In fact, I was too thin, but I felt hurt and insecure by his comment anyway. He quickly reassured me, "Elana, in Mexico, '*gordita*' is an affectionate term. It's like saying 'cutie.'"

That was just the first of many cultural nuances to which I have had to accustom myself since I met my husband. The next one was with my mother-in-law, who called me every day, three times a day. I felt like I was being interrogated by the KGB each time she called to ask me, "What are you doing? What did you do? What are you going to do?"

Later, I learned that my mother-in-law is just a gregarious woman who calls everyone that she loves and cares about. I learned that my responses really didn't matter, and the questions weren't really an interrogation, but a means of saying, "I'm here if you need me. I'm just checking in."

A hundred years ago, most people either married the "boy or girl next door," or they married a relative. They knew the culture and family of their spouse, and certainly spoke the same language. Now, with telecommunications and rapid transportation, matches have become multicultural. I have Canadian friends who've married French, Americans who've married Israelis, Brazilians who've married Spaniards, not to mention myself, an American who married a Mexican. Communication has become instant, but it's also become more difficult.

Through trial and error, and now years of experience, I've come to realize that communicating is not about talking and "listening;" it's about understanding. When you hear a loved one or friend say something to you that seems to be invasive or hurtful, ask yourself, "Does this person want to hurt me?" You know in your heart that the answer is, of course, no. So why did he or she say it? I don't know, but maybe we actually didn't understand what was said, and you have to know that it wasn't said to hurt you.

Sometimes we have to take a step back to try to understand other people and really hear what they are trying to tell us. Even if you do marry your next-door neighbor, each person is a world of his own, and brings his own language into any relationship. Relationships take work, and it takes time to learn the art of understanding. But if you start out by judging the other person favorably, you'll see your negative reactions fading away, and you'll have an easier time communicating.

The Grass is Greener

I make my family hearty, whole wheat bread and rolls. A lot of love goes into my baking, not to mention the healthiest ingredients that I can find. So when my son told me one day, "Mommy, I want you to *buy* me a roll for my lunch," I was heartbroken to say the least. Here my son gets organic, homemade whole wheat bread and what does he *want*? A store bought, plain *white* roll. Does this make sense to you?

"Of course," you tell me, especially when you find out that the person sitting next to him every morning on the school bus has in his lunch a store bought white roll. I didn't even bother to preach to him, "But my rolls are better. They are made with the best ingredients; they are healthier; they are homemade, etc."

I didn't bother attacking the store bought roll, saying "Those are empty calories; they taste like stale paper; *his* mother doesn't even know how to make bread!" – even though I really wanted to. All I did was tell him:

"I hear you. I know that you want the store's rolls." (First step, as I learned in my parenting class: validate the request.)

"I love you and I want to give you the best. This is the best for you and the store bought roll is the best for him. I don't buy white rolls. Period." (Second step, as I learned in my parenting class: make a general statement; state the ground rules without ordering or demanding.)

He hasn't mentioned it again and the subject was dropped. I did however buy him a whole wheat roll when I found one at the bakery. (Third step, as I learned in my parenting class: when you can comply, comply.)

Now, breads and rolls aside – this request and the arguments that I hear or see daily about always wanting what the other has, well, they depress me. For example, when there is only one green apple left in the refrigerator and my son starts to eat it. My daughter then throws a fit because she now wants it. (She didn't want it before he started chomping on it.) Or my daughter picks up a toy, my son then drops the *ten* that he was playing with and decides that the *one* toy my daughter has is the one that he wants. You get the picture. Why is it that children always want what the other one has?

I stop for a moment and think about what I just said. Are we adults any better?

"Why did he get the promotion and raise and not me?" "Why do I have to struggle for everything and for her it comes so easy?" "Did you see their new car? Why do I have to still drive this old jalopy?" "Everyone except for me gets to take a vacation."

Is it the nature of man to always want what the other has and to never be satisfied with what one does have? Based on this it appears that the answer is yes, but is there anything that can be done about it? Can we ever be happy with what we have?

First Step: Whatever I have only corresponds to *me*. Whatever anyone else has only corresponds to *them*. The Talmud teaches us that no one can touch what is designated for another person. If you know that the other person's possessions don't even correspond to you, then what is there to be envious of?

Second Step: Is the grass really greener on the other side? It certainly appears that way, but as the prophet says, "For a person sees the eyes and G-d sees the heart" (Samuel I 16:7). No one really knows the trials and tribulations of another person and I guarantee you that if you did, you certainly wouldn't want to change places.

The Talmud relates how the son of Rabbi Yehoshua ben Levi, Rav Yosef, was very sick. His heart stopped beating and he was clinically dead. He miraculously recuperated after his soul had entered the threshold of the world to come. His father asked him, "What did you see?"

Rav Yosef answered, "I saw the world upside down. The high were low and the low were high."

His father commented, "You saw a clear world (how things really are and not as how they appear)."

If we could really step into the shoes of another person, whether they be boots, high heels, or platforms, you would find them terribly uncomfortable. G-d gives every person what he needs and when he needs it. If you don't have it, then you really don't need it, and if you do have it, then it means that there is a purpose to your having it.

Third Step: It's not even mine to begin with; it's all G-d's. Now this one might seem hard to grasp, but I tell you it's wonderful, especially when your toddler is throwing a tantrum in the middle of the supermarket. At the moment when you most want to crawl into a hole due to embarrassment, look up to the Heavens and quietly say, "Remember G-d, he's not mine, he's Yours and I'm just watching him for You. Can you please help me with this?" You can now calmly smile at everyone and tell anyone who asks, "He's not mine, I'm just taking care of him." I assure you that your ego will no longer get in the way and you will find yourself calm and composed about the whole thing. You'll also have nothing to be jealous of when you see your friend's toddler behaving like a total angel because after all, her kid isn't hers either! So really, what is there to be jealous about anyways?

Seeing the Blessing

It's funny – I hate to shop and I never like buying things for myself, but when it comes to buying presents for others, especially my children, I am a compulsive buyer. We walked by a store with colorful candy dishes on display. There were adorable apple shaped containers. I looked at them; I looked at my children. Within minutes we had bought them and were talking about how we would fill them up with raisins and nuts.

Less than twenty-four hours later, one of my children had already broken the apple's top. It was broken in such a way that I knew I couldn't fix it or glue it back together.

My son, Avraham Nissim, spotted the apple container and picked up the broken top in his hand. "What happened?" he asked. "It broke," I answered as I braced myself for his reaction.

"Now we can put a spoon in it and use it for honey!" he exclaimed.

"May you always be blessed to see the world with those eyes," I praised him as I hugged him and gave him a kiss. The choice was his; he could have seen the broken top, focused on what was lacking and become angry, but instead he chose to see what he had in his hand, what was there and not what was missing.

~ ~ ~

In the text of the *Ethics of the Fathers*, the Sages state that those who have a good eye, a humble spirit and an undemanding soul are the disciples of our forefather Abraham. Abraham is the symbol of *chesed* (kindness). He was the man who waited in the sweltering heat for guests to arrive just three days after his own circumcision – despite his physical discomfort and advanced age. He is also the one to whom G-d said, "I will bless you, and I will make your name great, and you will be a blessing. I will bless those who bless you...and all the families of the earth will be blessed through you" (Genesis 12:2-3).

G-d gave our forefather Abraham the power to bless. The key to making oneself a recipient for blessing, or bounty, our Sages tells us is, "a good eye, a humble spirit, and an undemanding soul."

G-d came to Abraham and told him that He was going to turn him into a great nation. At this point Abraham didn't even have a child, let alone a nation! G-d told him to step outside and see beyond the stars. He told them that he (in other words, the Nation of Israel) had access to a reality that was beyond nature. Abraham, with his good eye and humble spirit, believed in G-d. He didn't dwell or focus on what he didn't have; he looked ahead to the future and only saw the potential – not just what was but what could be.

~ ~ ~

I just received our monthly credit card bill. On it was a month's worth of food shopping, as well as my utilities and phone bills. I looked at it. There were no luxuries; everything for me was a bare necessity. I gasped when I saw the total. *How are we going to make it?* I felt a moment of panic. This was the perfect moment to start thinking about everything that we "don't" have: "we don't have enough money, we don't have extra savings, I can't get a better job if I want to be at home for my children, I don't have, we don't have, I don't have."

I stopped myself.

"I have a family, I have a job, I have food in the refrigerator, my children are healthy, I have peace in my home. I have, I have, I have; most importantly I have G-d and He always takes care of me."

The same glass is either half-empty or half-full depending upon the perspective of the eye. As long as the soul is housed within the body there always exists the "what is," even when it appears that all that there is, is nothing. My grandfather would say that money comes and money goes. The one who is on top finds himself on the bottom and the one on the bottom finds himself on top.

~ ~ ~

The Talmud describes how Rav Chanina ben Dosa's daughter mistakenly filled the small oil lamps used for *Shabbat* candles with vinegar instead of oil. She realized her mistake too late to fill them with oil in time to light the candles for *Shabbat*. Rav ben Dosa told her to light the wicks which were sitting in the vinegar. The same G-d who made it so that oil can light can make it so that vinegar can light, he told his daughter.

What is the message for us? We should always look at what we have and whatever it is, with the right perspective, it can be seen as a potential blessing.

Open Your Mouth

"My L-rd, open my mouth, that it may declare Your praise" (Psalms 51:17).

It's a typical scene, a friend or a guest is visiting and my toddler strikes up a conversation with him. He excitedly tells the visitor something or makes a proclamation. The visitor turns to me clueless and asks, "What did he say?" I translate. We're all speaking the same language, but only I can decipher what he is saying. Only his Mommy seems to be able to understand and decode his words, know his needs and shed light unto his babble. Even his Poppy (Daddy), who absolutely adores him and wants to understand him, doesn't always comprehend and frequently turns to me with the same question, "What did he say?" What's so special about me that I have the capacity to understand what others don't and interpret when others can't?

"Blessed are You, L-rd who hears prayer" (sixteenth blessing of the daily prayer).

On more than one occasion someone has asked me how to pray. "How do I pray? What should I say? I'm not sure what to ask for… is G-d really going to listen to me anyways?" Before beginning the formal daily Prayer, a prayer which includes nineteen blessings, one must begin the Prayer with the verse from Psalms: "My L-rd, open my mouth, that it may declare Your praise." (This was instituted by the Sages. See *Berachot* 4b.) The way a person begins to pray is simply by asking G-d to open his mouth.

There are many factors which give me – my son's mother – the ability to understand him when no one else can. Love and patience are important factors. There's also the desire to comprehend. But grandparents and other relatives share this and yet they still don't know what the child is saying. It's something else. You see, I spend hours upon hours listening to my child. I now know how to read his expressions and his body language. I know my child because I am with my child.

When you don't know what to say or how to say it, watch a child and do the same. First you begin by opening your mouth. You let out a sound, a squeal or a babble. The babble turns into a toddler's words and the words turn into a child's sentences. Soon the sentences mature and communication develops.

When it comes to prayer, G-d is like a mommy. Not only does He love us and have infinite patience, but He knows us, and if we let Him into our hearts and lives, He becomes a part of us. The more we allow Him to enter, the more we talk to Him, the easier the words will flow and the more we will make ourselves understood.

The Power of Touch

Florence came to me for a stiff neck. As my hands carefully massaged her frail body, the words poured forth from her mouth. I touched her eighty-four-year-old hand and she told me a story. I caressed her arm and I found out that her husband had suddenly died in a car accident two years ago. Her only two sons also tragically died. She moved a year ago from her home in the States to Jerusalem to be with her only daughter-in-law and grandchildren.

My hands didn't stop as the touch of the skin touched the heart. Florence kept talking, I kept massaging. She told me that her daughter-in-law was leaving for a week-long trip. She had made arrangements for Florence. Florence wouldn't be left alone for a minute. But I heard Florence's voice filled with stress as she told me about the daughter-in-law's trip. At the end of the treatment Florence praised my touch, the work I did on her neck. "You are wonderful, but I still feel some pain. When will it go away?"

"Florence," I gently answered her. "The pain will go away when your daughter-in-law comes back from her trip."

"You heard that, hun?" She smiled as I gave her a hug.

~ ~ ~

There is nothing as delicious as the hug I receive from my three-year-old daughter. I adore holding her tightly, putting her head on my shoulder and breathing the sweet smell of her hair. I kiss those adorable cheeks and close my eyes to the touch of the Garden of Eden. For my eldest son, I ask permission first before planting kisses all over his face, as he grows and matures into a little man who might just possibly be embarrassed by his mother's touch. This doesn't stop him, thank G-d, from coming to me with a banged arm or leg for a healing massage, a soothing touch. I pass him something and I make sure to lovingly squeeze his hand. A child thrives on touch. Without food and water you can't live; without touch you can't grow. Sometimes, when I have no comforting words for my friends or students, I give them a hug which conveys more than words ever could.

As a massage therapist and reflexologist, I know a lot about the power of touch. Touch can heal, it can soothe, but when used improperly it can also destroy. I will never forget the painful touch I received at the age of fourteen. I was touched by someone whom I didn't know and whom I didn't want touching me; it was also in a place where I didn't want to be touched.

As a twenty-year-old I discovered a new aspect of touch. I was studying in Paris. There it seemed like everyone was always touching. To anyone you greet you give two kisses, one on each cheek. There was one exception: at the family whose home I spent every *Shabbat*. There the father never touched me, never greeted me with kisses or a handshake, and neither did his sons. The mother gave me plenty of kisses, but she never greeted her male guests with kisses or a handshake, and neither did her daughters. There was plenty of warmth. Their home was lively and loud. But the men were more reserved in their touch, as were the women. I found it interesting, respectful. Touch was powerful.

Two years later I stood under the *chuppah* (wedding canopy) with my *chatan* (fiancé) in Mexico City. When I first arrived in his native land a few months prior to our wedding, he told his male friends, "You can't touch Elana!" To his female friends he also said that he wouldn't greet them anymore with the customary Latin kiss. He explained to them that even casual touch between the genders was reserved for between husband and wife and close family members. On one's wedding night, the first time a groom and bride touch, the power of touch is then most clearly understood. I understood at last that touch was not only healing. It was not only soothing. And it did not only have the potential to be damaging. But more than anything – touch was holy.

In the Sanctuary of the Holy Temple stood the two *keruvim* – the mystical, golden cherubim. They were in the shape of a male and female embracing each other. The *keruvim* cleaved to each other in an embrace like a man and woman who love each other. This represented the love that G-d has for Israel. When the Nation of Israel would ascend to the Temple in Jerusalem for the three pilgrimage Festivals (*Pesach, Shavuot* and *Sukkot*), the curtain of the Holy Ark would be parted and they were shown the *keruvim* embracing. They were told, "See how you are beloved before G-d, like the love of a male and a female!" In the Holy of Holies, the holiest place on earth, was an image of a man and woman touching, demonstrating the holiness and purity that can be obtained in the touch of a man and woman.

I think back to all the religious people I encountered in my youth. I had no idea what they were doing. No concept of why the rabbi never shook my hand or the rebbetzin never greeted the male congregants with more than kind words and a smile, never a touch. Now I know. Now I understand. Touch is transcendental. When touch is lovingly and respectfully kept between husband and wife, it allows one to reach one of the highest levels of attachment and closeness, both to G-d and to one another. Pure and simple, touch is awesome; it's holy.

A Narrow Bridge

I have to admit, I'm easily brought to tears. I don't know whether it's because I'm overly emotional, overly sensitive, or both; but these eyes of mine, they fill like wells in a heartbeat.

I sat before one of my students. A woman who four months ago was living, or I should say dying, on sixty calories a day. Now, with a lot of help – I repeat – a *lot* of help, she's at her minimum weight, looks stunningly healthy, and has eyes that amongst their sadness also shine forth with life.

A guitar lay next to her. "Play me something," I requested. Transformation. I saw metamorphosis, thinking back to the girl who came to us four months ago and to the woman who picked up the guitar now.

"The entire world is a very narrow bridge. A very narrow bridge. And the principle is not to ever be afraid." She sang these beautiful verses of Rabbi Nachman of Breslov and I cried. I couldn't help myself. My eyes became wells of tears as I joined in with her, "The principle is not to ever be afraid."

A year ago I started working with young women who have eating disorders. It is not an easy job. I have moments where I want to quit. I tell myself, "I'm not qualified for this. I'm not strong enough for this. I just can't do it." My boss tells me, "If you don't, who will?"

At times it is one step forward and two steps back. What do I do with them? I teach them exercises, I practice reflexology on them. In between I always share with them a bit of Torah – it's not the body alone that is starving, but also the soul. I relate to them the words of our Holy Sages.

I take them to the graves of *tzaddikim* (righteous individuals) and share with them stories: stories of hardships and stories of survival. Everyone has her story; I have mine.

I explain, "The Sages tell us that the righteous fall seven times and get up." I relate in the words of my teacher, "It's not that the righteous are righteous because they are the ones who can pick themselves up – the fact that they fall enables them to become righteous." At times, the only way to ascend is by means of descent.

I tell myself, "The statistics are not good. The chances of full recovery are slim. G-d, I can't do this, but You can. With You there are no statistics, no numbers. Let me be Your messenger and heal these precious women." Suddenly I feel less afraid. Whatever I do, I am not a failure.

"The entire world is a very narrow bridge. A very narrow bridge. And the principle is not to ever be afraid."

~ ~ ~

Imagine our forefather Abraham with his wife Sarah. G-d came to him and told him, "Go. Leave everything that you know and go." "To where?" "To the place that I will show you."

They went, and what did they do? They revolutionized the world. Two people. The commentator Rashi explains that Abraham did acts of kindness and converted the men, while Sarah did acts of kindness and converted the women. What if Abraham had said, "I can't do it. I'm not qualified for the job"?

I remember when I was eighteen years old traveling alone in Europe. I arrived in Venice. I saw by the historic synagogues a sign that read, "Chabad. Kosher Pizza." I hesitantly walked in, "*Shalom Aleichem*! Welcome!" boomed a loud voice. It was not the first time, nor will it probably be the last time, that a friendly voice called out to me in some far-off place. His smile said it all. "What can I do to help you, my fellow Jew?"

Yes, what can I do to help you? I wish I had all the answers. I wish I had a magic wand that would make all the suffering and pain of my students go away. Unfortunately I don't.

I'm not a prophet, I'm not a magician, I'm just a simple Jew with a heart and two hands to extend to another. I'm probably not qualified, but then again, maybe it doesn't really matter. After all, the principle is "not to be afraid, at all...."

Strength or Desire?

You know that pile of laundry, the one that never ends. You wash all the clothes in the morning, and by nighttime the pile is there again. Oh, and those stacks of dishes, you know the ones – the ones that never end. You wash all the dishes in the sink, and within an hour the stack is there again. I sweep, I clean up. The kids make a mess. I sweep and clean up yet again. Inevitably, within a few minutes, there's that mess again. I'm tired. I just picked up. I look at the mess and say to myself with a sigh, "I have no strength!"

The phone rings. It's that lonely woman, the annoying one who calls me all the time to chat. She talks and she talks. I sigh under my breath, "I don't have the strength to listen to this!

My child is playing, "Mommy, Mommy! I want you to play with me." I think to myself, "I can't. I'm so tired. I have no strength." "Mommy, Mommy, I need… I want…" And I keep thinking to myself, "I have no strength! I need strength."

This time, the table is turned. I'm still cleaning, but I ask my son to lend me a hand and pick up the toys in his room, "Oh, I have no strength," he sighs to me. I'm taken aback. "What do you mean, you have no strength? You have strength to play, but not to help Mommy?" I mumble to myself, "If I offered him a treat, he would suddenly find the strength. It's not that there's no strength; there's no desire!"

I stop for a moment to think about what I just mumbled. The Baal Shem

Tov teaches us that when we see something in another person that we don't like, we need to first examine ourselves, because most probably we have that same quality. I go over the words "I have no strength." Is it no strength, or no desire? If I knew I was being paid big bucks to do laundry, would I find the strength? If I was preparing an important dinner for the royal family, would I find the strength to cook and clean? If a client called, would I suddenly find the strength to talk? I think that I would, because I would have desire.

If I could really internalize that playing with my children was as essential to their wellbeing as giving them food to eat and clothes to wear, then surely I would find the strength to sit on the floor with them and play with blocks.

~ ~ ~

From the codified books of Jewish law we learn that upon rising every morning, a Jew is supposed to wash his or her hands with a cup-like vessel. One pours the water over the right, then left; right, then left; right, then left. In the morning, we awake physically and spiritually refreshed and energized. We are alive! We have renewed strength, and it is as though we emerge newly born from the Creator's hand. We wash our hands, raise them and say, "I'm ready to serve You, G-d. I'm ready to raise my hands from their mere physical nature to their higher, spiritual purpose. I am ready to uplift the mundane and make it holy."

I go back to the words I grumbled about my son. I go back to the words and the prayers that I say when I am so tired. I remember the thoughts that I have when I'm doing the million and one tasks that I do at home, or the times when I'm asked for help and I really just don't want to. I think about how at times I almost feel resentful as I sigh, "I have no time! I have no strength! *Tatty* (Father)," I ask to G-d, "give me strength!"

What would happen if it all were to stop? What would happen if, G-d forbid, I was sick in bed, and had all the time in the world to do nothing? What would happen if, G-d forbid, I didn't have a husband to accompany, children to take care of, a home to clean, or work to do? What would happen if I didn't have anyone who needed me?

Instead of asking just for strength, maybe I can also pray for desire? "G-d, give me strength, which You do every moment of the day, and give me will, give me desire! G-d, help me to change my outlook and to change my attitude! Let me see the importance in what I do, and then I will surely want to do it, and find the strength to do it. Let me use my physical hands for all these 'mundane' tasks, and make them holy."

"*Tatty*," I tell G-d affectionately, "*Tatty*, don't stop. You gave me kids; bless me with more, and with the vigor to take care of them. You gave me a home to clean; give me one that's bigger, with more rooms. And also, You can give me cleaning help! Send me more patients to heal, and give me the tools that I need to help them. *Tatty*, I want more of everything that You know is good for me, and give me insight to appreciate it."

~ ~ ~

I get up in the morning. I wash my hands, pouring the water over the right, then the left; right, then left; right, then left. The ritual is repeated a little bit later, but this time I have my prayerbook and I am ready to start my morning blessings. I raise my hands up, and before I dry them, I say the blessing. I think to myself, "I'm a new creature, a new person. I'm ready to start this day. G-d, everything in my life, everything that I do, should be to serve You – giving it meaning and purpose. G-d, give me strength, and give me desire!"

Jealous of the Dog

I never had a pet, except for a fish that we named Maroc. Maroc was an amazing goldfish that lived six years, which is a pretty long time to live for a twenty-five-cent goldfish. Other than Maroc, we didn't have any pets.

Why didn't we have pets? For one thing, my mother has a lot of allergies – and dogs and cats come with fur. The other thing was that my childhood home was not suitable for pets. There were rooms where nobody entered, rugs on which nobody stepped, *objets d'art* that nobody could touch; you get the picture. I never had any friends over because my home was not even conducive to kids, let alone animals.

So imagine my surprise when my mother, at the age of sixty-six (she should live and be well!), called me to tell me that my parents got a dog. Not only did they get a dog, but they *love* the dog.

Now, I'm not the jealous type. I never was. I always had – and have – everything that I could possibly want, and I could clearly see that whatever wasn't mine didn't correspond to me. So it was strange, the lump I felt in my throat, the burning in my cheeks, the emotion that overtook me, as I spoke with my mother. I realized what this was. This was that feeling, that emotion. This was what they called… jealousy! "Mommy," I told her. "I was never jealous of Aaron (my brother), never jealous of Mark (my stepfather), never jealous of anyone or anything. But Mommy, I'm jealous of the dog!" Yes, I, a thirty-three-year-old mother of three, am jealous of a dog – which has a name, by the way: Simcha (hebrew for joy)!

"Don't worry," she laughed, "you have nothing to be jealous of."

I'm not so sure about that. You should hear the way my mother talks about this dog. My mother and Mark, they *love* this dog.

We had another conversation about Simcha a few days later. My parents are coming to visit us in the spring. They are looking forward to the visit, they tell me. We haven't seen them in a year and a half, but there is one concern. That's right, you guessed it: Simcha. What will be with Simcha? Do they take him, or leave him with a dogsitter at home? I, who have three children, but who never had a pet, can't relate to the dilemma. "You haven't seen your grandchildren in over a year, and you are hesitant to come because you don't want to leave the dog?" I asked in disbelief.

My mother's answer: "Elana, I love the dog. He makes me happy. He loves me. When I come home, he's so happy to see me…"

That last sentence got to my heart, "When I come home, he's so happy to see me…"

Was this the first time that my mother felt welcomed and greeted with sincere happiness? Can I ever remember, as a child, being excited as my mother walked in the door? Do I remember, as a child, being greeted with happiness and excitement as I came home from school?

Our Sages teach us to "receive every human being with a cheerful and pleasant countenance" (*Ethics of the Fathers* 1:15), and to "receive every human being with gladness" (ibid. 3:12).

How did Simcha know? Who was Simcha's rabbi, and was he attending one of those wonderful Torah classes?

As a *kallah* (bridal) teacher, one of the first things I tell a bride in preparation for her married life is, "Always greet your husband with a smile when he walks in the door!" It's one of those fundamentals. What I forget to add – but, thanks to Simcha, now I won't – is, "Always greet *everyone* with a smile and cheerful face!" Let your smile be the first thing that a child sees when he comes home from school; let it be the first thing your spouse comes home to, whether it be from work or from the supermarket; and let sincere gladness be the first thing that people encounter when they meet you. Imagine the *simcha* (joy) you can create just by following the sages' (and Simcha's) advice!

The Shul

She finally fell asleep, my newborn, who is always sleeping and yet whom I'm always putting to sleep. I'm sure you've done it a thousand times yourself. You rock, you nurse, you carry and sway. Your baby falls into a heavenly sleep. She looks so peaceful and content. You put her in the carriage or in the crib, and a minute later she wakes up and lets out a cry. The cycle repeats itself again and again. She doesn't want to be anywhere but in the comfort of your arms, hearing the beating of your heart, feeling the warmth of your skin.

~ ~ ~

When I was eighteen years old, I had an internship at an auction house in Geneva. I traveled across the globe, and for the first time, lived on my own. It was exciting, and I befriended many interesting people, yet I still felt very much alone. I called home, and my mother advised me, "Go to *shul* (synagogue); you'll meet other Jews." The idea didn't sound bad, but I didn't know where to find a shul. And anyways, so what if I went to a shul? How would that, and meeting other Jews, make me feel any less alone?

I walked on the streets one day, and saw a man sporting a black hat and dressed in a black suit. I immediately identified him as a religious Jew. I walked up to him with my heart pounding. I nervously asked him, "Where's the nearest shul?" Much to my surprise, it wasn't far from the hostel where I was staying, and I told myself I would go the following Saturday morning to see what it was like. I brought along a friend that I had made in the hostel, a non-Jewish German friend, who was also curious to see the shul.

We walked into the shul. We were instantly greeted by two lovely young women who handed us prayerbooks and motioned to where we could sit. I opened the prayerbook with its somewhat familiar Hebrew script, closed my eyes, perked up my ears, and realized they were praying in the same tunes that I was accustomed to hearing. I was thousands of miles away from my home, and yet I was near. After the service was over, the women invited us to a *kiddush* (*Shabbat* refreshments) and then to a *brit milah* (circumcision) that was taking place a few blocks away. We went with the crowd of people to celebrate the *brit milah* of a family I didn't even know. My friend was impressed by the hospitality and the warm greeting we received. "How lucky you are to have this, to be part of this," she told me.

To be part of this, to have this. The sentence resonated in my ears. This – this shul – a home away from home.

How did my mother know that in a synagogue I wouldn't feel alone? How did she know that in a foreign country, this would be the only place where I wouldn't be a stranger – and why had this secret always been kept from me? It took a German woman to point it out to me – a granddaughter of Holocaust survivors.

The shul that she was referring to has nothing to do with a building. It's the feeling of being amongst your own, even when you don't know anybody. It's experiencing and observing. It's practicing and doing rituals that have been done by your family for thousands of years. It's like tasting foods that you've never tasted, and recognizing them.

~ ~ ~

When my husband and I first moved to Israel, the security situation was extremely bad. We came on our own, leaving our family and friends behind. Everyone asked us, "How can you live in Israel, in Jerusalem? Aren't you scared? You don't know anyone; aren't you lonely?" Lonely, scared? But we're home.

Over the years, I've lived in many cities and have traveled to many countries. The first thing I do when I arrive in a new place is to seek out the shul. It's like a magnet pulling me towards it. Like a baby in her mother's arms, it's where I feel safe and find comfort. The prayers and fellow Jews are the beatings of the mother's heart. *You're not alone,* the heart beats. *You're a part of something; you have something.*

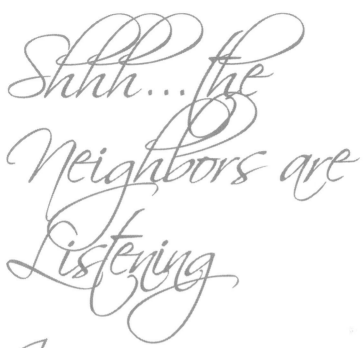

Shhh...the Neighbors are Listening

I had spent the past ten days at home with my sick son who was very cranky (and rightfully so). My baby was crying and I myself didn't feel well. My son started to cry and whine and have a tantrum – about what, I don't even know. I burst out screaming, "Will you stop crying? What is it that you want from me?" I lifted my head from his startled gaze and my eyes rested upon the open windows. Probably everyone in my apartment building had heard me scream. I instantly lowered my voice and told him in a near whisper, "Let's make a deal. Avraham Nissim will stop whining and Mommy will stop screaming." He nodded his head in agreement.

Shhh, the neighbors are listening, what will they think?

I grew up in a large house, oblivious to what was going on around me. Every scream, shout or negative comment stayed within the four walls of our home or trapped within my heart. We never worried about what the neighbors would think. When I was first married, we rented an apartment in a large apartment building in the heart of Mexico City. At two o'clock in the morning, I would awake to the sounds of people screaming below us. After two months, I told my husband I couldn't take it anymore and we moved to a different apartment, leaving behind a big deposit. It was worth it. I wonder to myself how many homes would be saved if only the occupants had thought to themselves, "Shhh, the neighbors are listening, what will they think?"

On occasion, by the time Thursday or Friday rolls around I'm so exhausted from the week, I can't even think about preparing for *Shabbat*. I have thoughts of serving peanut butter and jelly sandwiches or store-bought cold cuts instead of my usual home-cooked meals that are infused with love and holiness. Just then, the phone will ring, as it does almost every week, and it's someone asking to come over for a meal on *Shabbat*. I tell the caller "yes" and breathe a sigh of relief. Thanks to the *Shabbat* guest, my home will radiate, sparkle and shine and the smell of good food will fill it...after all, what would the *Shabbat* guest think?

Even when the windows are closed shut in the middle of the winter or during the week when we don't have a single caller, I say to myself, "The windows are open, what will the neighbors think. You might have an unexpected guest, what will he/she think?"

Have you ever noticed how easy it is to get upset with your family and how difficult it is to display the same anger for a stranger? How your home looks impeccable when you know that visitors are coming, and if not, it would look like a disaster? You might ask, why do you need the neighbors or a *Shabbat* guest to do what you should be doing anyways? Isn't it like living a lie or putting on a show? One might call it pretend or make-believe to always be thinking that someone is listening or that someone is visiting, but, in fact, it is reality. The first law in the famous compilation of codified Jewish law, the *Shulchan Aruch*, states, "*shiviti Hashem linegdi tamid*" – I am always dwelling in front of G-d.

The Talmud (*Berachot* 28b) relates that when Rabbi Yochanan ben Zakai was on his deathbed, his students asked him to give them a blessing. He told them, "Have the same fear of Heaven as you have of man."

"That's it, Rabbi? [Only the same, not more?]"

"*If only* it would be the same as it is for man!" he answered.

We seem to forget that we are never alone; we always have Someone listening and observing each and every one of our actions. I always tell the brides I counsel to speak in a tone with their husbands as they would if the neighbors were listening, to treat their spouses and future children with the same patience as they would a guest.

Once again my son taught me a valuable lesson and reminded me that everything I do does make a difference, because, after all, "Shhh, the neighbors are listening, what will they think?"

"*Shiviti Hashem linegdi tamid*" – I am always standing before G-d.

Knowing and Controlling

"Elana, if I only knew when I would become pregnant. Then I could wait. You can tell me that it will take a year's time, even two years. Whatever. But just give me a number and tell me that it will happen. I can handle that – waiting – as long as I know. But this not-knowing – that I can't deal with…"

"Elana, when do you think I'll give birth? Do you think it will be soon? Tonight? Tomorrow? When? If I could just know, I would be so much calmer. I could go on for another few days, if I just knew when…"

"When is this labor going to end? How much longer until I have my baby?

"Elana, when?" The famous question I hear all the time. And "How?" Women want to know. And they want to know now. Their knowing stems from a desire, a need to control. I wish I had the answers to give them, but maybe not knowing and relinquishing control is actually the answer.

~ ~ ~

And G-d commanded the man, saying, "Of every tree of the garden you may freely eat; but of the Tree of *Da'at* (knowledge) of Good and Bad, you must not eat thereof."… And the woman saw that the tree was good for eating and that it was a delight to the eyes, and that the tree was desirable for comprehension, and she took of its fruit and ate; and she gave also to her husband with her and he ate.… And G-d said to the woman, "What is this that you have done! … I will greatly increase your suffering and your pregnancy; in pain shall you bear children. And your craving shall be for your husband, and he shall rule over you" (Genesis 2:16-3:16).

What exactly happened here? Eve, the first woman of the world, ate from the Tree of *Da'at*. She didn't eat from the Tree of Life. She didn't eat from the tree of beauty, wisdom, or desire. No, she ate from the Tree of **Knowledge**. Eve wanted a specific type of knowledge. She wanted the knowledge that is only in G-d's hands. She wanted to control. Don't we all want to know and want to control?

"I feel so bloated, when are my menses coming already?"

"What is going on with my body?"

"When am I going to give birth?"

"What is happening with the baby?"

You want to get pregnant; you can't. You don't want to get pregnant; you become pregnant. You want the baby to sleep; she won't go to sleep. You want him to wake up; he won't wake up. You know what's best; you see with such clarity, but your husband won't listen to you or take your advice. Knowledge – that is control. This is what we all want, right? (I certainly do!) And yet the more we want to know, the less we do. The more we want to control, the less we can.

There's a woman who comes to me for a reflexology treatment for infertility. She has read all the medical literature and knows how to calculate her ovulation and how to optimize her chances of becoming pregnant, but she still cannot become pregnant. I tell her, "Stop being so smart! Stop trying to figure it all out. Stop trying to know so much! Babies are from G-d. Relinquish control to Him and work on having a loving relationship with your spouse and with G-d." She comes to me three months later with good news: Thank G-d, she's pregnant.

Another woman has read every birthing book and spoke with every mother that she knows. As her doula, I breathe with her, I dance with her, I massage her back. She wants to know every detail of what is going on: "What process of labor am I in? How long do you think it will be now?" And with all her questions and wanting to know, she stays closed. I whisper into her ear, "Let go. Stop trying to control your body." When I tell her that it doesn't really matter, when she lets go of the control and need to know, this woman opens up and calmly births her baby.

~ ~ ~

The sages say that only G-d holds the keys to birth, to the Revival of the Dead and to rain (all which have to do with growth and life). That means that no doctor or healer can tell you when you will become pregnant or when a treatment will work – it is purely in G-d's hands. When you are in labor, no doctor or midwife can tell you when you will give birth – only G-d knows.

As women, we have a *tikkun* (reparation) that we can do in order to rectify the sin of Eve: to relinquish the desire to control. To call out to G-d and let Him open up the door to salvation. When we do that, we convert the "curse" into a blessing.

The Sincerity of Simplicity

The woman on the bus motioned for me to come sit next to her. She wore a simple black shirt and shawl. Her legs were covered with opaque tights under her flowing skirt. I had no idea how old she was. She looked like she could be any age and she also looked timeless.

She smiled brightly at me. Her smile was contagious. She couldn't contain her excitement anymore and I put down my book to listen. She held out her hand for me to see what she was holding.

"My son sent me these!" They were vouchers for the supermarket. "I just got them and I quickly got on the bus to do a shopping for *Shabbat Kodesh* (the Holy Sabbath)."

Vouchers for the supermarket. This woman was grinning from ear to ear because she now had what she needed to buy food to honor the Holy Sabbath.

Simplicity. Sincerity.

I took my children to the toy store. It was my daughter's birthday. I held my breath as we walked there. How I would love to buy her anything that her heart desires; I touched the wallet inside my pocket and knew that it was nearly empty except for a few dollars. We walked past the electric toys, the fancy bicycles, the doll houses and the toys that can walk and talk. We arrived at the back of the store and I told her to pick out whatever she wanted. She grabbed a bag of seventy-five-cent marbles and a two dollar watch. I praised her for her excellent choices. She spent hours playing with her fascinating marbles.

Marbles that require no batteries and don't know how to make noise or light up. My daughter was thrilled with the gifts that cost her Mommy a few dollars.

Simplicity. Sincerity.

At our table was an international mixture this past *Shabbat*. Usually there is a common language (English or Hebrew) amongst our guests; but this time my husband and I had to wing it, speaking in three languages. At one point it became a bit complicated: by trying to please everyone and make everyone understand the conversation, no one was paying attention.

One of our guests, a professional cantor, got up and grabbed a book of songs. He opened his mouth and started to sing. All of a sudden there was harmony and everyone, including my two-year-old daughter who barely speaks a sentence, joined in by singing, humming, or clapping.

When there are no common words and there is lack of understanding, there is always the profound simplicity of music.

Simplicity. Sincerity.

My students ask me why I always look happy. My friends ask me the secret of the radiance that, thank G-d, shines from my children's faces. The answer is simple. It's all about simplicity. It's all about sincerity.

The Baal Shem Tov, the founder of the Chassidic movement, had a very dear disciple. One day, the man came into the Baal Shem Tov's presence intending to ask him a favor. He was taken aback by the cold reception that he received. The Baal Shem Tov was about to go on a trip and invited him to come with him, although still keeping his distance.

During the journey, in the carriage, the Baal Shem Tov suddenly broke the silence:

"Do you think that I don't know why you came to see me?"

The man began to tremble, sensing that his teacher was reading his mind.

"You came to ask me to teach you the language of the birds, didn't you?"

The disciple nodded. The Baal Shem Tov then began to teach him the keys to this secret science. In a very short time, the man began to understand the twittering of the birds in the forest through which they were passing. He heard everything, including great secrets and announcements about the future.

Suddenly, as they were approaching the end of their journey, the Baal Shem Tov passed his hand over his student's face. The man immediately forgot all that he had heard and could no longer understand the language of the birds.

The Baal Shem Tov then said to him, "If I had thought that you needed this knowledge to serve the Almighty, I would have taught it to you a long time ago. But it is not the case. You must serve G-d with the means that you already possess and be simple with the Almighty your G-d."

Simplicity. Sincerity.

We live in a world where everyone thinks that if you don't have a title before or after your name then you are a "nobody." We live in a world where if you don't possess the newest cell phone, computer, or electrical device, then you are not "with it."

Well guess what: the title, the object, the money – they won't buy happiness. As the famous saying goes, "When you have one then you'll want two; when you have ten you'll want twenty." I look at my finger, at my most precious piece of jewelry, the simple gold wedding band that my husband gave me.

Simplicity. Sincerity.

For it is with a simple, sincere and pure heart that we can not only reach the most intense levels of closeness to one another, but to our Creator as well. To reach the highest spiritual level one must focus on the brilliance in the simplicity and sincerity of the connection. As our Torah teaches us, if you want to *be* with G-d, "be *tamim* (sincere) with G-d" (Genesis 17:1).

Made in the USA
Columbia, SC
15 September 2020